# Spirituality in Education in a Global, Pluralised World

A particular problem associated with international research in the field of spirituality and education is the reluctance of scholars to agree on what spirituality means, with numerous descriptions increasing ambiguity and reducing the impact of research in the discipline. *Spirituality in Education in a Global, Pluralised World* argues that it is important to understand spirituality as a unifying concept that has the potential to be meaningful in its application to the lives of children and young people in areas of learning and wellbeing.

This book will clearly show how contemporary understandings of spirituality are quite distinct from understandings of religion and religiosity; that we need to examine the concept from Western, Eastern and indigenous perspectives to inform our understanding; and that it has a significant role to play in education to promote learning, social cohesion and wellbeing. Chapters also show why and how spiritual learning should be addressed across the curriculum, with implications for the design of learning programmes and environments.

This book, therefore, is aimed at a global market of academics and researchers interested in spirituality, religious and holistic education, moral development and wellbeing. It should also be of interest to educational policymakers, curriculum advisors and classroom practitioners.

**Marian de Souza** is Honorary Associate Professor at Federation University, Ballarat, Australia and Honorary Fellow at Australian Catholic University. She is also Chair of the International Association for Children's Spirituality.

# Routledge Research in Education

# Spirituality in Education in a Global, Pluralised World

Marian de Souza

Routledge
Taylor & Francis Group

LONDON AND NEW YORK

First published 2016
by Routledge

2 Park Square, Milton Park, Abingdon, Oxforshire OX14 4RN
711 Third Avenue, New York, NY 10017

*Routledge is an imprint of the Taylor & Francis Group, an informa business*

First issued in paperback 2017

*British Library Cataloguing in Publication Data*
A catalogue record for this book is available from the British Library

*Library of Congress Cataloging in Publication Data*
Names: De Souza, Marian.
Title: Spirituality in education in a global, pluralised world / Marian de
   Souza.
Description: New York : Routledge, 2016 | Includes bibliographical
   references.
Identifiers: LCCN 2015033276| ISBN 9781138804746 (hardback) |
   ISBN 9781315752761 (ebook)
Subjects: LCSH: Religious education—Study and teaching. | Religious
   education—Teaching methods.
Classification: LCC BL42 . D47 2016 | DDC 200.71—dc23
LC record available at http://lccn.loc.gov/2015033276


ISBN: 978-1-138-80474-6 (hbk)
ISBN: 978-0-8153-5916-6 (pbk)


Typeset in ITC Galliard Std
by Swales & Willis, Exeter, Devon, UK

# Contents

# Acknowledgements

The author gratefully acknowledges the following publications for granting permission to reproduce certain sections of the stated works in this book:

de Souza, M. (2014). Religious identity and plurality in Australia: Inclusions, exclusions and tensions. *Journal for the Study of Religion*, *27*(1), pp. 210–233.

de Souza, M. (2011). Promoting inter-spiritual education in the classroom: Exploring the perennial philosophy as a useful strategy to encourage freedom of religious practice and belief. *Journal of Religious* Education, *59*(1), pp. 27–37.

de Souza, M. (2005). Engaging the mind, heart and soul of the student in religious education: Teaching for meaning and connection. *Journal of Religious Education*, *53*(4), pp. 40–47.

de Souza, M. (2004). Teaching for effective learning in religious education: A discussion of the perceiving, thinking, feeling and intuiting elements in the learning process. *Journal of Religious Education*, *52*(3), pp. 22–30.

# Introduction

When I first began to research and write about young people's spirituality in the final years of the twentieth century, my interest was stirred by a frequent response that I heard from Year 12 students in Australia (17–18 year olds in their final year of secondary school): *I am spiritual but not religious.* The same response was echoed by a large number of the 220 Year 12 students, across twelve Catholic schools in the state of Victoria, who participated in my doctoral research in the mid-1990s in which I had been investigating their perceptions of their learning experiences in their religious education programme.

This was a phrase I had not heard before, possibly because my previous teaching and research studies had concentrated on musicology (jazz) and music education. I transferred to religious education for my doctoral studies. At that time access to the internet, with its breadth and speed of information, was rather different and less easy from what it is today. Hence, it was some years later that I discovered the widespread use of the mantra 'spiritual but not religious'. Today, a Google search indicates 57.2 million hits for the statement. Smith (2005) cites data which showed that 8 per cent of teenagers agreed that they were spiritual but not religious; 46 per cent said it was somewhat true and 43 per cent said it was not true at all (p. 77); and Harris (2014) states that 20 per cent of Americans claim to be spiritual but not religious (p. 6).

Not surprisingly, I wanted to better understand what the students were trying to convey to me. My research over the past two decades has thus examined contemporary influences on and understandings of spirituality, the relationship between spirituality and religion in pluralistic contexts and finally, the subsequent implications for curriculum and pedagogy.

This book is an attempt to reflect on and further examine my research journey into understandings of the concept of spirituality over the past twenty years and the role it has played and continues to play in education and in people's lives, both religious and non-religious. As a result, I have drawn on many of my earlier publications to revisit the ideas and discuss them within the context, trends and influences of contemporary society. In addition, I have drawn on other research that has supported or questioned some of my concepts and which has helped to further illuminate my initial understandings and applications of the spiritual dimension in life. My research took me into other areas, such as intuition, the role of non-conscious learning, concepts of spiritual intelligence, the dark side of spirituality and, more recently, some relevant discoveries in neuroscience which have further informed our understandings of spirituality.

In the late 1990s, I began a study of relevant literature which, then, informed a series of small research projects where young people from different backgrounds were interviewed to learn about their perceptions and expressions of spirituality. An additional aspect was to identify the differences between religion and spirituality. The findings, generally, supported other research that spirituality is about experiences and expressions of connectedness; that is, it pertains to the relational dimension of being. These topics provide the content of the first chapter.

I also discovered that academics and professionals from disciplines outside theology and religion were examining the role of spirituality in the physical, mental and emotional wellbeing of the individual. In particular, I became interested in neuroscientific research and the discovery of mirror neurons and the implications for the relational dimension of the individual. If mirror neurons indicate that the human person is programmed to be relational and empathetic, I argue that they provide us with physical evidence that the human person is, indeed, a spiritual being, since connectedness to the Other is implicit in our understanding of spirituality. These areas are the focus for the second chapter.

If we are spiritual people, and spirituality is an innate human characteristic, we need to find ways in which spirituality may be nurtured. Religious practices are seen as traditional forms of spiritual nurturance, as are family and community rituals and gatherings. However, in a contemporary world where traditional institutions have lost much of the leverage that they had in years gone by, and where family structures have changed beyond recognition, such influences have been seriously tempered by social media and technology. The third chapter, then, examines various factors and influences – in a society that is contextualised by a pluralised global world – which nurture or hinder spiritual growth amongst children and young people. It poses the argument that if we can promote understanding and inclusion of the Other who is different, there is a greater chance that social cohesion will result – which will enhance spiritual wellbeing.

One of the factors that impedes spiritual growth, but which receives little attention in education and other programmes that attend to the wellbeing of children and young people, is an identification of the human shadow. The fourth chapter looks at the implications of the shadow side of spirituality and argues for the need to incorporate strategies into education programmes that will assist young people to identify and embrace their shadow in their journey to wholeness.

Having established the significance that spirituality has in human life, the fifth chapter presents an approach to learning that recognises the child as a rational, emotional *and* spiritual being. Therefore, I revisit the learning approach I developed many years ago which addresses the spiritual dimension of education. It identifies the role of intuition, imagination and creativity as elements drawn from the non-conscious mind and which comprise the spiritual dimension of learning.

In particular, it recognises the complementarity of cognitive, affective and spiritual learning. Some guidelines are also offered as to how this spiritual dimension may be incorporated into everyday classrooms in learning and assessment programmes.

Finally, another aspect that relates to spiritual learning is that spirituality and religion have close links. In the past, there was a rather restricted understanding of spirituality as it became submerged in and confined to religious practice in the Western world. Acknowledging that religion and spirituality are two distinct but related concepts is an important consideration in contemporary research. More importantly, we need to recognise that while spirituality has gained popularity over religion in the West, the growth of religious plurality today heralds a new era when the role of religion in the lives of people should be acknowledged. This is particularly important in education since children and young people need to know and understand the beliefs and practices of other peoples so as to remove fear of difference and promote inclusive and empathetic attitudes and behaviours. The sixth chapter, then, focuses on the importance of learning about different religions. An approach that focuses on the spiritual dimension of different religions – an *interspiritual* approach – is discussed as a way forward towards social cohesion, thereby allowing today's students to learn about the religious traditions that have become features of the world in which they live. This is essential for any future encounter or engagement they are likely to have with the Other who is religiously different.

The epilogue revisits the main arguments through each of the chapters to provide a rationale as to why spirituality should be incorporated into and addressed in education programmes to enhance and promote social cohesion and spiritual wellbeing of all students, and why it should be an essential requirement for all educational programmes in the global, pluralistic world of the twenty-first century.

# Chapter 1

# Spirituality, children and young people

## Perspectives from research

In order to understand the role of spirituality in the learning process I needed to discover how contemporary perceptions of and attitudes towards spirituality impact on the lives of children and young people. Given the dominance of a secular culture and the receding influences of traditional religion, many young people have little experience of religious and spiritual practices. On the other hand, alternative practices, such as yoga, meditation and ecological concerns, have become widespread over the past forty years and they are easily accessible and attractive to young people in their search for meaning. This chapter, then, will explore the changed understandings of the concept of spirituality and the implications for the expression and practice of the spirituality of children and young people today.

## Concepts of human spirituality: Perspectives from West to East

Western culture, derived as it was from a 2,000-year-old Christian history and consciousness, traditionally treated spirituality as an offshoot of religion. Spirituality and religion were used synonymously so that spirituality came to have little life of its own (for instance, see Hughes *et al.*, 1995 and Ó Murchú, 1997 among others). In addition, with the birth of an industrial and technological age during the previous two centuries, the dominance of scientific and rationalistic thinking meant that spiritual matters became of less concern in human affairs. Indeed, in the years following the Second Vatican Council in the Roman Catholic tradition, mystical theology, which explored the spiritual realm in the Christian world, was not taught in Catholic seminaries (Johnston, 2000). At the same time, traditional religion slowly began to lose its foothold in society. People started drifting away from institutional Christian churches (Francis, 1989; Kay & Francis, 1996; Rymarz, 2006) and many found themselves floundering in the mass of information and misinformation generated by media and other outlets that purported to offer answers to the big questions. In describing this situation at the turn of the century, Carroll (1998) argued that the West is 'lost in a crisis of meaning' (p. 1). The reasons that have given rise to this situation is that answers to the big questions about the meaning of life have become swamped by a materialistic culture, leaving many individuals confused and unsettled as they struggle to find purpose in their everyday.

Ó Murchú (1997) recognises spirituality as more central to human experience than religion. His Christian viewpoint acknowledges that the spiritual consciousness of our time is about leaving behind the familiar – the era of 'mechanistic modelling, patriarchal control and the triumph of rationality' – and yielding to the deep yearning to outgrow, transcend and evolve towards the new, 'to outgrow the stultifying and crippling boundaries with which we have tried to hem in the human search for meaning over the past 300–500 years' (p. 14).

Tacey (2000) supports the notion of spirituality without religion but observes that while expressions of this 'new' spirituality is about connectedness to nature and the cosmos, it also draws on our religious history and tradition (p. 15). Lyons (2000) concedes that while links to an institutional church may have become somewhat problematic for many Christians, their relationship with Jesus remains an important one. He uses the metaphor of Jesus in Disneyland to discuss the commodification of spirituality, rather than religion, where a post-modern image of Jesus has become popular. In this guise, Jesus is seen as inclusive of outsiders and minority groups; he is critical of organised religion and promotes social justice. This image of Jesus, then, has been made into an icon to embellish T-shirts and other accessories or referred to in popular music and books. 'Jesus comes dressed up in the clothes of our own culture' (pp. 136–137).

Beaudoin (1998), a Generation Xer, concurs. He suggests that if we seriously explore the cultural symbols and practices of Gen X[1] we would find a people whose search for God remains at a personal level. Many engage in a serious study of the Christian tradition which then positions them to offer critical and constructive comments on Church teachings and practice. Beaudoin's opinion is that if the institutional Church wanted to attract Gen Xers, it needed to hear their voices and respond by bringing its 'practices and preaching back to its origins and its centre – Jesus' (pp. 64–65).

Certainly, the human search for meaning and transcendence has been the subject explored by many philosophers and theologians. Evelyn Underhill's thesis on mystical theology, written in 1910, argued that the human search is a distinctive feature of humankind:

> The most highly developed branches of the human family have in common one peculiar characteristic. They tend to produce – sporadically it is true, and often in the teeth of adverse external circumstances – a curious and definite type of personality; a type which refused to be satisfied with that which other men call experience, and is inclined, in the words of its enemies, to 'deny the world in order that it may find reality' . . . their one passion seems to be the prosecution of a certain spiritual and intangible quest: the finding of a 'way out' or a 'way back' to some desirable state in which alone they can satisfy their craving for absolute truth.
>
> (Underhill, 1993, p. 3)

While these views reflect a perspective influenced by Western Christian thought, Gilbert (2010, p. 5) points to the fact that the notion of returning to the Godhead is contained within different religious traditions where earthly life is seen as one of suffering. Thus, the human search for meaning is about returning to our origins. He describes, for instance, the concept amongst Muslims and Christians that suffering is attributed to the separation from God. Consequently, humans yearn to return to and be united with God. He discusses, as well, reincarnation amongst Buddhists and Hindus, where a breakthrough to freedom from the endless cycle requires an enlightened mind and doing good works. The common theme underlying these notions is that the goal is to escape this life and to return to an Absolute Reality.

Echoing Underhill's thesis nearly a hundred years later, Karen Armstrong asserts that 'religion was not something tacked on to the human condition . . . the desire to cultivate a sense of the transcendent may be *the* defining human characteristic' (2009, p. 19). She further argues that the Ultimate Reality is not a personalised god. Rather, it is a transcendent mystery, the depths of which can never be comprehended. It is Armstrong's contention that – while different faith traditions have their own 'unique genius and distinctive vision: each its peculiar flaws' – there are some fundamental principles common to most faith traditions: 'when one loses all sense of duality and is "oblivious to everything within or without"' (p. 31). Thus, Armstrong speaks of the self-forgetfulness that is experienced by people who become so practised in their skill that it becomes second nature to them – the depth of their absorption unifies them with whatever they are doing. Citing Zhuang, an important spiritual figure in ancient Chinese history, she says it was 'an *ekstasis* that enabled you to "step outside" the prism of ego and experience the divine' (p. 5). She goes on to say this was the way in which individuals were able to discover that the transcendent dimension in their lives was not something 'out there', but something that they drew from the core of their existence (ibid.). Furthermore, Armstrong refers to the fact that, historically, we can find evidence that many men and women have had experiences which allowed them to transcend the ordinariness of their daily lives:

> Indeed, it is an arresting characteristic of the human mind to be able to conceive concepts that go beyond it in this way. However we choose to interpret it, this human experience of transcendence has been a fact of life.
>
> (Armstrong, 1993, p. 6)

Importantly, Armstrong does admit that not all people will recognise this transcendent dimension as divine; for instance, Buddhists do not attribute it to a supernatural force but, rather, recognise it as a natural aspect of being human. Nonetheless, Armstrong stresses this human need to reach out to something beyond as a 'yearning for the absolute' when people 'sensed its presence all around them, and went to great lengths to cultivate their sense of this transcendence in creative rituals' (2009, p. 23). Like others, Armstrong recognises that people have different names for this reality: God, Dao, Brahman or Nirvana (p. 5).

This argument is reinforced by Nakagawa who refers to D.T. Suzuki's discussion on the Eastern perspective in 1963:

> Eastern perspective is different from the Western perspective that is based on 'dualistic divisions' of things. It refers to the state of 'unitary One' – *Tao, li, t'ai chi,* absolute Nothingness, absolute ne, Emptiness – before a dualistic division takes place . . . The 'unitary One' does not mean the union of the two separate realms such as subject and object, or God and human, but the undifferentiated primordial state prior to division of any kind.
>
> (Nakagawa, 2000, p. 10)

Simply put: Western thinking seeks a *unio mystica* between God and human while Eastern thinking is based on the non-dualistic ground of Being prior to dualism (ibid.).

Dualism has, without doubt, been central to Christian theology and doctrine. Nonetheless, many Western Christian mystics – for instance, Bede Griffiths, Meister Eckhart, Thomas Merton, Teresa of Ávila, Teilhard de Chardin – found a transformation in their perceptions and experiences of a God 'out there' to a sense of oneness and union with God. This is captured by Robinson's (1963) classic discussion on God in Christianity, where he describes how the theologian Paul Tillich influenced him to speak of God 'with a new and indestructible relevance and (which) made the traditional language of a God that came in from outside both remote and artificial' (p. 22). To Robinson, Tillich had moved away from the understanding of God as a separate being. Rather, Robinson says Tillich spoke of God as 'the infinite and inexhaustible depth and ground of all being' (p. 46), as Ultimate Reality.

Significantly, the Western Christian concept of a God 'out there' made God a distant figure for many, known only through the description offered by others rather than through personal experience. This distant God in his heaven, implicit in the Christian tradition of the West, was often reflected in literature and the arts; for instance, in Browning's line from the poem *Pippa Passes*: 'God's in his heaven, all's right with the world.' The comfort, consolation and intimacy that humans find in tangible relationships may remain missing in such a relationship. A distant God for many, then, persists as an intellectual concept of an Unseen Presence, a presence that they may be unable to experience through their physical senses which define them in their human reality – and therefore, for some, this Unseen Presence may remain a relatively elusive Unknown Presence.

Davies (2006) illuminates this relationship in his examination of different experiences of mysticism, which he defines as 'an experience of God' (p. 1) – or what some may refer to as experiences of transcendence. The most common within the Christian context is through attendance at a church service. Here, the experience of God is mediated through communal liturgy, prayer and ritual – but, nonetheless, it is real and meaningful for the individual (ibid.). The second most common form is when an individual's relationship with Jesus is illuminated by the Scriptures and Church teachings and is so profound that it finds expression in a 'visionary and particularly intense form of Christocentric spirituality' (p. 2). Interestingly, Davies identifies an influence of the secular world in this second form since the visions are described through the use of romantic and almost erotic imagery and language. Davies goes further to suggest that the visions may have been prompted by the medieval practice involving severe forms of mortification which weakened the physical body, thereby increasing the susceptibility of the individual to visionary experience. Davies contends that these two forms were reflective of a particular time and setting within the Catholic world, but the third form is not so restricted. It is found amongst mystics of many different traditions and it takes the shape of 'a direct and unmediated experience of God in which the soul rises or is raised beyond the material world to share, briefly, in the glory of the Godhead' (p. 3). To sum up, Davies calls the first form of mystical experience the mysticism of the sacrament and liturgy; the second is a Christocentric spirituality; but the third:

> aims specifically to transcend images and to enter the 'darkness' and the 'nothingness' of the Godhead itself in a journey which leads the soul to the shedding of all that is superfluous, contrary or unequal to God as he is in his most essential Being.
>
> (Davies, 2006, p. 4)

According to the third form, then, we find a sense of union with God, the unity and oneness that has been described by others from both Christian and non-Christian, Western and Eastern worlds. That this concept of oneness can be found across Western and Eastern thinking suggests that it not only transcends cultural and religious preconceptions but, potentially, has significance and relevance for the human search for Ultimacy or Absolute Reality, or the host of names found across the human world for a Transcendent Other, or for deities that are believed to be incarnations of the Transcendent Other.

Certainly an idea of oneness may be found embedded in the philosophies and practices of many Christian writers. For instance, Thomas Merton speaks of a thread of unity that runs through his thinking and writings:

> What every man looks for in his life is his own salvation and the salvation of the men he lives with. By salvation I mean first of all the full discovery of who he himself really is. Then I mean something of the fulfilment of his own God-given powers, in the love of others and of God. I mean also the discovery that he cannot find himself in himself alone, but that he must find himself in and through others.
>
> (Merton, 2005, p. xv)[2]

Chittister (1991) too speaks of humankind as a people who lack awareness and a sense of balance which has 'frayed' our wholeness (p. 69) and asserts that

'Benedictine spirituality asks us to recognize our connectedness . . . calls us to be mindful' (p. 70). She acknowledges the dualistic feature apparent in traditional spirituality when it is packaged through religious frameworks which substitute religious formulas for spirituality:

> Real spiritual wisdom knows that spirituality is not packaged and not processed and not produced for the mass market. Real spirituality is something that brings us now in touch with God here. It does not take formulas or *imprimaturs*. It takes consciousness . . . We have all been taught, whoever we are, that God is just a notch beyond and above and unlike ourselves. It is time to find out where God really is for us.
>
> (Chittister, 1991, p. 206)

Further, Paul Nangle conducted a doctoral study into the contemporary understandings and practices of spirituality of the Irish Christian Brothers in Australia. He concluded that a concept of universal connectedness provided a foundational basis for the perceptions and expressions of spirituality of many of the Brothers he interviewed (see Nangle, 2014, pp. 242–246).

Another advocate is Bede Griffiths, whose exhaustive study of Western Christianity and Hinduism led him to discuss a new vision of reality. He noted that a universal wisdom, or perennial philosophy, prevailed from about 500 CE to approximately 1500 CE, which explained that 'the material world was pervaded by, and would find its explanation in, a transcendent reality' (1989, p. 11). He echoed Armstrong and Nakagawa when he recognised the different names by which this reality was known: in China as the Tao, in Mahayana Buddhism as the Void or *Sunyata*, in Hinduism as Brahman, in Islam as the *al Haqq* or the Reality and in Christianity it was known as the Godhead or Supreme Being (ibid.). It was Griffiths's contention that a transcendent reality had been studied with some accuracy for many years in the East. However, it was done in a manner that differed from the rationalistic, objective scientific approach that was later developed in the Western world, and which gave no credence to an Ultimate Reality. Griffiths felt that some of the problems in the world today were a result of a rather restricted view, and if humankind was to survive, it needed a change of heart where science was to become subordinate to wisdom:

> The discursive reason which seeks to dominate the world and imprisons the human person in the narrow world of the conscious mind must be dethroned, and must acknowledge its dependence on the transcendent Mystery, which is beyond the rational consciousness.
>
> (Griffiths, 1976, p. 19)

Ultimately, Griffiths is claiming that there are things beyond the scientific mind so that a Western rationalistic, reductionist, objective approach to understanding the world would not provide all the answers. Nor could it express the ultimate meaning and purpose of life which always appears out of reach but 'is the "Ground" of all existence, that from which all things come, to which all things return' (1976, p. 19). While Griffiths's thought was influenced by his religious thinking, there are others from different backgrounds and disciplines who would support his stance. Willis Harman, for instance, points out that knowledge systems, even the sciences, are parochial precisely because they are shaped and, subsequently, reinforced by the characteristics of the society that produces them:

> We have the kind of society we have in part because of the fruits of science and technology. But the converse is also true: We have the kind of science we have in part because of the particular nature of the society in which it was developed.
>
> (Harman, 1998, p. 22)

I recall a conversation that illustrates Harman's argument at a very simple level. I had just returned from presenting a paper at a spirituality conference in São Paulo where a presenter from the United States spoke of his research into reincarnation, which was focused on children's memories of past lives. On my return home, I was in discussion with another colleague, an Anglo-Australian member of a religious order, who became quite sceptical as I spoke about the evidence this academic had presented to affirm the fact of reincarnation. She asked: 'And where was this research done?' When I said that much of it had been conducted in India, she smiled knowingly and said, rather dismissively, 'Oh yes, of course'. On reflection I realised I should have asked her, 'And where do the apparitions of Mary [perceived as the Mother of God in Christianity] occur?' Because, of course, Mary does not appear in cultures and regions where no one knows about her. The belief that she has appeared to someone is supported by a communal belief that she is the Mother of God and, within the community, there exists a religious history of her apparitions. Thus, the apparition is validated by the belief system. In a Western culture where, generally, people do not believe in reincarnation, if a child starts talking of a past life, parents and other adults will attribute the stories to imagination and fantasy. On the other hand, in a culture that supports the concept of reincarnation, a child's account of memories of a past life is likely to be taken more seriously and investigated. Therefore, the belief system of both cultures, respectively, supports that particular experience within each culture, whether it is an apparition of Mary or whether it is a memory of a past life. While this anecdotal evidence is rather ordinary, it does demonstrate Harman's thesis that the beliefs and practices in any system are generated and continue to be supported because those same beliefs and practices are foundational to the life and existence of the system.

Harman's (1998) critique of the modern scientific worldview identifies its neglect of a critical area of human life – that of choosing and implementing fundamental value commitments. Thus, Harman argues, science has given little consideration to the subjective experience that is an essential part of being human, 'for it is in this realm of the subjective, the transcendent, and the spiritual that all societies have found the basis for their deepest value commitments and sense of meaning' (p. 24). Therefore, differing worldviews which originate from diverse cultures and regions are not wrong; rather they are complementary. Ultimately, Harman's contention is that Westerners who have been educated in a scientific/ technological world tend to assume with some confidence that their scientific view of reality is the correct one and superior to a pre-scientific or primitive understanding. However, they must also recognise that others may see reality through different cultural windows which accentuate other qualities and elements in human experience. Certainly, a combination of perspectives is required if a holistic view of reality is to be realised. This may encourage individuals to derive meaning from the totality of human knowledge and experience, while also emphasising an underlying connectedness and unity.

There are many other instances when an understanding of spirituality intersects Western and Eastern worldviews. In discussing the word 'spirit', Wong (2005) suggests that the word *qi* may best describe Chinese spirituality and he shows an alignment with the Greek *pneuma*, Hebrew *ruah*, Sanskrit *prana* and Latin *spiritus*, all of which may be interpreted as 'wind', 'breath' and/or 'spirit'. Citing Lindqvist (1991), Wong identifies the three roughly horizontal strokes which compose the pictograph for the Chinese character *qi* as 'representing parallel layers of clouds arising from the condensation of moisture, thus denoting "air, vapour or gas"' (Wong, 2005, p. 154). He notes that the later addition of a pictograph for rice, which was inserted under the horizontal strokes, was probably intended to show 'the vapours rising out of a saucepan of boiling rice' (ibid.). These vapours may be interpreted as 'breath' which, in many cultures, is used metaphorically as the energy of life or spirit. However, Wong further ascertains that *qi* is a term that is central for the two dominant intellectual traditions in China that influence all aspects of life: Daoism and Confucianism. He argues that while a multiplicity of terms have been used to translate *qi* into English, it is often left untranslated, which would imply that while there are some commonalities, there are also significant differences. The differences, it would seem, are related to the differences noted by Nakagawa (2000) between Eastern and Western perspectives as discussed earlier because, as Wong asserts, *qi* is all-encompassing; it may not be relegated to matter alone, nor must it be confined to spirit. Citing Tu, in order to give emphasis to his argument, Wong says:

> The dichotomy of spirit and matter is not at all applicable . . . the most basic stuff that makes the cosmos is neither solely spiritual nor material but both. It is a vital force. This vital force must not be conceived of either as disembodied spirit or as pure matter.
>
> (Tu, 1998, cited in Wong, 2005, p. 155)

Finally, it is pertinent to note here that much of New Age and/or alternative understandings of contemporary spirituality in the West actually tend to sit astride both Eastern and Western perspectives where there is a focus on unity, oneness and the interconnectedness of all things. This has become evident amongst those scientists who have been examining new paradigms which reflect spirituality, although it is equally evident that there are many scientists who reject religion and a notion of God or a greater power beyond the physical world. Interestingly, many of the latter reside amongst other public intellectuals when making disparaging comments about religion and God, because they continue to frame their arguments in institutional religious language, often with specific references to religious texts from mainstream religions such as Christianity.[3] Hay (2006) commented on this tendency amongst the participants of his research studies: 'It was striking to see how often they continued to use orthodox religious language – and this included people who were very remote from the church' (p. 56). Their arguments often tended to reveal a lack of recognition that religion and spirituality were not one and the same (p. 48). Of course, there are always exceptions. One instance is the self-declared agnostic Carl Sagan who, though critical of formal religion which promotes a personal God, recognises a link between science and spirituality:

> Science is not only compatible with spirituality; it is a profound source of spirituality. When we recognize our place in an immensity of light-years and in the passage of ages, when we grasp the intricacy, beauty, and subtlety of life, then that soaring feeling, that sense of elation and humility combined, is surely spiritual.
>
> (Sagan, 1996, p. 29)

Many quotes as well have been attributed to Einstein, which suggest that he recognised something 'other', a spirit of things, which had little to do with formal religion.[4]

However, the former group of scientists are the ones that concern us in this discussion, since their focus on interconnectedness and a sense of oneness suggest their awareness of the spiritual dimension of life. While an extensive discussion of these alternative views is beyond the remit of this chapter, a few pertinent ideas and arguments will help to inform this discussion.

One well-known researcher in the field is David Hay, who began his professional life as a zoologist but who, in his later years, developed an interest in spirituality. The opening lines of his book, appropriately titled *Something There* (2006), reveal the fascination he has for this other dimension:

> It's to do with transcendent or spiritual experience . . . like the Wordsworthian idea of a presence rolling through all things, an un-named power, God or the gods. Or it could just be the wisdom of the unconscious . . . the point about it is that it feels as if it is coming from somewhere else, or outside.
>
> (Hay, 2006, p. ix)

Hay's significant contribution to the debate is that spirituality is primordial; it is natural to the human condition and relationality is its essence:

The physical and emotional intimacy of relationship both inside and outside the womb is intense and it is immediate. It is very obvious that the biological process of becoming a human being is the extreme opposite of an isolated, abstract affair. It is here, in this most natural of processes, that relationship and relational consciousness is made manifest as the primordial mode of being-in-the-world.

(Hay, 2006, p. 141)

Another well-known scientist who has moved the science/religion/spirituality argument forward is Laszlo (2008). He contends that a fundamental factor of the new paradigm in the sciences does not pertain to technology. Rather, it confirms something that has been experienced and understood by much of humankind, particularly traditional and Indigenous people. This key aspect is the close connection people have to one another and to the cosmos. It is something that has been neglected and even denied by people who live in a world dominated by rational, scientific thinking, because they have not yet found a rational scientific explanation for it. Lazlo argues that, for a long time, this knowledge has been largely intuitive but, with expanding scientific frontiers, it is now being confirmed, particularly with quantum physics, which 'began to indicate that the "oneness" people sometimes experience is not delusory and that the explanation of it is not beyond the ken of sciences' (p. 3). Laszlo reminds us of how important it is for people to rediscover this wisdom because he believes it is vital for the continuation of human civilisation and, possibly, the survival of the human species. He emphasises his argument by revisiting and extending the Delphian oracle: 'Know thyself as part of an interconnected rapidly changing world' (ibid.).

Similarly, in the preface to the thirty-fifth anniversary edition of his book, *The Tao of Physics*, Capra (2010) argues that his philosophy 'engenders a profound sense of connectedness, of context, of relationship, of belonging' (p. 8). He proceeds to identify the commonalities between spirituality and ecology by arguing that 'the experience of being connected with all of nature, of belonging to the universe, is the very essence of spirituality' (ibid.). Thus, the fundamental basis for Capra's thesis is that:

Connectedness, relationship, and community are fundamental concepts of ecology; and connectedness, relationship, and belonging are the essence of religious [spiritual][5] experience. I believe therefore that ecology is the ideal bridge between science and spirituality.

(Capra, 2010, p. 9)

Other well-known scientists whose ideas may be recognised as belonging to an alternative worldview are Rupert Sheldrake and Ken Wilber. Their writings (for instance, Sheldrake, 2012; Wilber, 1998; 2006) would support the argument that scientific inquiry is reductive and objective and rests on the assumption that science can provide all the answers. Both of them, in turn, argue against this belief that has been pervasive in Western societies throughout the past two centuries; and both explore the possibility of a complementary relationship between science and spirituality.

On the other side, writings from a theological and religious stance which have looked at links to science come from people like Thomas Berry, Brian Swimme, Matthew Fox and Bede Griffiths, amongst many others. While there is, certainly, a wealth of literature that focuses on different understandings and perceptions of contemporary spirituality, the above discussion has drawn on just a select group of writers and their perspectives of a transcendent reality. They come from different regions and a range of contexts that encompass Christian, secular and New Age spirituality. Although restricted, this selection is sufficient for the purpose of this chapter since they present some insights that bridge religion and spirituality which have been influential in informing contemporary understandings of spirituality in the Western world. In later chapters we will engage with other perspectives, also derived from scientific fields, which will be relevant to other aspects of contemporary understandings of spirituality. Finally, to conclude this section, a quote from William Bloom on contemporary spirituality:

> Contemporary Spirituality emerges from all the diverse traditions in our global village. It approaches spirituality with a multicultural and interfaith attitude, and recognises the difference between spirituality and religion. It is centrally concerned with individual spiritual experience as the starting point for exploration and development. Its values and beliefs are holistic, recognising the intimate interdependence of all life.
>
> (Bloom, 2009)

It is quite probable that the widespread interest and the abundance of literature over the past few decades have been motivating factors for educators to investigate the role of spirituality in the lives of children and young people. The next section will examine a selection of specific research studies from Australia, Britain, Canada and the United States to identify findings that are relevant for the ideas and arguments that are offered in the later chapters. The discussion will be restricted to these countries since they share much with one another in terms of culture and education systems and, therefore, the key factors that emerge in the studies should have relevance for the lives of children and young people in each of these countries. As well, it is more than possible that they will raise pertinent issues for children and young people elsewhere.

## Some relevant research studies into children and young people's spirituality

An early study that informed and influenced my own work was the research conducted by David Hay and Rebecca Nye, which was reported in their book *The Spirit of the Child* (1998). Hay and Nye's research involved thirty-eight primary school children, aged between 6 and 11, and in her discussion of the findings, Nye articulated the concept of relational consciousness:

- An unusual level of *consciousness* or perceptiveness, relative to other passages of conversation spoken by that child.
- Conversation expressed in a context of how the child *related* to things, other people, him/herself, and God [emphasis in the original text].

(Hay & Nye, 1998, p. 113)

Around the same time, religious educators Harris and Moran claimed that spirituality was alive and well amongst the young people with whom they worked. The characteristics they identified were:

its connectedness, its relational and communal character, which is in contrast to a privatized and individualistic spirituality. The impulse towards connectedness places the practice of justice in a special and privileged place, with justice understood as 'fidelity to the demands of all our relations'. Such justice includes not only our relations to other human beings; it includes our relations to the nonhuman universe as well: to the other animals, the trees, the ocean, the earth, and the ozone layer

(Harris & Moran, 1998, p. 46)

Furthermore, an Australian study into young people's perceptions of the future conducted by Richard Eckersley discovered that:

their dreams for Australia were of a society that placed less emphasis on the individual, competition, material wealth and enjoying 'the good life', and more on community and family, cooperation and the environment. Some expressed their wishes in terms of a greater recognition of the 'natural', 'human' or 'spiritual' aspects of life.

(Eckersley, 1997, p. 245)

A few years later, Eckersley (2004) observes that we are currently living in a world of 'promises, perils and paradoxes' (p. 211) where amazing scientific and technological discoveries are living alongside an upsurge in religious fundamentalism. Thus, Eckersley recognises the emerging links between science and religion (see Chapter 12, pp. 211–228) and notes that, while science had generated our current culture which emphasises materialism and individualism, the movement towards recognising our connectedness and interdependence with the world around us is providing a more spiritual and communal perspective.

Another perspective on understanding spirituality and its importance in well-being came from an Australian evaluation report (O'Connell Consultancy, 2000) that was produced in response to six cases of youth suicide in the Hume Region in 1999. It identified the difference between religiosity and spirituality (p. 11) and the need to address the spiritual dimension of young people's lives that is beyond the physical dimension of human existence. Spirituality was perceived as 'aspects of connection including to significant other adults, peers and parents, faith or belief in something larger than the self, and high self-esteem are all aspects of spirituality' (ibid.). This was further acknowledged at the 10th Annual Suicide Prevention Australia National Conference,[6] in Brisbane in June 2003, where the main theme was 'The role of spirituality in suicide prevention' and where related themes of identity, belonging and meaning were also discussed.

What was significant for me was that the findings by Eckersley (1997) and O'Connell Consultancy (2000), which came out of the Australian secular context, both identified spirituality as an aspect of humanness which needed to be addressed in the promotion of an individual's wellbeing. What is more, the description of spirituality was aligned with the concepts that were also used by people coming out of a religious framework as discussed above – that is, spirituality was about connectedness and relationships.

An explanatory note is needed here for those who are not quite familiar with Australian secularity. Australia was born at the height of the European Enlightenment and as Gascoigne (2002) claims, the values, reason and scientific progress, which reflected that period, fostered a distinctly secular influence during the formative years of White Settlement in Australian history. Alongside this was the direction and authority of nineteenth-century Irish Catholicism brokered by the Irish Catholic bishops who were concerned about the large number of Irish who were settled in Australia. Not surprisingly, then, early Australian culture and identity emerged with dualism as an essential feature: British Protestantism influenced by the Enlightenment as one strand and Irish Catholicism as the other. Evans (2010), in a national report to the International Academy of Comparative Law, noted this element in the Australian psyche when she stated that Australia is a broadly secular state with Christian influences (p. 87) and that Catholic-Protestant sectarianism has, for some time, played a divisive role in Australian public life. However, she acknowledges that while religious arguments and commitments have often had some airing in Australian political and public life, they have rarely been given the prominence that they might attract in other countries (ibid.). One outcome of this dualistic feature is that the Australian Constitution, which clearly separates religion from public life, nonetheless has a clause in Section 116 which recognises that the individual is free to follow and practise a religion. Some Australian states also specifically protect the individual's right to religious freedom.

A further outcome of this dualism is that, on the one hand, religious education is not offered as part of the core curriculum in government schools – but some voluntary faith-based programmes are allowed as an extra. On the other hand, faith-based schools have been receiving government funding since the Whitlam Government in the 1970s and they have the freedom to teach their faith traditions as part of their core curriculum. In general, many Australian children who attend state schools do not receive formal learning about the religious and/or the spiritual dimensions in life.

To return to the concepts of spirituality discussed earlier, these were some of the writings that informed my initial research into spirituality; therefore I began from the foundational idea that spirituality was about a deep connection that the individual experienced to others in the world and for some, to something beyond the physical world. Further, it appeared that attention needed to be given to the quality of these relationships if spirituality was to be nurtured and allowed to grow.

### Findings from some early research in Australia

I then embarked on a series of small research projects that examined perceptions, expressions and experiences of the spirituality of young people. The first, in 2000, was a collaborative project (Engebretson, de Souza & Salpietro, 2001) funded by the Australian Research Council Small Grant Project Scheme and it explored the religiosity of two groups of adolescents at either end of the middle school spectrum, seeking to understand the ways in which they commonly perceived and expressed spirituality. The focus on the middle years was a response to the era when research studies indicated that many students experienced a sense of frustration and, indeed, alienation during these particular years (Braggett, 1997) and schools were being called upon to discover ways in which to address problems associated with this age group. I should note here that these young people would now be young adults and their current perceptions and experiences will provide a point of interest for contemporary studies, given the political contexts, characterised by cultural and religious diversity and prejudice, within which children and young people are growing up today.

Drawing on the literature and some informal discussions with students, five categories emerged that related to the ways in which young people thought about and expressed their religiosity and spirituality, and these provided the structure of the open-ended questionnaire that was used:

1   Mystery and awareness of a Supreme Being or Power. (This category contained questions about the student's awareness of a transcendent dimension in life.)
2   Inner peace and emotional wellbeing. (This category contained questions about the student's awareness of their own identity, and their reflections on meaning.)
3   Values and justice. (This category sought to discover the extent to which the student's spirituality was coloured by an awareness of justice.)
4   Relationships. (Here the students were asked to reflect on the important relationships in their lives in terms of their spirituality.)
5   Influence of a religious tradition. (This section sought to discover the links, if any, between religiosity and spirituality in the lives of the students.)

In the end, 240 Year 6 students (aged 11 to 12 years) and 338 Year 9 students (aged 14 to 15 years) completed the questionnaire. Of the 578 students, 472 indicated they were Catholic, 52 were from other Christian traditions, 17 were from non-Christian traditions and 35 stated they had no religion. Two students did not respond to this question.

The findings indicated that a large majority of students displayed a fairly positive spiritual dimension to their lives in terms of the quality of their relationships and the connectedness they experienced. They also showed that there was a distinct decline in positive responses to the impact of their respective religious traditions and teachings between the primary (more positive) and the secondary (less positive) students. As a result, there was a certain tension as students moved away from the impact of their immediate relationship circle of family and close friends in primary school to the wider circle of societal influences as they passed through their teenage years. For some of the Year 9 students, seeking alternative answers to their questions, particularly ones that were more suitable to their own levels of intellectual and emotional maturity, was part of their passage to young adulthood. The research also identified a crucial issue for some young people who did not appear to have a significant person in their network of relationships to whom they could turn or confide in times of distress. This is an important finding for any parent or professional working with young people and shall be discussed in later chapters.

Since this study focused on children in Catholic schools where religious education is part of the core curriculum, it was not surprising to find that many were positive about their own spirituality in terms of connectedness to the Other[7] in the human and non-human world. This was despite the fact that many in the older group yielded less favourable responses to questions related to church attendance and other religious practices, thus reinforcing the fact that religious institutions were losing their hold on their communities, particularly younger members.

A second qualitative study in 2002 (see de Souza, Cartwright & McGilp, 2004; de Souza 2003a) set out to investigate the spiritual wellbeing of a group of 16- to 20-year-old young people who lived in regional Victoria. The intention was to move the study beyond those young people who belonged to a religious tradition. The first step was to identify a range of different organisations that existed in the regional town from which young people could be included to form a small sample group. In order to access these young people a number of relevant educational institutions and other organisations were approached through an initial telephone call and a follow-up visit. Twenty-two young people aged from 16 to 20 and one young person aged 15 from across these institutions agreed to participate in the research. They came from a range of backgrounds: some were in secondary schools, some attended alternative educational programmes, some were seeking work and some were in traineeships/employment.

The research instrument was a semi-structured personal interview that lasted approximately 45 minutes. A list of focus questions was drawn up that concentrated on the relational dimension of young people's lives and the influences that determined their values and actions, which contributed to their self-esteem and self-worth. Accordingly, there were items included across four broad relational areas which indicated the individual's sense of connectedness – that is, to the Self, to others and to the physical and non-physical world. The participants were also invited to offer their perceptions of how their corresponding experiences might help them to interpret life's meaning and purpose:

1   Relationship to oneself – their self-esteem and awareness of their own iden-
    tity and the impact this may have on their attitudes, values and behaviour.
2   Relationship to others – who is important/influential in their lives, how does
    this affect their values; for instance, does it promote action for community
    and social justice?
3   Relationship to the world – how do they respond to nature and creation,
    music and beauty? What do they value in the world, what are their interests
    and how do they spend their free time? How do they respond to action for
    the care of the world?
4   Relationship to a Supreme Being or Power – do they have a sense of mystery
    and wonder, what is the purpose of life, death, joy and suffering? Are they
    aware of a transcendent dimension in their lives; do they desire time for quiet
    reflection and inner space?

The findings revealed different levels of connectedness that the participants experienced to the Other and this was reflected in their values and dreams for the future and their sense of wellbeing. There were quite significant differences between the background of the participants, ranging from some who were attending private faith-based schools to one, a 20-year-old, who had been homeless at the age of 14, lived on the streets of Melbourne and, subsequently, spent some time in jail. This meant that there were different levels of maturity in their relationships and sense of connectedness. Nonetheless, a common factor could be seen to emerge, where most showed some awareness of their lives as a journey. Some reflected on the difficult relationships they had experienced in their early years which, they believed, had led to alienation and disengagement with their families and communities. More importantly, it became clear that they had a particular relationship to at least one person, whether parent, grandparent or friend, that ultimately led them to re-engage with their communities and reshape their values and dreams for the future. The fact that someone cared enough to always be there for them provided them with a sense of belonging and a realisation that they should care for themselves and take responsibility for the direction of their lives.

The responses of these young people showed them to be at different levels of connectedness and spiritual maturity and certain features characterised these different stages. At the first stage, where most of them were located, their sense of connectedness was intertwined with the Other in their immediate world. For some, however, their connectedness stretched to include the Other in the wider world. Their sense of identity and self-esteem corresponded to the stage at which they found themselves, as did their attitudes, actions and behaviours. Their family and friends were important and they appreciated time spent with them; but they also spoke of their need for 'space' and 'quiet times'. Accordingly, they mentioned activities that they resorted to as outlets for individual creative expression. Significantly, their perceptions of the important times in their lives were linked to their rites of passage within their families and communities. An unexpected response – given that many of the participants did not belong to a religious tradition and religious influences had not been part of their lives – was that nearly all of the participants spoke of their sense of, and a connection to, a presence outside their physical world. Indeed, so as not to influence the responses, the researchers had taken care not to speak of God, but instead alluded to the possibility of 'something out there' or the existence of a 'Supreme Being'. Nevertheless, in the words of one 15-year-old who had left home at 13 because of an abusive situation and who had no links to a faith tradition:

> I feel that God is there . . . it's not something that is just decided in my head, it's a very real thing for me . . . I think God speaks to us in many ways and a lot of that is through other people . . . if I am going through a hard time and my friend will say something and I think, 'yes, that's it', I think that's God using them . . . I believe that God has great things in store for me.
> (From the unpublished transcript of the research project 'Perceptions of their spiritual wellbeing of 16–20-year-old young people in a regional centre in Victoria': de Souza, 2003a; de Souza *et al.*, 2004)

It is possible, of course, that this young person, despite no formal religious instruction or influences, had absorbed the trappings of a Western culture that is dominated by a Christian worldview so that in many areas of her life, especially in the various media outlets which are so influential, there are often references to God. Hay (2006) identified a similar element in his research; that is, 'the importance of the cultural context in which an experience (any kind of experience) occurs for the construction of meaning' (p. 12). Thus, for young people who are trying to make meaning of challenging or difficult life experiences, a beneficent God-like figure, guiding angels and spirits or heroes fighting evil creatures from beyond the physical realm, form an attractive proposition. Indeed, this kind of attraction could account for the large following of films and TV series that suggest such possibilities.[8] Erricker *et al.* (1994) noted in their research into children's worldviews that this was an element of informal learning and argued that teachers need to 'affirm the wisdom they [children] acquired elsewhere and assist them through difficult passages in their experience' (p. 4).

A third smaller study, also conducted in 2002, provided yet another dimension to understanding young people's spirituality (de Souza, 2003b). In this case, ten fourth-year pre-service religious education students volunteered to take part in the research. They each participated in an in-depth interview in the last few weeks of their university course. The aim was to discover their perceptions of the elements that had nurtured their own spirituality and sense of the sacred. There was some expectation that these young people who had made a deliberate choice to become religious educators would provide further insights about the spiritual dimension in their lives. A list of focus questions was given to the participants some days before the interview, which allowed them time for reflection:

*A sense of values – one's longings and ideals:*

- Consider the values that are important to you. How are these reflected in your relationships, actions and decisions?
- Who or what helped you develop these values?
- How important is it for you to share these values with others, and how would you do it?

*A sense of purpose – a reason for Being:*

- What fires your passion, what are your dreams?
- Who or what influences you in making important decisions?
- From where or whom do you draw your strength?
- Reflect on some significant moments in your life – what made them significant?

*A sense of the sacred:*

- What do you understand by sacred?
- What people, places, objects, etc. inspire in you a sense of the sacred? Would you like to elaborate on this?

In general, the findings reflected how the relational dimension of their lives was a vital factor in self-awareness and how their connectedness with family and close friends had contributed to their sense of self and to becoming whole people. Of interest was that only one made a direct reference to religious practice as an influential factor in their spiritual journey, but all spoke of experiencing a Transcendent or Divine Presence in their everyday lives. As we had hoped, there were levels of maturity and stability that were evident in these participants' stories which could have been attributed to the fact that as pre-service religious educators they had been encouraged to reflect on their lives as a spiritual journey. However, the limitations of language, it appeared, made it difficult for each student to speak of deeply meaningful experiences which had stimulated a response from the depth of their soul. This highlighted the fact that in a secular education system and society, where people do not speak readily of sacred and spiritual experiences, appropriate language or space is not easily available to allow such discussions to take place. Nonetheless, these participants reinforced the idea that connectedness was an essential factor in their spiritual wellbeing and their relational experiences reflected a level of maturity and wisdom.

In drawing conclusions from these studies, I realised that there was more to the notion of relational consciousness as discussed by Hay and Nye (1998) in relation to understanding spirituality. What our research studies had shown was that there was a distinct movement in levels of consciousness that was reflected in the connectedness young people experienced. This was particularly obvious because we found that some participants across the various studies responded in the same way to a specific series of questions. For instance, two of the studies were conducted around the time of the Tampa incident in Australia in 2001.[9] There had been a succession of boats containing asylum seekers arriving on the north-west coast of Australia for months and this had whipped up a frenzy amongst politicians whose negative pronouncements about 'boat people', 'queue jumpers' and 'illegals' were frequently portrayed in the media. Between the media and the politicians, the campaign to vilify and malign asylum seekers had been successful, and it had generated a deep fear of the otherness of the Other amongst a large number of Australians – encapsulated clearly by the then prime minister, John Howard, who stated, 'We don't want people like that' – thereby emphasising the 'us and them' attitude which had become dominant.

It was this scenario that was used to draw responses from the participants in two research studies and the majority from both studies answered in a rather predictable fashion – they repeated the negativity they had read or heard in their homes, on the street and in the media. In each group, however, there was a small minority whose connectedness to the Other had moved beyond their immediate circle of family, friends and community. These participants appeared to feel levels of empathy with people who were quite different from themselves – such as asylum seekers. However, the most interesting and significant responses were from those participants whose reflexive responses had echoed the majority but who had paused midstream, considered what they had said, and changed to show more empathy and acceptance.

## Shift of consciousness: A contemporary spiritual paradigm

It was the responses from these participants in my early research that led me to the idea that there was a certain movement in the consciousness of these young people that had shifted upwards and outwards from their initial experiences of feeling connected to the people around them who lived and shared similar life-styles. It was almost as if their relational awareness had moved through different layers, one emerging from the other, thereby providing a second layer and so on. It was at the first or depth level that young people experienced a sense of belonging within family and community. However, as other layers were superimposed but also encompassed what was there before, these experiences grew to connect with friends, groups and networks as the individual moved beyond the familial environment to include wider social contexts. A sense of belonging provides individuals with a sense of self and place. They develop an identity as family member, friend, member of a team and eventually, member of the wider society. A sense of belonging helps to ground the individual by providing a particular way of being in the world which, in turn, helps individuals to make meaning of their life experiences and gives them a sense of purpose, including a sense of responsibility to the group to which one belongs. Furthermore, it helps them determine how they will respond to or act in different situations and towards the Other. Such connectedness is concerned with the relational dimension of human lives that is instrumental in guiding individuals' actions/achievements and reactions/responses and, finally, their way of engaging with the world. Therefore, such expressions may be recognised as spirituality. Expressions of this relational dimension, then, become expressions of spirituality.

It is important to note that positive experiences of connectedness, especially in the early years of childhood, provide the individual with a secure sense of identity and belonging as well as self-awareness and self-esteem. If the individual is grounded in the wellbeing that this foundational base provides, it is more likely that he or she will be encouraged to reach out into a wider circle, to express feelings of empathy and compassion for the Other who is different. For some, this may stretch beyond to the awe and wonder generated by experiences of mystery and transcendence in the human and non-human world.

While most of the participants across the studies displayed these attitudes and traits, there were some among them who had more negative experiences during their childhood which had led to alienation, confusion, despair and a lack of purpose. These may be recognised as the darker side of spirituality and I shall discuss this in Chapter 4. However, their respective stories reveal that it was a specific relationship that helped them to start believing in themselves and turn their lives around.

The findings from these studies which indicated the value of experiences of connectedness and the relational dimension in human spirituality had significant implications for the direction of my ongoing research, and I will discuss them in more detail at the end of this chapter; but for now, it is relevant to look at other pertinent studies that have been conducted over the past decade.

Another research study in Australia that focused on the spirituality of children was conducted by Hyde (2008). Hyde's doctoral study was informed by Hay and Nye's (1998) themes of spiritual sensitivity – awareness sensing, mystery sensing and value sensing (p. 87) – and set out to examine the spiritual dimension of children's lives to discover characteristics of their spirituality. It involved three Catholic primary schools in Melbourne, respectively located in an inner city, a suburban area and a rural area. Thirty-six children participated in the study: two groups of six from each school. One group consisted of Grade 5 students, approximately 10 years of age, and the second group were Grade 3 students, around 8 years in age. Hyde's visits to each school comprised of two-hour sessions per week over a period of five weeks. There were three meetings with each participant which lasted between 45 minutes to one hour. During the meeting the children were involved in activities as well as responding to questions and other stimuli. Hyde's findings identified four spiritual characteristics:

- The felt sense, which was about what was happening in the here and now and how the child drew upon bodily wisdom as a perceptive way of knowing (p. 93).
- Integrating awareness, which suggested children could operate at two levels of consciousness. One kept them absorbed on the task at hand but, at another level, they engaged in a free-flowing conversation with other students (p. 104).
- Weaving the threads of meaning allowed children to connect disparate information to compose a view and understanding of their world, which also influenced their relationships with the Other in the human world and, sometimes, in the non-human world (p. 122).
- Spiritual questing occurred when the student explored new and, perhaps, more authentic ways of connecting with the Self, others, the earth and, for some, with God (p. 138).

Hyde also identified two factors that appeared to inhibit children's spirituality:

- Material pursuit, where children showed a valuing of things above people. Hyde felt that this encouraged the child to focus on satisfying the desires of the outer/physical Self so that materialism and consumerism dominated their worldviews, thereby promoting a disconnection with the Other (pp. 156–157).
- Trivialising was a conscious or non-conscious strategy that allowed the child to mask their inner feelings and to outwardly show an attitude of complacency. Thus, some issues and feelings would be ignored and become part of the child's shadow (see Chapter 4 for more discussion of the shadow). Hyde observed that this was an action taken by children if they felt insecure and vulnerable in the group and, not surprisingly, led the child to experience a loss of meaning and purpose (p. 157).

For most parents and professionals who work with young children, it is not difficult to recognise these characteristics that Hyde noted, particularly the factors that impede children's spirituality in a context that is driven by economic and scientific rationalism and which neglects the spirit of the child.

Another Australian study conducted by Mason, Singleton and Webber (2007) examined the spirituality of adolescents and young adults (13–25 years) who were identified as 'Generation Y'. The lens through which the spirituality of these participants was examined and interpreted was distinctly Christian and was reflected in the definition of spirituality that was offered: spirituality is a conscious way of life based on a transcendent referent (p. 39). The study examined the participants' worldviews and values; sense of meaning and purpose; ways in which they found peace and happiness; their involvement in traditional religions and alternative forms of spirituality; and social and other influences that shaped their outlook and lifestyle. The findings revealed three types of spirituality amongst the participants: Traditional Spirituality, which included a belief in God and was discussed mainly in Christian terms; New Age Spirituality; and Secular Spirituality, which appeared to indicate a lack of belief in or doubt about God (pp. 301–304).

Also drawing on the research project conducted by Mason *et al.*, Hughes (2007), a senior researcher in the Christian Research Association which had partially funded the study, offered another interpretation: that essentially, the findings revealed that neither traditional religious frameworks nor alternative forms of spirituality were particularly important to young people. Existentialism appeared to be foundational to the way in which they viewed the world. Of importance were the relationships around which their lives revolved and which provided them with fun and excitement and which made their lives worthwhile. They wanted a peaceful and secure world where there was justice for all and care for the environment. Hughes, therefore, claimed that 'young people are rooted in this world in the present moment. For many, the idea of a spiritual dimension means little' (p. 200).

What is interesting here – if one examines the characteristics that Hughes identified – is that they are clearly linked to the relational dimension of young people's lives; that is, relationships to the Other in society and the world and to the environment. I would claim that this is, indeed, the essence of spirituality. However, for Hughes, spirituality is about a relationship with God. Thus, the lack of reference to God amongst these young people could have prompted Hughes to claim that they were not interested in the spiritual dimension of their lives. Nonetheless, Hughes does identify signs of spirituality since most of the young people, while unsure, were not closed to the idea of the existence of God and he made the following observation:

> In the depth of personal relationships, young people reach out beyond themselves. While they enter relationships with personal intentionality, they experience something in those relationships that transcends their individualism . . . this retreat had moved students beyond their own preoccupations with body image, with style and fashion, with success and failure. They had listened to each other. In 'I-Thou' experiences, to use Buber's term, they had been touched by something that transcended them.
>
> (Hughes, 2007, p. 200)

Therefore, it is possible that if Hughes had examined spirituality as relational rather than as a relationship to or belief in God, he would have recognised that the spiritual dimension in the lives of these young people was alive and well, since they expressed a connectedness to and care for the Other in society and the world and to the environment. This is one of the problems with traditional understandings of spirituality when it is used interchangeably with religion and religiosity. In addition, it continues to arise when an understanding of spirituality is restricted to interpretations in religious frameworks, rather than in an arena encompassed by the breadth and depth of human experience.

Arguably, the 2007 study by Mason *et al.* may not claim any generalisability about its findings in relation to Gen Y (13–25 year olds) since it was not made clear whether the background of the participants in fact reflected the rather large number of social and religious cultures, as well as youth sub-cultures, that characterise and influence the beliefs and values of Gen Y, or whether the group was composed largely of young people who, at some time in their lives, had exposure to the teachings of the Christian tradition.

Mason *et al.* reinforced the findings from a much earlier study (Crawford & Rossiter, 1993) which concluded that young people were at a high water mark of secularisation, so that their way of making meaning and developing purpose in their lives and their perceptions of traditional religion were different from previous generations. Finally, Crawford and Rossiter identified that they had a different approach to understanding and forming their identities and that relativism, indifferentism, the privatisation of beliefs and religion as an option were all traits of young people in the 1990s.

Other studies of the spirituality of children and young people echo the concept of connectedness and relationality, although many of these were linked to exploring religious influences on children's way of being and thinking. For instance, Erricker *et al.* (1994) found that children used their relationships with family and friends to develop their own individuality and self-esteem and to make sense of the whole mixture of beliefs, desires, emotions and intentions (p. 6). In this, they support Donaldson's (1987) claim that the growth of consciousness corresponds to the growth of the intellect as well as the individual's ability to control their own thinking (p. 123).

Moving across the Atlantic, a discussion of the spirituality of American youth within a religious framework comes from Smith (2005), who claims that many teenagers are very involved in religion, that their religious beliefs and practices are important parts of their lives and that faith provides them with guidance and resources for knowing how to live well (p. 4). Smith argues that if we get a picture that American youth are not religious it is because surveys usually neglect the religious aspect of their lives (ibid.) when, in fact, 'the vast majority of US teenagers identify themselves as Christians, either among the broad array of American Protestant denominations or as Catholic' (p. 68). His analysis of some relevant survey findings points to the fact that for the majority of US teenagers, expressions of religion and spirituality are part of their family life. He goes further to assert that it is only 'a very small fraction of American teenagers' who are spiritual seekers along alternative pathways, and that the claim that many American youth are being influenced by these non-religious worldviews has been 'greatly overstated' (p. 78).

A somewhat different picture of American young people is provided by Moore and Wright (2008) who, together with a collection of academics from practical theology, set out to identify 'life-giving elements of religions and culture, and critiquing that which thwarts life' (p. 2). The authors examined religious and cultural effects that were life-affirming and which affected the spirituality of children and youth, that is, 'the paths of hope in the lives of young people, in their spiritual traditions and communities, and in the world as it is' (p. 3). They identified several influential themes that engendered both positive and negative experiences apparent in young lives today, including: giftedness and the need for self-expression; experiences of marginalisation linked to gender and race issues;

the lack of traditional family and community mentoring and religious influences; the benefits and problems of multiple identities; and the impact on their lives of social problems, such as violence, a media-dominated materialistic culture and poverty (see pp. 7–11).

There would appear to be a distinct difference in the perceptions of Smith (2005) and the authors contained in Moore and Wright's collection (2008), with the former being quite upbeat and optimistic about the religious influence on the spirituality of American youth as compared to the latter group, who identify many problems for children and young people's spirituality in what they describe as a troubling world. Importantly, however, one may discern an underlying theme in all the writings, where connectedness and supportive relationships provide the keys to nurturing and to positive expressions of spirituality, whether these come from the religious practices of the family and community or from other sources within society. The authors in the latter group also identified various contemporary elements that hindered young people's spirituality or their way of Being in the world, thereby affecting their identity, self-esteem and wellbeing.

Two other research studies, based in Canada, come from the respective fields of Christian youth work and sociology. While these do not specifically investigate spirituality, they do look at the relational dimension of young people's lives and their wellbeing; therefore, they are pertinent to this discussion. The first is from Overholt and Penner (2005), who draw on the findings from three surveys into young people in Canada by the sociologist Reginald W. Bibby from over a period of approximately sixteen years to discuss strategies that they believe will be relevant to youth workers across Canada and the US, regardless of any particular religious framework. Of the nine themes listed (p. 3) the first is about relationships, where the two most important interpersonal values for teens are friendship and being loved (p. 138). However, it is significant to note, for the purposes of this discussion, that all the themes are linked to expressions of relationality and connectedness – they are about an individual's awareness of and response to something other which is outside themselves, whether this is framed by community or culture. Alternatively, the responses could have been to something deep within themselves, whether they were aware of or conscious of their inner lives, and the impact it may have on their outer actions, personal identity and self-worth. The role of non-conscious learning and its effect on spirituality will be discussed in Chapters 4 and 5.

While Overholt and Penner's research was informed by Bibby's data collected between 1984 and 2005, Bibby's (2009) later survey, *Project Teen Canada 2008*, was once again able to identify friendship and being loved as the most valued characteristics (p. 39) among the 3,600 15 to 19 year olds who participated in the study across Canada (see p. 214). He also found that, despite the fact that four in ten people were involved in a faith tradition, there were growing numbers who, rather than turning to religion, were turning to each other to help them deal with the issues in their everyday as well as in their search for answers to ultimate questions (p. 209). Further, Bibby noted the cultural and religious diversity (p. 126) and the positive interaction between people of different cultures (p. 128): '95% of close friends are *found at school,* regardless of one's birthplace and parentage' (p. 129). Amidst these findings, it is possible to discern the importance of relationships and experiences of connectedness amongst the participants, which are important factors in their sense of wellbeing. Other findings from this survey identified the fragmented lives of young people (p. 186) and some negative impacts from overuse of technology and social media (p. 187). These aspects will be discussed in Chapters 2 and 3.

Yet another research study (Collins-Mayo *et al.*, 2010) that was motivated by a distinctly Christian worldview concentrated on those young people who were both 'unchurched' and 'dechurched' (p. 3). The researchers were social and youth workers who investigated the views of 300 young people from 8 to 23 years of age who were involved in one of 34 Christian youth and community outreach projects around England over a five-year period, from 2005 to 2010. They described Christian consciousness as young people's knowledge and understanding of Christianity, one that publicly offered religious and moral worldviews. They found that the participants had an awareness of Christianity in relation to their own sense of personal spirituality, religious identity and faith (p. 29). Data were collected through structured questionnaires and semi-structured interviews which were designed to elicit information about young people's religious identities, their beliefs and values, and whether their involvement in Christian youth work had assisted them in their search for meaning in Christianity or other religious frameworks (p. 29). Given the focused selection of participants, the findings showed that there was a 'Christian heritage' (p. 116) to the spirituality of these young people; and their concern for the ethical wellbeing of themselves and others appeared to be drawn from Christian thinking as well. Furthermore, while many young people were not involved with the Church, they had some appreciation for its role in society and also for church buildings. Finally, relationships with family and other adult mentors were important to them (pp. 116–117).

An additional conclusion that may be drawn from the findings of this study is that it distinguished particular expressions of young people's spirituality within a religious framework. Implicit in the findings are the importance of relationships for the participants; these also provided them with a worldview that guided their moral understanding and concern for the wellbeing of themselves and others. Moreover, by finding themselves in a community that shared their values and ethical concerns, these young people were able to experience a sense of belonging and having a place within the group. Therefore, while the study by Collins-Mayo *et al.* into the faith of Generation Y was distinctly linked to religious influences and worldviews, there was, again, an underlying theme of connectedness and the relational dimension of young people's lives which reflected their worldviews and expressions of spirituality.

Finally, to bring this discussion of research and literature in spirituality to a close, I would like to examine some additional perspectives, namely from the fields of health and wellbeing. Culliford's (2011) thesis on the psychology of spirituality contends that spirituality is about wholeness. He argues that the fragmentation of contemporary life provides an incentive for the individual to rediscover the 'essential qualities of indivisibility and non-separateness' and to recognise that adversity is the beginning point for spiritual development (p. 32). Aligning spiritual development with Fowler's stages of faith development, Culliford argues that we are each born with a spiritual core or 'true self' – which he names the 'pristine ego' – which very soon becomes obscured by the 'everyday ego' (ibid.) and it is necessary that both these halves are reconciled in order to experience 'a homecoming' and to find the Authentic Self, where the whole brain works as one. Culliford argues against any attempts to analyse spirituality but, rather, he suggests that various themes may be used to identify spirituality, for instance: joy and wonder; meaning and purpose; God, religion and belief; love and wholeness; an inner source of knowledge; and universality and reciprocity – what goes around must come around (pp. 53–54).

To sum up, Culliford supports the notion that spirituality is innate to the human condition (we are born with it) and that while the inner Self co-exists with the outer Self, the latter dominates, thereby creating the dualistic nature that so often is perceived as a characteristic of the human person. Finally, it may be observed that the themes Culliford identifies are, indeed, responses of the individual to something other than Self – to the inner Self, to the Other in community, to the Other in the physical world and/or to a Transcendent Other. Hence, we have the notion of relationality emerging again as these themes are no less than expressions and experiences of connectedness.

A complementary view about spirituality in health is offered by Hvidt (2013), who provides a lucid account of health-related research literature on meaning and coping and identifies the growing references to spirituality as something distinct from religion. He argues that the distinction was first made by French Catholic theologians in the 1930s with the creation of a dictionary of spirituality which was meant to focus on the ascetic and mystical dimensions of religion (p. 111). Noting that Jesuit theologians made distinctions between the doctrine of faith (theology) and the life of faith (spirituality), Hvidt contends that, historically, the real distinction lay between theology and spirituality – and it is only in the latter part of the twentieth century that the distinction was transferred to religion and spirituality. He attributes three reasons for this: the spread and influence of Eastern spirituality, which is also linked to New Age spirituality; spirituality has become a commodity in the search for happiness and wellbeing; and the relativisation of religious beliefs, which provides individuals with a wide selection of belief systems from which to choose (see pp. 111–112).

With Hvidt, we find distinctions between theological influences, which perceive spirituality as the practice of faith or the life of faith, and Eastern or New Age spirituality, which are seen as not quite the same thing. It is almost as if there is a hierarchical structure for spirituality where spirituality that is derived from religion – in particular, Christianity – is somehow more authentic than alternative versions, which are seen as linked to a materialistic, consumeristic world. Such an attitude towards spirituality is found amongst some theologians and religionists, where there is a sense that true spirituality belongs in the religious domain and is about a relationship with God or a Supreme Being, something beyond the physical world. Such an attitude also implies that one is only spiritual if one has a relationship with God, a supernatural being who exists beyond the physical realm. If anyone claims a spirituality outside this category, it is deemed as flawed or even fraudulent.

I have difficulty accepting this viewpoint. If, as I have been arguing, spirituality is an essential element of Being, *all* people are spiritual and while, for some, their spirituality may be grounded in this world, for others, spirituality soars beyond the confines of the material and physical realm in which we live. Such an understanding of spirituality includes all of humankind, including religionists and non-religionists, and is much more wholesome and holistic and has certainly much more relevance for a global pluralistic society that contextualises the lives of so many people in today's world.

It must be noted that one reason why Hvidt and others tend to reject the more recent use of the term 'spirituality' is because it has become overused and applied to so many different aspects of life that its meaning has become confused and infused with ambiguity. The lack of clarity that envelops the term has posed some challenges in relation to the validity of research and practice because of the uncertainty associated with interpreting the concept. I agree with Hvidt and others that the imprecise explanations and ambiguity of the term does present some problems and, perhaps, it is time to look more carefully at the concept and try to capture it more accurately. Accordingly, I will attempt to do this in the next section in order to explain how the concept is being used and applied in this book.

## A concept of contemporary spirituality and a spiritual continuum

It is plain from the preceding discussions that the concept of spirituality retains a certain ambiguity amongst scholars, religionists and practitioners. There appears to be intense reluctance in trying to pin it down and define it. It is possible that the reluctance is linked to the fact that, for many, spirituality has something to do with 'spirit', a 'going beyond' the physical world of humans into the realms of mystery and unknowing. In a contemporary world that is dominated by scientific reality and technology and consumed by material possessions and longings, the language needed to speak about mystical experiences and other worldliness has been lost. Consequently, the language to discuss spirituality has become confused. Concern is expressed that any attempt at defining spirituality may reduce the concept to only a part of what it is and that something may be left out. Accordingly, researchers and scholars invariably begin their presentations by explaining that they are not defining the concept. They then proceed to 'describe' how spirituality is being used in their research and produce a list of words – for instance, joy, delight, wonder, awe, truth and honesty, search for meaning and purpose, sacred spaces, self-discovery, sacred journeys and pilgrimage, kindness, care and compassion, empathy, dreams, freedom and self-transcendence, sacred rites and rituals and other religious activities and so on. Of course, by focusing research on one or more of these elements, the process remains reductive and the study, rather than being about research into spirituality, becomes a study of joy, wonder and so on. While these are recognised as spiritual expressions or experiences, they do not constitute the Whole. Under these circumstances, research into spirituality remains problematic.

If however, we accept the notion that spirituality pertains to and is implicit in the relational dimension of Being, we would need to allow that the individual's response to people and things that compose the Other – that is everyone and everything that is other than Self – can translate into experiences of joy, delight, wonder, awe, truth and honesty, search for meaning and purpose, sacred spaces, self-discovery, freedom and self-transcendence. Alternately, the response may originate from the dark side of spirituality and generate experiences of doubt, suffering, hurt, anger, dishonour, cruelty, alienation, disenchantment, despair and so on. What is important to note is that all these experiences have been, generally, recognised as either positive or negative elements in relationships or experiences of connectedness. They have also been alluded to as features of the light and shadow sides of spirituality and both aspects need to be recognised and addressed in any programme or practice that aims to nurture the whole person. The shadow side of spirituality is expanded upon in Chapter 4.

If we go further, we may detect in individuals the capacity to be self-reflective alongside the potential to develop a consciousness of the fact that they are relational beings who belong to and are a part of the Whole. We may also understand that their journey of self-discovery that reaches into the core of their Being – where they discover the common elements which bind them to the Other – also generates a journey outwards to rediscover the Other. I recall, when I was trying to articulate this insight that came from my early research (de Souza, 2003a, pp. 276–277), finding myself going to Merton, who clearly encapsulates this notion: 'I must look for my identity not only in God but in other[s]' (cited in Del Prete, 2002, p. 165) where 'the process of inner transformation that leads to self-discovery is simultaneously a process of discovering our deep relatedness to others' (ibid.). In other words, as an individual reaches the wider circle, they enter another realm of spiritual maturity or another level of consciousness, and the extended relationship they experience with the Other at this level may help them to go deeper within themselves to understand or, possibly, become aware of a less familiar part of their Being; that is, they may recognise that the Other is, in some way, the same as themselves. Thus, the widening circle of connectedness to the Other brings a deepening knowledge with a heightened awareness of the inner Self and encourages a deeper connectedness to the Self.

The culmination of the journeying may lead the individual to connect so deeply to the Other that the boundaries between Self and Other disintegrate and the Self merges into the Other. This is a point of Ultimate Unity, where the Self has moved beyond the duality implicit in a relationship and experiences a sense of oneness and union with the Whole: 'To be what we are requires that we realize our oneness, our existence in an "original unity"' (Del Prete, citing Merton, 2005, p. 165). Thus, the end point in human spiritual growth, the realm of Ultimate Unity, is where the individual has reached a level of consciousness or awareness that has sometimes been referred to as *Unity Consciousness* (Wilber, 1999, p. 440),[10] *Supermind* (Ghosh cited in Maitra, 2000, p. 56)[11] or *Cosmic Consciousness* (Bucke, 1901). The movement towards Ultimate Unity is an ever-swirling spiral built with layers of connectedness/relationships which span a lifetime – the spiritual journey.

A further consideration of this movement in spiritual consciousness suggests that as a new layer of relational awareness is superimposed on previous layers, it may be aligned with another level of spiritual growth in terms of reaching another level of consciousness[12] that raises awareness of the relational dimension of Being. With each accruing layer or level of consciousness, the sense of connectedness continues to be extended to the wider world and beyond. Each layer brings with it a learned wisdom, empathy and compassion, which are expressed by the ways in which the individual interacts with others and the wider world. This connectedness or relationship is significant in shaping the individual's sense of identity, as well as their perceptions and actions. If the connectedness is positive, it will provide the individual with a sense of self and place in their community and the world; in other words, the sense of belonging which is a vital factor for the well-being and positive growth of most humans. This, in turn helps to give them a sense of meaning and purpose. If the connectedness or relationship is such that it impedes the flourishing of the individual and prevents them from becoming the person they are meant to be, it will cause damage and generate feelings of alienation, self-hate and despair – therefore creating the shadow side of spirituality.

Finally, I suggest that every human person is somewhere along this continuum and there is always the possibility that, as they travel, they may sometimes experience a mystical state where they may glimpse and/or experience moments of deep sacredness and transcendence in their everyday. If they reach the end of the continuum they reach the point of Ultimate Unity, which is also the point of enlightenment.

I felt affirmed in the conclusions I had drawn from my research when I read Newberg, D'Aquili and Rause's (2001) discussions from their investigations in neuroscience. They describe a similar continuum in relation to experiences of unitary states that mystics may have and discuss the neurological changes that take place in the human brain as people move along this unitary continuum. One end of the continuum reflects the everyday experiences of most people, where they continually interact with others who compose the world around them. They realise that they are connected to others at some level, but experience the world as something apart from themselves. Sometimes, they may have experiences of transcendence when they respond to beauty in art or nature or, indeed, to the happiness they may experience in someone else. At such times, the boundaries separating the Self and Other disappear and they feel a sense of complete union with everything. However, these are temporary and, in due course, they return to their normal state of being an individual, distinct from the Other. In other words, their individual identities set a clear boundary between themselves and everyone else. Newberg *et al.* make it clear that these transcendent states are not religious experiences but, in neurological terms, they are similar to many unitary experiences produced by religious activity. As the individual progresses along the unitary continuum, the separation of the Self and the Other becomes less distinct and the unitary states become more intense, characterised by feelings of awe and rapture. The other end of the continuum is marked by profound states of spiritual union similar to that described by the mystics. Newberg describes this as a 'state of pure mind which consists of an awareness beyond object and subject. It is a state of Absolute Unitary Being, the ultimate unitary state' (pp. 115–120). It is my contention, then, that the movement towards Ultimate Unity may be aligned with Newberg *et al.*'s movement towards Absolute Unitary Being, which signals corresponding changes in the brain. Thus, it would seem that there is physical evidence reflecting spiritual growth that is expressed by increasing depths of connectedness between the Self and the Other.

## Concluding thoughts

This chapter has explored a wide range of perspectives of spirituality from different cultural, religious and regional settings. In many instances, Christian religiosity was the foundational basis from which much thinking and research originated. Nonetheless, this thinking and research has been contextualised by the secular and religiously diverse fabric of wider society and, given the fact that various aspects of religion have, in many countries, become part of the public discourse since 9/11, it is almost certain that secularity and plurality would have had some influences on the understandings and expressions of spirituality. More importantly, the children and young people with whom most professional people work today come from this diverse context and it provides a reason why an understanding and identification of a spirituality that transcends religious and cultural diversity becomes a significant factor that needs to be recognised and addressed.

Accordingly, I have drawn together different research findings and interpretations from the literature to provide an understanding of spirituality that aligns with both Eastern and Western thinking and experiences, and which is also applicable in religious and secular cultures. It is holistic, rather than reductive, and it considers objective and subjective experiences. This concept of spirituality which has been foundational to my research over the past twenty years is based on the understanding that spirituality is an innate human trait which pertains to the relational dimension of life and may be observed and experienced through the expressions of connectedness between the Self and the Other. For some, the relational dimension is grounded in their physical existence but for others, it soars beyond into the non-human world, reaching out to a Transcendent Other. This is the understanding of spirituality that will be used in these chapters and it provides the basis for the discussions that follow.

The next chapter will explore contemporary social and political contexts that have been influential and have implications for the spirituality of children and young people.

## Notes

1  For the purpose of this book, baby boomers refer to those born after the war to around 1960. Generation X (Gen X) refers to those born in the 1960s through to the mid-1970s. Young people and youth refer to the next generation born from the mid-1970s to the late 1980s.

2  This is quoted directly from Merton's thesis and the lack of inclusive language is reflective of the period. I have chosen not to make these changes in the quote.

3  For instance, note Laurence Krause's arguments on a recent Q&A programme screened on Australia's ABC TV. At one level he refers to the wonder that scientists experience, which is divorced from the God factor. At another level he articulates his disbelief in God using traditional religious language and concepts. Thus, he does not acknowledge that the different names and forms attributed to an understanding of God may, indeed, refer to the same "something other" (Hay, 2006) which many people around the world believe they have experienced. Krause's arguments can be viewed on iview.abc.net.au/programs/qanda/FA1407H022S00.

4  A Google search of the words 'Einstein and spirituality' indicate 818,000 hits. Of course, many of these websites do not reference their sources. Others do, but still others will critique some of the references. However, the fact remains that they provide some evidence of Einstein's awareness of a spiritual dimension to life as apart from religious doctrine, which was compatible with the inspiration and wonder of scientific thinking and discovery.

5  I have added the word 'spiritual' here.

6  See www.abc.net.au/religion/stories/s972766.htm (retrieved 13 October 2015).

7  Throughout this book, I use 'the Other' as a collective noun to personify all others, that is, everyone and everything that is other than the Self.

8  For instance, see the following websites: www.imdb.com/list/ls055036091/; www.sundance.tv/series/the-writers-room/blog/2014/04/top-10-supernatural-tv-series

9  A full account of this incident by Julian Burnside, AO QC, a well-known barrister, human rights and refugee advocate in Australia, is available at www.futureleaders.com.au/pdf/Julian_Burnside.pdf.

10  Wilber (1999) describes Unity Consciousness as the point where a person's identity is with the All, i.e. with absolutely everything.

11  Sri Aurobindo Ghosh identified five levels of consciousness above the mental, namely: the Higher Mind, the Illumined Mind, Intuition, Overmind and Supermind.

12  For instance, some well-known writers who discuss the concept of different levels of consciousness, which move the individual closer to the point of transcendence or enlightenment, are Sri Aurobindo, Ken Wilber and Teresa of Ávila.

# Chapter 2

# The empathic mind
## Essence of human spirituality[1]

In the previous chapter, I examined some of the aspects of contemporary spirituality that require attention in any study of the subject. First, there is the research literature that has attempted to illuminate new understandings of spirituality; and second, there are the perceptions and expressions of spirituality amongst young people, which may be deciphered today within the context of these new understandings. This chapter turns the attention to some findings in neuroscience about the connectedness an individual feels towards the Other; therefore, it helps to clarify and re-articulate our understanding that spirituality is relational and, also, that spiritual growth may be aligned with the heightening of the individual's awareness of him or herself as a relational Being – which leads to expressions and practices that reflect deep connectedness to the Other.

Spirituality, which was once restricted to theology and religion, is now a subject for discussion across many disciplines and professions that encompass aspects of human health and behaviour. In some traditional frameworks, generated by theological and religious perspectives, spirituality is about the human person's relationship with a divine mystery, known as God. This tends to be exclusive: it excludes those whose Reality is firmly grounded in the here and now and who are not believers in a God who dwells outside the physical realm. It suggests that spirituality is something learned or a gift given to a chosen people. Perspectives from other disciplines may be quite different and yet influenced by this traditional notion. For instance, Hollingsworth (2008) acknowledges that spirituality 'defies definitional consensus' (p. 838) and refers to the abundance of meanings that are consistently applied to the concept. Her own preferred construct is the ongoing relationships which the Self has with the Other and with that 'which we deem sacred' (ibid.). She adds that 'the term *sacred* may refer to a divine being, divine object, Ultimate Reality, or Ultimate Truth as perceived by the individual' (p. 839). Accordingly, it is possible to detect an influence of traditional religious understandings of spirituality in Hollingsworth's definition.

I believe that a restricted understanding of spirituality is problematic in our contemporary world. For instance, in the West, there are many people who identify themselves as non-religious and who do not believe in God or a Divine Consciousness/Energy. To put some figures on this, Newberg and Waldman

(2006) point to an assessment done by Phil Zuckerman from Pitzer College which concluded that between 500 million and 750 million people across the world do not believe in God (p. 217). They also quote from a 1991 survey which yielded figures of the number of atheists in Western countries. At the top of the list was an astonishing figure indicating that 88 per cent of the population in East Germany were atheists. In the 2011 Australian Census there were just under 4.8 million (22 per cent of the population) who indicated no religion. The people who composed this number were atheists, agnostics, freethinkers, social-ists, rationalists, humanists and people who stated 'No denomination' and 'No religion'. A further notable fact revealed in the census was that the number of people reporting no religion in Australia had increased substantially over the past hundred years (Australian Bureau of Statistics, 2014). Moving across to Britain, the UK Census from 2011 indicated that those indicating no religion are the second largest belief group; at 26.13 per cent of the population they encompass a collective that is about three and a half times as many as all the non-Christian religions put together (British Humanist Association, n.d.).

Given these figures – and if we also examine positive and negative spiritual characteristics such as truth, justice, beauty, freedom, caring, joyfulness, mys-tery, awe, wonder, empathy and compassion, *or* suffering, hurt, anger, alienation, despair and so on – we find these traits in all people, religious *and* non-religious. Therefore, defining a concept of spirituality that is more inclusive and which has meaning for all people becomes an important component for future research, practice and applications.

My research, which follows on from others, views spirituality more inclusively. It is seen as an essential part of the human condition which may not be confined to the religious dimensions of human life or, indeed, restricted to an understand-ing that it reflects a relationship with God. Instead, spirituality is understood as a raised awareness/consciousness that individuals may have of themselves as rela-tional beings; that is, an awareness that the Self is part of the Whole, which also comprises the Other and, for some, includes a Transcendent Other.

Such an understanding of spirituality is significant when we turn our atten-tion to the discovery of mirror neurons, since they provide physical evidence that an individual's response to another's emotions or actions stimulates movement in his or her brain which mirrors the oscillating movement in the other's brain. This discovery is significant if we consider that a fundamental element of human spirituality is connectedness.

This chapter, then, examines relevant research relating to mirror neurons to discuss possible implications for the spiritual lives of children and young people. It also focuses on the concept of empathy as a human experience which corre-sponds directly to the action of mirror neurons, and investigates how the highly materialistic and consumeristic influences that dominate the lives of young peo-ple today can lead to empathy erosion. Finally, attention is given to the links between the erosion of empathy and the problematic issue of school violence and bullying.

## Mirror neurons and human spirituality

Mirror neurons were discovered by Italian neuroscientist Giacomo Rizzolatti and his team in the 1990s. Since then, the main focus has been on the use of these neurons in clinical work with patients displaying neurological disorders and little, if any, attention was given to how they may impact on other dimensions of Being. More recent studies though (Iacoboni, 2008; Rizzolatti & Sinigaglia, 2008, Keysers, 2011) have concluded that there is a level of interaction between mirror neurons and human empathy. Thus, when we are confronted with another person's distress and we find ourselves saying, 'I really do *feel* your excitement or your hurt and anger', neurologically speaking, we actually are equipped to do just that. Iacoboni (2008) contends that we react to a movie character's distress, chivalry and so on, precisely because the mirror neurons in our brains recreate for us whatever we are actually watching and lead us to literally experience the same feelings that the fictional characters are experiencing (p. 4). He extends this discussion to claim:

> 'Vicarious' is not a strong enough word to describe the effect of these mirror neurons. When we see someone else suffering or in pain, mirror neurons help us to read her or his facial expression and actually make us feel the suffering or the pain of the other person. These moments, I will argue, are the foundation of empathy and possibly of morality, a morality that is deeply rooted in our biology.
>
> (Iacoboni, 2008, p. 5)

Cozolino (2006) offers a succinct description when he says that mirror neurons 'provide us with a visceral-emotional experience of what the other is experiencing, allowing us to know others from the inside out' (p. 59). Previously, the Theory of Mind, coined by David Premack and Guy Woodruff at the University of Pennsylvania in 1978 (see Boyd, 2008, p. 370), explained how the human person had an ability to understand that another person had a mind, a way of thinking, feeling and behaving which was different from their own. It furthered our knowledge about social intelligence and social cognition, and it also suggested that humans had some degree of empathy if they had this capacity to understand that another person's thoughts and feelings were different from their own. Mirror neurons, it appears, goes beyond this to provide us with access into another person's brain so that we are actually tuned into their thoughts and experience their feelings. This is an exciting discovery for any professional and/or researcher whose intention is to find ways to promote the cohesiveness and wellbeing of societies which are composed of diverse communities, because it suggests that mirror neurons have major implications for the relational dimension of human lives.

According to Iacoboni (2008) it was Vittorio Gallese who first proposed a role for mirror neurons in both understanding and empathising with the emotions of other people (p. 108). Iacoboni agrees with Gallese and points to many empirical studies in neuroscience over the past decade, where the findings from evidence collected by using a range of different methodologies support the claim that there is a distinct link between mirror neurons and empathy (p. 109).

Extending this discussion, the eminent neuroscientist Vilayanur Ramachandran (2012) observes that the significance of mirror neurons is that they are not just motor-command neurons because they appear to have predictive power; that is, they allow a person to read another's mind and they can figure out what the other person is about to do, as if 'mirror neurons are nature's own virtual-reality simulations of the intentions of other beings' (p. 121). When Ramachandran mentions experiments which indicate the ability of these cells to empathise with others, he refers to them as 'Gandhi neurons' because they 'blur the boundary between self and others' (p. 124). Newberg, D'Aquili and Rause (2001) also speak about the blurring of boundaries between the individual and others as they progress along a unitary continuum (p. 115). While Newberg did not mention mirror neurons, it is possible that they have a role in effecting the momentary feelings of transcendence and unity that individuals may experience in their everyday or, in reverse, they may be activated because of such experiences. These are the moments when a person may lose their sense of self in response to something that inspires wonder, awe, rapture, liberation and/or great joy and the Self becomes encompassed by the Whole.

Another pertinent point made by Ramachandran (2012) is the consideration that this particular aspect of mirror neurons – that is, the ability to empathise with others – could become a problem if there was nothing to prevent individuals from blindly imitating every action they see or literally feeling someone else's pain. Certainly, social processes and communications would become quite chaotic and people's sense of self would become quite confused if such were the case. Accordingly, Ramachandran speculates that that there may be a frontal inhibitory circuit that suppresses the inclination to automatic mimicry when it is inappropriate, thereby allowing the individual to 'enjoy reciprocity with others while simultaneously preserving their individuality' (p. 125). This theory is supported by both Iacoboni (2008) and Keysers (2011).

In further deliberations, Ramachandran (2012) discusses the human characteristic that allows the individual to be introspective and to have self-awareness. He proposes that it is possible that mirror neurons turn inwards to enable a representation of one's own mind:

> with the mirror-neuron system thus 'bent back' on itself full-circle, self-awareness was born . . . Science tells us we are merely beasts, but we don't feel like that. We feel like angels trapped inside the bodies of beasts, forever craving transcendence. That's the essential human predicament in a nutshell.
>
> (Ramachandran, 2012, pp. 260 and 291)

Thus, according to Ramachandran, self-awareness is the trait that makes us distinctively human but it also appears to activate in us a desire to be something more than merely human. He alludes to the fact that self-awareness is often used interchangeably with the word 'consciousness' (p. 291) and asserts that, once this human trait evolved, a natural progression was for the individual to start pondering on where they had come from. This search leads us 'to our peril – into metaphysics, but as human beings we cannot avoid doing so' (p. 292). Acknowledging that self-awareness and consciousness have been difficult concepts to study, Ramachandran suggests that one approach to understanding this human trait is by studying the inner mental life of neurological and psychiatric patients, but he concludes with the sobering thought that we need to accept, with humility, that we will probably never have the answers to questions about our ultimate origins, no matter how far we are able to extend our knowledge of the brain and the cosmos.

Given Ramachandran's assertion, we can understand that mirror neurons have a distinct role in both helping an individual retain a sense of self – thereby preserving their individual identity and providing degrees of separation from the Other – but, at the same time, they are instrumental in enabling and maintaining relationships precisely because they create a level of unspoken communication between any two individuals. He argues that our awareness of the Self and the Other 'co-evolved, enriching each other enormously and culminating in the kind of reciprocity between self-awareness and other-awareness seen only in humans' (p. 260).

Later research suggests there are different types of mirror neurons. Apart from the visual mirror neurons, as indicated by Ramachandran, which allow the individual to see another person's visual and conceptual stance, there are also auditory mirror neurons (Keysers, 2011) and sensory mirror neurons (ibid.; Ramachandran, 2012). Keysers (2011) confirms the notion that other people's emotions become our emotions almost as if what is happening to others actually envelops us without any conscious action or control on our part. Instead, it is largely an automatic and intuitive response. He further claims that this 'feat of our brains, the emotional connection with others is, to a large extent, what makes us human' (p. 8) without which our social lives and social networks would break down, since the success of our personal and professional relationships depends on our ability to read the emotional states of others – including when they may try to hide an inner turmoil that is devouring them. Keysers contends that: 'Mirror neurons "mirror" the behaviour and emotions of the people surrounding us in such a way that the others become part of us' (p. 10). He determines that the discovery of these shared circuits means that we have to change the way in which we think about ourselves in relation to others, because we are not strictly separated from them: 'In all these shared circuits, neurons that deal exclusively with the self coexist with neurons that respond similarly to self and other' (p. 221).

Another view is offered by Metzinger (2009) who believes that the discovery of mirror neurons is an indication that empathy is a natural phenomenon which we have acquired, one step at a time, through our biological evolution. He uses the metaphor 'Ego Tunnel' for conscious experience (p. 6) and argues that because of mirror neurons we can consciously experience another human being's thoughts and movements as meaningful. However, the process requires interaction between our conscious and non-conscious minds because 'whenever successful social understanding and empathy are achieved, we share a common representation: of one and the same goal state in two different Ego Tunnels' (p. 170).

From the research perspectives presented here it would seem that the discovery that mirror neurons have an implicit role in the relational lives of humans does support the notion that humans are biologically programmed to reach out to the Other and, if that is so, one can expect that experiences of connectedness are essential for each individual's wellbeing. This supports our knowledge and understanding of human history as well, which has shown that humans appear to favour a way of life which is about gathering together in groups for reasons apart from physical security. The sharing of values and a way of being in the world with others brings more than physical security and convenience. These factors develop a sense of belonging which leads to identity formation in the individual which, in turn, encourages a sense of loyalty to the herd/clan, thereby inspiring feelings of responsibility to and protection of the group. Thus, it is the holistic experience of being part of a group with the sharing of each other's values, attitudes, feelings and a way of being in the world that becomes an essential component in the physical, mental, emotional, social and spiritual wellbeing of individuals and communities.

As with most ideas in the human world, there are differing views about the role of mirror neurons in generating empathy. Dossey's (2010) philosophical stance questions whether mirror neurons can explain the '*conscious experience* of empathy or any other complex social emotion' (p. 106). He argues that the neuroscientists may have it backwards: we do not know if it is mirror neurons that send empathic messages to conscious awareness and that, in fact, it may be 'the felt experience of empathy that causes the empathy neurons to light up' (p. 107).

Regardless of whether it is mirror neurons that cause empathy or whether, as Dossey suggests, it is the felt experience that activates the neurons, in the end, Dossey recognises that empathy is an essential human experience and makes a perceptive observation in his final estimate when he reflects that the significance of the mirror neuron hypothesis is that it offers an alternative view to one that perceives humans as totally selfish and self-absorbed creatures. Rather, it suggests that 'we are equipped for empathy, compassion, altruism, and cooperation, in addition to being biologically geared for competition, procreation and survival' (p. 116).

While some of the arguments and references to relevant studies have been explored in the preceding discourse, the purpose here has not been to examine different perspectives about the role of mind, consciousness and the brain; nor has the aim been to present an extensive exposition on mirror neurons. More exactly, the objective here is to specifically explore the implications of a particular claim: that it is possible that mirror neurons provide physical evidence that the human person is programmed to be empathetic. Here we may understand empathy as 'the vicarious socio-emotional response that is induced by the perception of another individual's affective state. It entails feeling an emotion that is similar to the one likely experienced by the other person' (Roth-Hanania, Davidou & Zahn-Waxler, 2011, p. 448).

My position is that empathy is absolutely foundational to successful human relationships and the corresponding expressions of connectedness. Accordingly, empathy may be recognised as a distinguishing human trait that is the experience and expression of the relational dimension of Being – that is, human spirituality.

## Empathy

As noted earlier, when people of different cultures, religions and worldviews become next door neighbours – whose lives are contextualised by a shrinking world owing to the impact of the speed of travel, social media and the internet – it can lead to misunderstandings and prejudicial attitudes and behaviour which are propelled by fear and ignorance of the Other. The result has been a rise, both in Australia and elsewhere, in the palpable expressions of distrust, wariness and verbal – sometimes physical – abuse towards somebody who is culturally, religiously and racially different. As a result, there are regular news headlines around the world that reveal the tension and violence between particular ethnic communities and the lack of inclusive and empathetic attitudes.

Baron-Cohen (2011) recognises that there has been an erosion of empathy around the globe. He notes that, generally, empathy erosion can be caused temporarily by destructive emotions such as deep resentment, revenge or blind hatred or an effort to protect. Alternatively, with some individuals, the lack of empathy can stem from serious pathological and psychological problems, in which case such individuals stay at a level of having no empathy. Baron-Cohen concludes that when people 'objectify others' (p. 1) in order to commit horrific acts of cruelty, they are experiencing an erosion of empathy; he uses Buber's *I and Thou* relationship to demonstrate the contrast between:

> the Ich-Du (I-You) mode of being (where you are connecting with another person, as an end in itself) with the Ich-Es (I-It) mode of being (where you are connecting with another person or object, so as to use them or it for some purpose).
>
> (Baron-Cohen, 2011, p. 5).

Accordingly, when we are in the I-It mode, we remain single-minded and self-focused so that we relate to other people and things as if they are just objects to be used for our sole purpose. Most people will experience this state where they lack empathy at the times when they are pre-occupied and their attention is completely focused elsewhere. However, this is usually a temporary lapse and, at such times, it is unlikely that our lack of empathy will have any negative effect on the Other. However, if we move from a single-minded focus to a double-minded focus of attention to the Other, it means that we are tuning into someone else's mind and thinking and feeling what they are thinking and feeling at the same time. Therefore, when empathy is switched off, we think only about our own interests, but when it is switched on, we focus on other people's interests too (p. 10).

Baron-Cohen then proposes a definition of empathy where he identifies two stages, recognition and response (p. 11). Thus, the identification of the thoughts and feelings of another person must happen before any response can take place. Both stages are required for an act of empathy to be enacted.

Baron-Cohen proposes an empathy spectrum beginning with zero degrees at one end. This would explain the atrocities that frequently comprise our daily news because they are usually committed by people who reflect zero degrees of empathy. At this end of the spectrum any feelings for the Other border on the non-existent, so the perpetrators are not really affected by the distress and/or the calamity they cause. Feelings of guilt or remorse are not part of the equation. However, in the case of most individuals, their levels of empathy may vary depending on their circumstances and/or emotional states, so that they may move up and down the spectrum. It is possible for anyone who is in a negative emotional state to be at zero degrees, but this is usually a momentary lapse and they will move up again in time. This does entail that they will be capable of insensitive and possibly even mean and cruel acts or attitudes towards another during this lapse, but they will experience regret and/or remorse at their actions when they move back up from zero degrees. Nevertheless, it is important to recognise that for some individuals, their particular psychological or medical conditions will ensure that their empathy remains stable at zero degrees; for instance, a sociopath or a person who is high on the autism spectrum.

I believe there is a distinct alignment between the relational/spiritual continuum, which I proposed in Chapter 1, and Baron-Cohen's empathy spectrum. The first is underpinned by an awareness of one's relationality, which is heightened as one moves along the continuum; while the relational experience of recognising and responding to the thoughts and feelings of another is foundational to the second. For both, the expressions of connectedness to the Other through actions and behaviour will correspond to where the individual stands on each continuum. When people are treated as if they were just objects, it can be the most degrading experiences they will have. Regrettably, our history is smeared with instances of people's inhumanity to other human beings and to other living creatures. We take away any semblance of human dignity when we ignore their 'subjectivity, their thoughts and feelings' (Baron-Cohen, 2011, p. 5). Human empathy involves 'the direct experience of another's emotional state' which would necessitate 'emptying one's mind of self-regard and avoiding being distracted by one's own emotional state, which must be completely quiescent' (Culliford, 2011, p. 216). As such, empathy should be recognised as an essential characteristic in the forging of the connectedness that the Self may feel to everything that is other than Self. Hence, it becomes an essential characteristic of human spirituality.

## Empathy and early childhood

If we accept that the human person is biologically programmed to be empathetic it would be fair to assume that babies are born into this world deeply connected to everything, and this is why they seem to respond, without discrimination, to people around them. In the past, babies were considered to be completely self-centred and unable to look or feel things from another's perspective. Goleman (1989) refers to studies by Hoffman (1984; 2000), a psychologist at New York University, to argue that from a few months after birth through the first year of life, infants have been shown to react to the pain of another as though it was happening to themselves. For instance, if they see another child get hurt and cry, they also begin to cry. Hoffman's findings, in fact, suggest that it is in the second year that children develop the capacity for authentic Other-oriented empathy, but before that time, their response to the crying of another baby is more likely to be empathic distress, that is, the empathy is actually self-focused because the baby is not yet able to distinguish Self from Other so they see the pain as their own. Another way of understanding this theory is that, rather than being self-focused as previously understood, the baby's connectedness to the Other is so deep that it is beyond relationality and, therefore, they are born in union with the Other. The duality that is evident in human nature is something that develops as babies become more aware of their surroundings and they begin to identify the Self.

Goleman (1989) cites Marion Radke-Yarrow, who claims that 'from around 14 months to 2 or 2 ½ years, you see children feel their own fingers to see if they hurt when someone else hurts their fingers'[2] – which supports Hoffman's findings that in their second year, babies begin to distinguish that the pain they see in someone else is actually not theirs but someone else's pain. It also points to the beginning of a movement from a position of deep connectedness, where one experiences being at one with everything that is Other, to a separation of the Self from the Other.

More recently, Roth-Hanania et al. (2011) alluded to the fact that there were only a few studies which had actually focused on empathic responses from babies in the first year of their lives. This realisation prompted them to develop a research project to examine the responses of 8- to 16-month-old babies to the distress of others. They found that there were some levels of empathy towards others amongst babies before their second year, which included an affective component where feelings were shown through facial expressions, calls and cries and actions reflecting concern. There was also a cognitive component, which included 'inquiry behaviour, attempts to comprehend the victim's state through non-vocal explorations, vocalizations, or both'. As a result, from 10 months through to 12 months and 14 months, young children started showing interest and concern in and for other children (p. 451). Roth-Hanania et al. also found that prosocial behaviour, which would reflect attempts to comfort a victim, were rare during the first year of life, but increased in frequency into the second year of life (p. 452). Their conclusions indicated that babies in their first year could understand the internal states of others and were able to comprehend their emotional states – at least that of distress – and were also able to respond to others with 'emotional attunement' (p. 455).

These research findings provide us with important new insights about the ability of babies to be empathetic. From their very first months, they imitate facial expressions of other people and take on their emotions, which Gopnik (2010) recognises as a kind of empathy in human babies.[3] Another pertinent finding from Gopnik highlights the fact that the tribal characteristics of human nature begins early so that, already by the age of four, children identify with belonging to their own group:

> The human impulse to depersonalize 'the others' seems as deep as the impulse to care about the people closest to you. Reestablishing that sense of personal intimacy with the 'others' may be one of the best ways of bringing about global moral change.
>
> (Gopnik, 2010)

Drawing on these research studies, we find a clear indication that babies are, indeed, connected to the world around them and, therefore, to the people who compose their worlds. In the early stages of their lives their connectedness is so deep that they are unable to separate Self from Other. However, within the first two years of their lives, the research shows that both mental and physical development, combined with a socialisation process, begins to impact on children's connectedness with the Other and moves them towards a state of awareness where self-identity becomes their foremost priority.

The Theory of Mind (Premack & Woodruff, 1978, cited in Boyd, 2008), discussed earlier, suggests that by four years of age, children have realised their separate identity from the Other and that their mind is different from the Other. In addition, as their social world starts to expand beyond the family circle, their openness to the Other and their sense of freedom, curiosity and adventurous spirit are often stifled through the efforts of their parents and other significant adults to protect them from anticipated dangers. They are also taught to conform to the expectations of the society in which they live in order to provide them with a smooth path to acceptance and inclusion. This helps to reinforce their innate desire to belong and be with others who are the same as themselves. Logically, then, children move towards group formation and membership which requires loyalty and allegiance so that both elements become instilled in the child's psyche.

The sense of belonging to a particular group is often strengthened by a dominant child or leader in the group, emphasising the perceived differences of those who do not belong as undesirable. Law (2006) suggests this is one of the strategies used by leaders in communities and governments to create barriers between 'us and them' and to promote allegiance to the leadership (p. 30), but it is a tactic that is also adopted by children and teenagers when they aim to effect loyalty and, indeed, submission from the group they want to dominate. Thus, children who desire acceptance by and belonging to the group begin to develop more exclusive attitudes and become less accepting of those who are not the same as themselves. In addition, by the time they are a few years old, children's identities are already being shaped by a progressive culture of compartmentalisation: they become, for different periods of time, a member of a family, playgroup, classroom, sports team and so on – and they learn appropriate behaviour and expressions for each of those identities.

As Elliott and Lemert (2006) claim, the creation of one's Self – that is, one's identity – is the result of one's social interaction so that 'it stands to reason that a Self can never be a once-and-for-all thing' (p. 21) because it continues to shift and transform in response to our changing external environments. Furthermore, they state: 'Ours is an era of identities individualized, and our current fascination for the making, reinvention and transformation of selves is, in some sense or another, integral to contemporary living' (p. 53). Thus, the multiple identities that children create for themselves, today, have some implications for the connectedness they may feel towards the Other, because there is always a chance that the needs and desires of one identity may clash with another. If the individual is well grounded as a whole person, they should be able to resolve the inner turmoil caused by conflicting identities, which also has some relevance for the nurturing of their spiritual wellbeing.

## The erosion of empathy

The many influences that shape children's identity today may not always nurture the relational dimension of their lives; instead, they may cause an erosion of empathy. Such influences create tension and distress and, ultimately, affect spiritual wellbeing and the ability to have enhancing relationships with the Other. A powerful and persistent facet of society which has been impacting on the relational lives of children and young people for many years now is media and technology. Images and sounds are beamed into the intimacy of family lives; and when the messages subtly and explicitly raise the spectre of the otherness of the Other, thereby encouraging divisiveness in society, it is not long before children and young people begin to display comparable attitudes. Such attitudes usually prevail when there is an economic downturn affecting employment opportunities, as has happened in the recent past. More recently, we have experienced a generation of children who have grown up against the backdrop of the country's involvement in the Iraq War and the rise in the number of refugees, asylum seekers and terrorists, all of whom are treated as the Other.

No doubt there is a long-term impact on the empathy of young children who have heard, through their most impressionable years, the voices and attitudes of leaders and other powerful people declaiming the undesirability and unacceptability of the Other. Quite possibly, these early learning experiences of intolerance have been stored in their non-conscious minds only to emerge unexpectedly when conditions appear favourable for their display. The role of non-conscious learning will be examined in more detail in Chapter 3.

Other external influences on children occur during their primary and secondary school years, when they are exposed to expanding contexts and new ways of thinking and perceiving the world. These factors can either increase their sense of wellbeing by emphasising their similarities to the mainstream group, or they can trigger insecurities and confusion if they find themselves on the other side – the ones who are different and therefore who have difficulty in being accepted. The opinions they hear through the media and their families can, as well, prompt them to turn on people who previously had been regarded as just another class-mate. In other words, their natural tendency to be empathetic can be eroded through an inundation of and exposure to prejudicial views that seek to provoke attitudes of 'us and them' in their worlds.

In more extreme situations, resentful and intolerant attitudes towards 'them' – that is, people whose religion and culture place them outside mainstream society – can be sparked by specific incidents and transform simmering fear and resentments into actions of hostility and aggression. In some school situations, where there has been a rise in bullying and violence in recent years, the question of identity and belonging becomes even more of an issue. This was reflected by Mansouri *et al.* in their 2009 report, *The Impact of Racism on the Health and Wellbeing of Young Australians*, involving eighteen schools across Australia and 823 student participants. The majority of the participants were middle and senior secondary school students, that is, from Years 9 to 12 (aged 15 to 18 years) with only around 5 per cent of participants coming from junior secondary level, that is, Years 7 and 8 (approximately 12 to 14 years). While the students' ethnic, cultural and religious backgrounds came from sixty different countries, 60 per cent of them had been born in Australia. The study found that 70 per cent of the participants had experienced racism and the most frequently cited response to racism were feelings of anger, frustration and of not belonging to the local community (p. 10). Interestingly, the research team also recorded that another frequent response to an experience of racism was that it made the person stronger, and they concluded that this was in line with the growing literature on the psychological and mental impact of racism, whereby more pronounced levels of resilience are reported as ways of resisting and countering discrimination and marginalisation (ibid.).

In addition, the researchers found correlations between experiences of racism and lower scores for health and wellbeing (p. 11). Overwhelmingly, the researchers found that students from migrant backgrounds were the most likely to experience racism, and that the incidents of racism grew exponentially in relation to how long they had lived in the country, with those who were second generation having fewer experiences of racism.

Findings from a study in the US mirror those from the Australian research in linking higher incidences of bullying with ethnicity. Peguero (2008) notes that previous research indicated that different levels of school violence were often linked to race and ethnicity, for instance, 'immigrant children with thick or heavy accents or with low English-speaking capabilities are often subjugated to negative treatment such as discrimination, ridicule, and harassment from other students, teachers, and school administrators'. He offers the definition of school violence-related outcomes as incorporating 'student victimization, both property and violence, student fear, and formal disciplinary school sanctions as new forms of detrimental outcomes linked to school violence', and points to evidence that 'the detrimental effects of violence, victimization, and student fear are found to be damaging to children's development'.[4] Thus, Peguero confirms that immigrant children with poor English language skills are more likely to experience bullying and violence at school as well as formal disciplinary school sanctions.

These findings are relevant to many contemporary societies which are ethnically, religiously and culturally diverse – and they need to be addressed. However, apart from problems associated with cultural and religious diversity (which will be addressed in Chapter 3), there are other elements in contemporary life that act as impediments to the development of empathic attitudes and behaviour which, thereby, reduce the potential for children to forge deep connections. One that has been particularly pervasive is the impact of social media. While this is a relatively new phenomenon – so there is not enough knowledge about the long-term effects it may have on the developmental lives of children and young people in terms of their physical, mental, emotional and spiritual capacities – it does feature prominently in the lives of our young, and some early research findings suggest that regular use of social media may obstruct the development of empathy and connectedness.

## Social networks and technology: Nurturing and impeding empathetic relationships

I have previously referred to the issue of multiple identities that begin in childhood and which have become quite evident amongst children and teenagers today. Another significant influential factor is the rapidly expanding, technologically driven, social networks. The identities of many children and young people are constantly being shaped by the latest communication gadget or software – mobile phones, iPads, Facebook, Myspace, Instagram and so on.[5] While I acknowledge that there are many positive aspects of media and technology in education and in improving health and lifestyles, I would like to look at some of the less enriching aspects that affect the lives of children and young people and the corresponding effects for their wellbeing – physically, emotionally and spiritually.

To begin with, in looking at some comparative statistics on the use of social media amongst children and adolescents across the US, Australia and Britain,[6] we find that social media does help children connect with the Other. It can improve their confidence and also their communication, social and technical skills (O'Keefe & Clarke-Pearson, 2011; Pitman, 2008; Rideout, 2012). Nonetheless, most research studies also identify many concerns about the other, non-enhancing effects. For instance, in a 2011 paediatric report that investigated the impact of social media on children and their families in the US, the authors found that 22 per cent of teenagers logged onto social media sites more than ten times a day; 75 per cent of teenagers owned mobile phones; 25 per cent used their phones for social media; 54 per cent used them for texting; and 24 per cent used them for instant messaging (O'Keefe & Clarke-Pearson, 2011, p. 800). These figures led the authors to acknowledge that much of this generation's social and emotional development occurs while they are on the internet and using mobile phones, and they caution that 'because of their limited capacity for self-regulation and susceptibility to peer pressure, children and adolescents are at some risk as they navigate and experiment with social media' (ibid.).

Australian statistics released in 2013 indicate that 23 per cent of 8- to 9-year-olds, 45 per cent of 10- to 11-year-olds, 69 per cent of 12- to 13-year-olds, 86 per cent of 14- to 15-year-olds and 92 per cent of 16- to 17-year-olds use social networking sites. Furthermore, 60 per cent of 14- to 17-year-olds said they felt good at using social media and around 45 per cent said it helped them feel close to someone else. The report also found that incidents of cyber-bullying increased with age so that 21 per cent of 14- to 15-year-olds and 16 per cent of 16- to 17-year-olds indicated that they had experienced this form of bullying (Australian Communication and Media Authority, 2013).

Finally, in 2014, Rhiannon Williams, a reporter for *The Telegraph*, a British newspaper, presented findings from *The Social Age*, a study conducted by knowthenet. org.uk, which indicated that 59 per cent of children are social networking by 10 years old and that 21 per cent had posted negative comments, starting from an average age of 11, while 26 per cent had 'hijacked' another person's account and posted without permission. Some 43 per cent had messaged strangers, starting from an average age of 12 (Williams, 2014). Williams also quotes the child psychologist from knowthenet.org.uk, Dr Richard Woolfson, as saying that as a result of social media, young people have blurred the boundaries between their public and private lives, and this increases their vulnerability to cyber-bullying and other dangers from online users. He noted as well that social media sites provided children with access to information and images which were not always appropriate for their age group and which, therefore, they would not have the emotional maturity to handle (ibid.).[7]

These statistics across three Western cultures indicate the increase in the usage of social media by children and teenagers and also the shared concern across these cultures about the possible negative impacts, for instance, cyber-bullying and online harassment, sexting, privacy concerns and the influence of advertising (O'Keefe & Clarke-Pearson, 2011; Pitman, 2008). Other problems relate to Facebook depression (O'Keefe & Clarke-Pearson, 2011) and social networking or internet addiction which involves excessive computer use, thereby affecting daily life (Griffiths, 2012; Karaiskos *et al.*, 2010; Andreassen *et al.*, 2012). Although these reports indicate that children, generally, did feel good about using social media, the problems identified by health professionals suggest that many are not mentally or emotionally prepared for some of the outcomes linked to its use.

In Britain, writing for *The Telegraph*, Graeme Paton (2012)[8] refers to findings by the Office for National Statistics which indicate the positive effects of video games and social networking in enhancing existing friendships and allowing shy children to communicate. He mentions too the negative effects if young people are exposed to technology for too long during the normal school day. He also cites the claim from the neuroscientist Susan Greenfield that one consequence of social media is the decline in physical human contact, resulting in many children having difficulty in formulating basic social skills to emotional reactions.

More recently, during Greenfield's visit to the University of South Australia as part of the South Australian Government's thinkers-in-residence programme, she claimed that the use of digital technologies is rewiring the human brain (reported by ABC journalist Gary Rivett, 2014).[9] Greenfield argued that for those who have already developed their own sense of individuality through their accumulation of a vast number of experiences and memories, which have enabled them to develop conceptual frameworks and attitudes, these new influences may not be problematic. However, for a young person who has not yet been grounded in a robust identity or developed effective interpersonal skills, long hours in front of a screen can be detrimental in reshaping the brain. For instance, they may grow up with short attention spans, have a real need to conform to their peers and lack an ability to discern the impact of their actions. Furthermore, while children in the past used their imaginations, today, when they sit in front of a screen, they become passive receivers, faced with a menu of choices provided by someone else. They are inundated with a never-ending source of information and they have little ability to do anything with it. Greenfield asserts that we were raising a 'generation who are completely self-centred, with short attention spans, not very good at communication, rather needy emotionally and with a weak sense of identity' (ibid.).

Zull's (2002, pp. 31–33) discussion, many years earlier, echoed Greenfield when he recounted a similar problem with one of his students. Zull described him as a 'latchkey' child who had spent an inordinate amount of time in front of the TV when he was growing up and had memorised huge amounts of information, but was unable to produce logical arguments or structure coherent paragraphs. Thus, the student had not used his amassed information to create ideas or actions. He greatly enjoyed the acquisition of information but it had become an end in itself, rather than a means to progress his thinking and learning by utilising that information. Zull speculated that such students do not use the idea and action parts of the brain effectively, and rely almost totally on their sensory and memory brain. He concluded that a balanced use of all parts of the brain are essential if information is to be transformed into knowledge, so that passive learners become active learners.

A further study that detects similar problems related to young people's use of social media and the internet reinforces the findings from other studies. Sagiolou and Greitmeyer (2014) recognise that Facebook use is being increasingly researched by psychologists since it is the most popular online social network; but they also acknowledge that there is still scant knowledge of the psychological underpinnings and consequences. They claim that the research literature shows that only 9 per cent of Facebook activity involves communication and the rest 'consists of mainly non-interactive processes such as directed or random consumption of social content' (p. 359), and that this passive consumption of other people's activities often provoke feelings of envy which, in turn, impact negatively on individuals' satisfaction with their own lives. Another identified outcome is social grooming, where individuals want to know what is happening in other people's lives as this provides the foundations for social gossip (ibid.). Sagiolou and Greitmeyer base their own study on the fact that not enough has been discovered about the impact of Facebook use on the emotional states of individuals, other than the tendency to produce negative emotional states. Their hypothesis was informed by Csikzentmihalyi's (1992, 2002) study, which found that the individual's sense of wellbeing and life-satisfaction was derived from finding meaning in work or leisure activities. Accordingly, they conducted three separate studies to discover if Facebook activity was actually meaningful for its users, and to identify the corresponding emotional states immediately after Facebook use. The findings from their first two studies show that internet browsing without resourcing any social networks does not dampen people's moods, but negative emotional consequences could be attributed specifically to the use of social networks (Sagiolou & Greitmeyer, 2014, p. 361).

The conclusions from their three studies led Sagiolou and Greitmeyer to claim that there is a causal relationship between Facebook use and experiencing negative moods immediately afterwards. The mood decline occurs because people feel as if they have wasted time and have engaged in something that is only a little meaningful by being active on Facebook. Their third study indicates that people continue to use Facebook despite the mood decline and the lack of meaning associated with the activity, because they mistakenly anticipate that their time on Facebook would be a positive experience (p. 362). Thus, an underlying incentive to use Facebook might be triggered by the expectation that it will make the user feel better which, in turn, is motivated by the need for social grooming. The experience can encourage a false expectation of positive feelings and overlook the fact that previous time spent on Facebook led to feelings of envy, insecurity and time wasted (ibid.). Sagiolou and Greitmeyer conclude that large numbers of young people engage every day in an activity that then ends up having little meaning for them and which, ultimately, has a negative impact on the way they feel (ibid.). However, they acknowledge that there is not, as yet, research that indicates the long-term impact that Facebook use has on wellbeing. The fact that there are indications it can produce negative emotional states immediately after use means that more research is needed, especially as it can be an excellent tool for social networking and helping individuals stay connected.

To sum up, the research findings from several projects across different Western countries regarding the use of social media and the internet have identified the rise in instances of cyber-bullying. In fact, cyber-bullying has become a serious problem in the lives of children and young people and it highlights how empathy erosion can happen in young lives which are being besieged by technology.

Indeed, for many young people, their sense of self is dependent on their popularity and status amongst their peers and it becomes important to have a large network of friends on Facebook, or to whom they can text, tweet and so on. Greenfield makes this point about social media, whereby young people have friends they do not actually know so that the 'friends' become more of an audience and the individual is prompted to create an artificial identity in an effort to win peer respect and approval (cited by Rivett, 2014). Greenfield further offers the caution that the audience can turn nasty, which can be distressing for the individual, because they are not constrained by face-to-face communication. Thus, one downside to this aspect of social networking is the facelessness that results when experiences of connectedness are actually 'distant connectedness' (de Souza, 2009) or what Turkle (2011) calls being 'alone together'.[10] This is akin to the superficiality noted by Ulf Hannerz that occurs in relationships young adults may develop through global networking (cited by Elliott & Lemert, 2006, p. 6):

> It seems, rather, that in the present phase of globalization, one characteristic is the proliferation of the kinds of ties that can be transnational; ties to kin, friends, colleagues, business associates, and others. In all that variety, such ties may entail a kind and a degree of tuning out, a weakened personal involvement with the nation and national culture, a shift from the disposition to take it for granted: possibly a critical distance to it. In such ways, the nation may have become more hollow than it was.
>
> (Hannerz, 1996, pp. 88–89)

The 'critical distance' that Hannerz refers to as a result of globalisation would appear to have the same impact on human relationships as the notion of the 'distant connectedness' of human relationships that are conducted through technological devices. Both serve to reduce human experiences of connectedness to something less than what it could be.

Nonetheless, having access to a parallel universe offers the temptation to move away from the real world to exist in a kind of cyber-reality of hearing and vision which does not involve eye contact or physical touch (Rivett, 2014). Of course, these are elements that are essential aspects of human connection and communication in the real world and are essential if genuine and sincere experiences of connectedness are to be achieved. Donath (1999) highlights these aspects: 'In the disembodied world of the virtual community . . . many of the basic cues about personality and social role we are accustomed to in the physical world are absent' (p. 27). With such anonymity, identity becomes ambiguous and the individual has the freedom and flexibility to create a desirable persona, which is a step or two removed from the 'real me', and this virtual identity, or identities as the case may be, become just one of the multiple identities to which children and young people lay claim in the contemporary world. What can become an issue is the likelihood that the virtual identity may become so attractive that the individual will spend more and more time online in this role which, eventually, could stunt their physical, mental, emotional and spiritual growth and development and ability to cope in the real world. Donath offers further insights on the difference between a virtual community and a community grounded by its physicality when she speaks of 'an inherent unity' that composes the physical Self. However, in the intangible, virtual world, the individual can create as many electronic personas as they wish, since these are not tied to the physical Self (ibid.).

What is needed here is the recognition that technology and social media provide children and young people with a refuge, especially if they experience insecurity and a lack of safety in their real world. In a virtual world, a child is in control and can create new identities and exciting scenarios through which they can play out all their desires and aspirations and, perhaps, confront and conquer their fears. Not surprisingly, when they are 'unplugged' from their virtual world, their Reality returns them to a dreary and unprotected place where they do not have the physical, mental, emotional and spiritual strengths to engage successfully with whatever challenges they encounter. Consequently, they may mentally and emotionally retreat from their real world and the subsequent experiences of isolation and disconnectedness can lead to alienation and disenfranchisement, or even radicalisation as discussed in Chapter 3.

Moreover, the ability to create multiple online identities may, ultimately, create some tension and anxiety at a non-conscious level as they lose sight, at a conscious level, of the person they are meant to be. Alternatively, they may experience disappointment because they realise that in the real world, they are not the person they want to be. Turkle puts this succinctly:

> As we distribute ourselves, we may abandon ourselves . . . In all of this, there is a nagging question: Does virtual intimacy degrade our experience of the other kind and, indeed, of all encounters, of any kind?
>
> (Turkle, 2011, p. 12).

In the end, these experiences associated with disconnectedness are very likely to result in feelings of spiritual distress and affect the physical, mental and emotional health of young people. Certainly, as humans, we are physical beings and it is through our senses that we engage with others to establish and maintain relationships. Through seeing, hearing, speaking to and touching another, a particularly human dimension of communication is created. Our physical senses are important elements in helping us understand and truly connect with and respond to one another and, as we have discovered, mirror neurons most likely do have an important role in this process. The many studies cited by Iacoboni (2008) indicate that when we are able to experience the feelings that other people are feeling, we find that we are also able to respond more compassionately to their emotional states (p. 114). However, when we communicate through a technological device, such as social media and the internet, the intimacy generated through our physical senses, and which is important to and enriching in human relationships, may be lost. The distant connectedness impedes our ability to 'read' another's face or really hear the emotions in another's voice. Certainly, we are unable to look a person in the eye or reach out and physically hug another in an offering of sympathy, comfort and/or compassion. Thus, the distant connectedness engendered through the process of communicating through technology promotes the possibilities for 'dehumanization and objectification that are present when the "zone of intimacy" becomes a line before which is "us" and beyond which is "them"' (Hess, citing Hundeide, 2012, p. 412). One outcome from this scenario is that it has provided some young people with an ideal avenue for cyber-bullying and there is much evidence of the increasing instance of children and teenagers being victimised by this form of bullying.[11]

## Empathy erosion in cyber-bullying and school violence

Bullying and cyber-bullying have become serious problems in schools in Australia and elsewhere. A search on Google Scholar for related articles on bullying and violence in schools reveals the following: since 2010, there have been 21,600 articles on school bullying and violence and, more specifically, 13,700 articles on school bullying and violence in Australia. The rise in the number of articles reflect the professional concern that has been generated by the increased incidents of bullying and violence amongst young people; as such, Baron-Cohen's (2011) discussion of empathy has relevance here. For instance, cyber-bullies act furtively and anonymously. Therefore, they have little or no opportunity to physically *recognise* the distress of their victims as shown through face and body. Thus, the first element of empathy is missing and, logically then, the second element – which involves a response – cannot follow. Generally, bullies and those prone to causing physical, mental and emotional abuse objectify their victims, thereby dismissing their value and feelings as individuals. They clearly display the 'single-minded attention' rather than the 'double-minded attention' as discussed by Baron-Cohen (p. 10). Their own interests and goals become all-encompassing and there is little or no empathic recognition of the Other. Their empathy has been eroded (p. 4), thereby reflecting Buber's I-It relationship, since the relation to Thou is direct:

> The primary word I-Thou can be spoken only with the whole being. Concentration and fusion into the whole being can never take place through my agency, nor can it ever take place without me. I become through my relation to Thou; as I become I, I say Thou. All real living is meeting.
>
> (See Glatzer, 1966, p. 48)

To be sure, bullies have been ably assisted by social media and telecommunication to invent and access particularly sinister and menacing ways of reaching their victims because of the anonymity provided; and the possibility that these individuals will be outed and have to face up to their victims is greatly reduced. More importantly, the bullies can remain relatively complacent since they do not physically witness, at the moment of impact, the distress they are causing which would be expressed on the victim's face or through the emotional turmoil in the victim's voice. In other words, the 'distant connectedness' implicit in technological communications does not allow mirror neurons from being activated for simulated facial feedback. Iacoboni (2008) claims that this simulation process happens automatically and without conscious effort and it allows a person to walk in another person's shoes (p. 120). This means that a cyber-bully's mirror neurons will not trigger a spontaneous, empathetic response precisely because they cannot physically see their victim.

Without empathy, children and young people have difficulty relating to others and this can lead to them craving attention or trying to dominate others, both of which are identifiable traits of a bully. Accordingly, raising the awareness of children and young people that they are spiritual beings whose essence is connectedness to everything other than Self may be a promising starting point in intervention programmes to prevent school violence and bullying. With the knowledge we have of the imitative action of mirror neurons, it is possible to develop activities to promote empathy amongst school children. Furthermore, we also need to recognise that at the point of enacting the role of cyber-bully, the individual's empathy levels have probably been suspended so that they would be placed low on Baron-Cohen's (2011) empathy spectrum. However, once they have regained some distance from the act, it is possible for them to recover a higher degree of empathy. This knowledge and understanding of empathy does provide a foundation upon which schools and other professionals can develop anti-bullying programmes, which may involve encouraging bullies to face up to the distress they have caused. If they have moved back up the empathy spectrum there is a greater likelihood that they will feel a sense of shame and remorse, which may prompt them to engage in restorative action.

Also relevant are the links between the imitative action of mirror neurons and the increased incidents of violence amongst children and young people. Iacoboni (2008) cites research where the findings consistently indicate that if children watch a short violent movie, it will result in imitative violence amongst them. Moreover, this happens from preschool years through into adolescence and across gender, regions and race (p. 206). He concludes that media violence *does* lead to imitative violence (p. 207).

Further, Carnagey, Anderson and Bartholow (2007) point to decades of research which have demonstrated that exposure to violence on television can cause increases in aggression. They discuss examples of direct links between Clint Eastwood's 'Dirty Harry' film character with subsequent copycat killings, and between violent video games and many of the school killings in the US (p. 178). They also cite the results of a comprehensive review of the effects of violent media from 2003 which found 'unequivocal evidence that media violence increases the likelihood of aggressive and violent behaviour in both immediate and long-term contexts' (ibid.). Carnagey *et al.* conclude that video games are more potent at instigating violence than film and television because of the interactive element. Players are able to immerse themselves in video games to engage in 'virtual violent actions, receive direct rewards for those actions, closely identify with the characters they control, and actively rehearse aggressive behavioural scripts' (p. 179). Additionally, Carnagey *et al.* refer to recent research in social neuroscience which illuminates our knowledge about the connection between exposure to violent media and the specific neural structures linked to emotional regulation, memory storage and retrieval and executive functioning (p. 180).

More recently, research findings from Anderson *et al.* (2014)[12] confirm these earlier findings. They conclude that:

> *Media violence is an important causal risk factor for increased aggression and violence in both the short- and long-term.* Moreover, media violence is one of the few known risk factors that parents, caregivers, and society in general can reduce at very little cost.
>
> (Anderson *et al.*, 2014; their italics)

As we have seen, while research over the past decade has provided concrete evidence of the effects of exposure to media and technology on subsequent violent actions, Iacoboni (2008) acknowledges that more research is needed before conclusions can be reached about possible links between the imitative capacity of mirror neurons in persuading perpetrators to commit violent acts. He does insist, though, that they will further inform our understanding about the *hows* and *whys* of imitative violence in the human world. Finally, he recognises that with a powerful media and an economy-driven culture riddled with consumerism, the eradication of screen violence is not going to happen any time soon. Instead, parents, educators and other concerned professionals will, once again, have to find ways to deal with the problems generated at the wider societal level in order to ensure the wellbeing of their children and young people.

## Concluding thoughts

This chapter has highlighted an area of research that has significance for the way we care for and educate our young, but which rarely gets a mention in teacher training programmes or in professional development programmes for classroom practitioners: that empathy is implicit in human spirituality. It has examined, as well, the particular features in contemporary society that may either nurture or impede empathy and revealed corresponding outcomes when these factors come into play. It has identified the need to address this new learning in educational settings.

One strategy could be to help children develop an awareness that they are relational, not isolated, beings. Programmes and learning tasks that promote a sense of connectedness will involve the activation of motor neurons which may, in turn, nurture feelings of empathy towards the Other. Such programmes would have significant value in multicultural and multi-religious societies, where connectedness and empathy need to be foundational factors in order to promote social cohesion and the wellbeing of both community and individual.

Further, educating children to understand different cultures and belief systems that have become part of the societal fabric may go a long way to promoting empathy and removing the fear of difference. This is particularly relevant since we now know that children are born with a tendency to be empathetic. Therefore, finding ways to nurture their spirituality by redesigning educational environments and programmes may be one step forward in the process of growing inclusive and compassionate young people.

In addition, educators should utilise and empathise with the rich heritage and wisdom of different traditions and cultures that compose the pluralistic, globalised world, and which are so often evident in contemporary classrooms. By providing opportunities for students to explore, through shared stories, experiences and vision, the mystery and wonder that accompanies the search for meaning by people from varied backgrounds, teachers can engage the rational, physical, emotional and spiritual dimensions of learning. If students – through the action of their mirror neurons – discover that their stories resonate with others, this will, potentially, raise their awareness of their connectedness with the Other which, in turn, should promote a feeling of empathy and enhance the spiritual dimension of learning.

These are just some of the factors that point to the need for new learning structures and spaces, and for programmes to be embedded in whole new frameworks which are more meaningful and relevant to the lives of children and young people today, and which may help them develop into active, thoughtful and empathetic citizens in their future communities.

## Notes

1   This chapter draws on an earlier article: de Souza, M. (2014a). The empathetic mind: The essence of human spirituality. *International Journal of Children's Spirituality* *19*(1), pp. 45–54.

2   Retrieved on 8 April 2015 from www.nytimes.com/1989/03/28/science/research ers-trace-empathy-s-roots-to-infancy.html?pagewanted=2.

3   Retrieved on 8 April 2015 from www.huffingtonpost.com/alison-gopnik/ empathic-civilization-ama_b_473961.html.

4   Retrieved on 17 April 2015 from onlinelibrary.wiley.com.ezproxy2.acu.edu.au/ doi/10.1111/j.1746–1561.2008.00320.x/full.

5   Citing some research from ComScore, Carpenter and Ferguson (2009) indicate that Myspace.com attracted more than 114 million visitors in 2007, a 72 per cent increase from the year before, and Facebook attracted 52.2 million visitors, a 270 per cent increase (p. 192).

6   Comparisons between these three countries are useful since they have links through some shared elements in their cultural, historical, religious and political heritage and, in the contemporary world, have much interaction and interchanges that do impact on their children and young people.

7   Retrieved on 14 April 2015 from www.telegraph.co.uk/technology/news/ 10619007/Children-using-social-networks-underage-exposes-them-to-danger. html.

8   Retrieved on 13 April 2015 from www.telegraph.co.uk/education/education-news/9636862/Overexposure-to-technology-makes-children-miserable.html.

9   Retrievedon13April2015fromwww.abc.net.au/news/2014-11-20/neuroscientist-warns-young-brains-being-reshaped-by-technology/5906140.

10   The title of Turkle's book is *Alone Together: Why we Expect More from Technology and Less from Each Other* (New York: Basic Books, 2011).

11   For instance, a search on Google Scholar on 18 April 2015 came up with 12,700 results to the prompt 'cyber-bullying'.

12   *SPSSI Research Summary on Media Violence*. Retrieved on 19 April 2015 from www.spssi.org/index.cfm?fuseaction=page.viewPage&pageID=1899&nodeID=1.

# Chapter 3

# Social and political contexts
## Influences on spiritual wellbeing

Following the discussions in Chapters 1 and 2, which focus on the relational dimension of the human person as being the essence of human spirituality, this chapter focuses on another area that has significance for the spirituality of children and young people: certain influential elements that reside within today's social and political contexts. Accordingly, it will examine the spiritually nurturing and alienating factors that characterise contemporary communities, such as religious and cultural diversity, the significance of identity in plural societies, and the combination of religious and political aspects that can lead to terror. These features may either promote or impede the connectedness experienced or expressed by individuals and communities, ultimately impacting on their spiritual wellbeing.

## Background

The global nature of human society over these past decades has created a paradoxical situation that, at once, unites and alienates people. On the one hand, far-flung incidents at one end of the world can become significant events for people who live a long way away. This reinforces a sense of belonging to the species called humankind. On the other hand, the immense movement of people across the globe has meant that the monocultural, monoreligious and monolinguistic fabric that encompassed most Western societies has been transformed to incorporate a variety of cultures, religions and languages which live next door to each other. Many people become fearful when confronted with such diversity on their doorstep. Politicians and others in authority often manipulate such fears by fostering deep feelings of loyalty to the group, its leadership and its beliefs. While this serves their own ends, it also promotes divisions in society (Law, 2006, p. 30). Thus, tensions arise where the otherness of the Other becomes a stumbling block in the creation of a harmonious, cohesive society.

In addition, many countries have experienced the underlying threat of home-grown and foreign terrorist activity, much of which has been linked to fundamental, political elements in Islam. And yet, evidence of concern, compassion and connectedness that rise to the surface regularly in response to the plight of victims of natural disasters and human atrocities demonstrate our basic human decency and dignity. Just one example is an incident that reflects both the dark side of human spirituality – that which reflects fear of difference – and the light side of spirituality, which promotes wellbeing through an expression of compassion, inspired by a sense of connectedness. In December 2014, there was a siege in a café in Sydney, Australia. The perpetrator was a Muslim and it was immediately identified as a terrorist attack. As the news spread through various media outlets, a woman travelling on a suburban train noticed a young woman in front of her remove her headscarf. She felt so much compassion for this young woman who had been prompted to remove any signs of her religious identity that she offered to walk with her when they got off the train. It gave rise to the hashtag *I'll ride with you* on social media: 'There were 40,000 tweets using the hashtag #Illridewithyou in just two hours, according to Twitter Australia; 150,000 in four hours' (BBC Trending, 2014).[1]

The shadow of fear because of the expected repercussions for Muslims in the community was reflected in the act of a woman removing obvious signs of her Muslim identity. If we consider spirituality as relational, acts and behaviour related to expressions of connectedness reflect human spirituality. Thus, we find at that particular moment that the woman's fear, because of her connection to Islam, was an experience that diminished her. Although momentary, her connectedness to her faith was a dark experience. From the same incident we have another individual who was moved to a sense of compassion, something which can only be felt because she experienced a connectedness to another human being in distress. Her reaching out to the Other is a positive expression of spirituality, one which would have been an enhancing experience. Incidents like this compose the everyday lives of individuals everywhere and they continually mirror the human spirit in both light-filled and dark experiences.

Another example of how the plight of the Other may inspire a collective consciousness of feelings of connectedness was the global outpouring of concern and pleas for clemency for two convicted young men from the Bali Nine as they awaited their death sentence. While these examples were given much media coverage, there continue to be countless, unremarked examples of kindness, caring and consideration for the Other in the everyday. This innate element – the reaching out to the Other prompted by a sense of being connected – is a quality that underlies human acts of hope, care and kindness as one person offers help and comfort to the Other and, perhaps, the act may sometimes be inspired because an individual recognises the Self in the Other. Significantly, though, this element in human relations is often disturbed or distorted by social and political contexts.

## Some features of contemporary Australian society

Over the past decade there have been significant events that have contributed to, manipulated and provoked particular human attitudes and behaviours. This is the period of time comprising the first years of the twenty-first century where the incident known as 9/11 fashioned the ebb and flow of human relationships, globally, politically, socially, religiously and culturally. It has certainly dominated the landscape of these early years, but an additional occurrence was the global financial crisis. While this did not have the same impact on Australia as it did on Europe and America, there has been evidence of a steady rise in unemployment especially amongst the young, often leaving them disillusioned and desperate.

More significantly, the disparity between the rich and the poor has become more pronounced, which should be of much concern in Australia. Generally, while Australians through the boom years of the post-war period of the twentieth century saw themselves as an egalitarian society, my own observations when I arrived in the country in 1969 were that, in fact, there was a distinct class structure that was heavily disguised by the relative affluence of the working classes. Some elements that provided evidence of different social classes were the large independent school system, elitist private clubs and certain residential suburbs that were populated by the wealthy. Nonetheless, for many Australians who, at that time, had received a better education and entertained more affluent lifestyles than their parents, the trappings of the wealthy did not appear to put a dent in their optimistic view of a classless society. My conclusions are reinforced by Hugh Mackay, a well-known social researcher and commentator in Australia:

> Living in a society which strove for almost universal home ownership and car ownership, and which seemed to have achieved a widespread sense of being 'comfortably off', Australians living in the second half of the 20th century generally lost interest in the question of social class.
>
> (Mackay, 1993, p. 133)

Mackay, who has over the past three decades periodically surveyed Australians across the country to determine their quality of life and wellbeing, describes the particularity of Australian egalitarianism as being a situation where the 'rich and poor no longer seemed to count as reference points for defining a structure of social class' (ibid.). Rather, his observations led him to understand Australian egalitarianism as based on a self-perception that the society was largely composed of a middle class and – despite the obvious economic differences between groups, generally speaking – Australians had obtained a level of economic prosperity which meant that a sense of envy of the rich was not particularly strong. Nor did those who were more prosperous attract deferential behaviour from others. Instead, there was a feeling that power, influence and wealth were available to anyone who was prepared to work for it (p. 132). Mackay claims that Australians have remained comfortable with the idea that while there are rich and powerful people in the community, generally, everyone shares in the common way of life (p. 135).

One exception that Mackay noted amidst all this general sense of equality and fairness was the plight of Indigenous Australians. They continue to exist, in the eyes of many Australians, as a sub-class. If there was such a thing as a lower social class in Australia, it would comprise the homeless, the unemployed and the dispossessed – and these are characteristics often associated with Indigenous Australians (p. 141).

Another dispiriting element that has emerged over the past decade is the decrease in fulltime employment for many young people and a raised consciousness amongst many Australians of the widening gap between the 'haves' and 'have-nots'. In a later commentary on Australian life, Mackay (2007) examines this trend and makes specific note of the word 'entitlement' that has crept into political and social jargon: 'an explicit sense of entitlement has begun to emerge among members of Australia's burgeoning wealth class' (p. 109). He asserts that it has become 'an accessory to power, wealth, status or fame' leading to a rather delusional sense of being titled – that is, being a person of superior rank to others (ibid.), and notes that this sits rather oddly with the cultural heritage of an Australian society which was built on dreams of egalitarianism.

Mackay's thesis is supported by the findings of an Australian Government report on social inclusion in 2012. It concluded that, in general, Australians are prosperous, faring well and express satisfaction with their lives. Nevertheless, it also identified levels of inequality, particularly amongst 15- to 24-year-olds who make up more than a quarter of all long-term unemployed Australians (Australian Social Inclusion Board, 2012). Long-term unemployment for young people will, inevitably, dent their sense of self and their place in their communities and it impacts on their hopes for their future. This, then, diminishes their spiritual well-being. A resulting loss of confidence and self-esteem may be reflected by the increasing numbers of young people suffering from mental health problems. For instance, Mission Australia's (2014a) report on the mental health of young people identified that one-fifth of the participants suffered from mental health and had concerns about depression and suicide.[2]

## Experiences and perceptions of young Australians of their wellbeing

Since 2002, Mission Australia has annually conducted a survey to gauge the well-being of young people.[3] It aims to discover what concerns young people on a personal and national level, what they value and who they turn to for help. In 2014 it focused on young people's engagement in community activities, their feelings about the future and their aspirations (Mission Australia, 2014b). Much care was taken to ensure that the respondents would represent the diversity of Australian society – culturally, geographically and socio-economically – including young people in detention and those who are homeless or are at risk of being so. In 2014, 13,600 young Australians aged 15 to 19 took part in the survey and a summary of the findings showed that while a large majority (eight out of ten young people) valued the concept of achieving a successful career, six in ten did not believe that they would be able to achieve this. There were, as well, high levels of stress and anxiety found among school leavers, especially girls. A large majority, 80 per cent, recognised the benefits of having a good education in order to get a job; but half of the participants acknowledged that their access to the good jobs would be affected by their residential location. Finally, home ownership was something they all strived towards and they also felt that, despite the rising costs and falling rates of home ownership in Australia, they would be able to afford to buy their own home (ibid.).

Overall, then, these participants displayed a combination of hopes for a positive future while also experiencing high levels of stress and anxiety. They had conflicting expectations for their future in terms of economic related factors, including achieving the Australian dream of home ownership. In addition, a significant number of young women indicated that they were overwhelmed by trying to cope with stress, because they felt their gender would have a role in whether they would achieve their aspirations.

The concerns of these young people do suggest that there are undercurrents that lie not too far beneath the façade of the buoyancy and sensation of a good life that is usually associated with living in Australia. On the surface, it could be expected that within the affluent and secure existence that contextualises the lives of most mainstream young people, they would have opportunities to pursue their dreams and develop their potential to become the people they were meant to be. However, the responses of these participants point to the fact that there are significant other pressures in contemporary society that impact harmfully on their mental, emotional and spiritual health.

Moreover, it might be expected that the positive attributes of an affluent society would also encourage an environment where the spiritual wellbeing of its members could flourish. As Maslow (1968, 1999) observed, when individuals have their physical, safety and social needs met, they become more focused on their spiritual needs, thereby they begin to search for answers to questions of meaning which, potentially, may lead a person to self-actualisation. However, the boom years of the late-twentieth century coincided with a period when the traditional influences of family and religious communities were dwindling, so that spiritual searching at a personal level became a characteristic of this period in Australia and other Western societies. Too often, this leads to less than positive results, especially when young people – whose grounding has been in a materialistic and mostly existential world – leave themselves open to commercial and other forms of exploitation as they drift down one avenue or another, seeking answers to their big questions. The creation of safe and inclusive spaces for young people to seek and find answers needs to be considered by parents, educators and other professionals who work with and care for them. Recognition needs to be given to the fact that spirituality has become a topic in the public domain in many Western societies – as shown, for instance, by an interest in Eastern religions, meditation and yoga practices. However, we need a word of caution here. The term 'spirituality' has also become used indiscriminately to promote many different practices, and such usage merely demonstrates the lack of cohesive understanding and the ambiguity that surrounds the concept.

Given the discussion of the various elements that comprise the global and domestic setting of children and young people's lives, it is not surprising that they may, on the one hand, be filled with possibility and potential for human flourishing. On the other hand, the lives of many young people may shimmer with fear, suspicion, distrust, anxiety, hostility and an overt tension founded on a concept of 'them and us' – all of which can override the natural human instinct to reach out and connect with the Other. In particular, three interconnected aspects of contemporary living have implications for the spiritual wellbeing of children and young people:

- Issues related to plurality, including racism.
- The accompanying focus on identity.
- The juxtaposition of religion and terror.

The relevance and implications of these are discussed next.

## The divisive elements of plurality, identity and terror

In the early years of this century, people around the world were confronted with the event that has since become known as 9/11. It certainly may be described as the crucial event that has determined social, political, religious and global relations throughout the first fifteen years of the twenty-first century. Around the world, concentrated television coverage of the event exceeded any coverage for terror activity that had previously, or since, happened in other countries. The images of those planes flying into the Twin Towers would have had considerable impact on the non-conscious minds of the young and very young who, in watching them alongside their parents, would have been left with not only the visual memories but also an absorption of the accompanying emotions of shock, horror, alarm and disbelief. It can be without doubt that the far-reaching consequences of that event are still being played out some fifteen years later in many parts of the world.

The widespread terror activity and the ongoing conflict in many Muslim countries has resulted in large numbers of displaced people, refugees and asylum seekers who have resorted to sometimes desperate measures to relocate themselves in affluent, democratic and peaceful Western nations. The increased surveillance and security measures with the corresponding rise in the fear of terrorist activity have, as well, affected the lives of millions of people around the world as they go about their daily business. Furthermore, there has been the birth of a phenomenon that has come to be known as *Islamophobia* across many countries, thereby reducing the quality of daily life for many Muslim people who, previously, had been peaceful and non-threatening members of Western communities.

These features of the contemporary world have had serious implications for the sense of connectedness which is an essential element in the spiritual wellbeing of people and their communities as indicated in Chapter 1. As a result, problems generated by misunderstandings, ignorance, fear of difference and faulty communications have created the very tangible situation of 'them and us' divisions in what were once relatively homogenised societies. These issues create obstacles to the efforts to grow communities that may experience wholeness, social cohesion and spiritual wellbeing; and while they are issues for Australia, they have relevance for other countries which share issues related to cultural and religious diversity that affect social cohesion.

### A divided society: Historical influences

The first two hundred years of life in Australia since White Settlement gave rise to cultural patterns and practices derived from the Anglo-Saxon/Celtic world, which included the adoption of English as the spoken language. Nonetheless, despite the apparent homogeneity of Australian society, there were always divisions. Most obvious were the differences between the European and Indigenous people, owing to the attitudes of white supremacy that were a distinguishing trait of the colonial era; and, even today, there are lingering effects of this legacy so that the health, social wellbeing and longevity of Indigenous Australians are continuing areas of concern. A report published in February 2015 by The Close the Gap Campaign Steering Committee, which examined the health of Indigenous people in Australia, revealed that the findings of the *National Aboriginal and Torres Strait Islander Health Measures Survey* (the largest biomedical survey ever conducted among Aboriginal and Torres Strait Islander people) were critical (Holland, 2015). The survey identified high levels of undetected treatable and preventable chronic conditions that impact significantly on life expectancy.

Equally as worrying are the problems that beset the lives of Indigenous children and young people. A report on the detailed *Western Australian Aboriginal Child Health Survey*, about the social and emotional wellbeing of Indigenous children (Zubrick *et al.*, 2005), found that nearly 25 per cent of Indigenous children and young people, many of whom had been forcibly removed from their families, were perceived as being in the high risk category of having emotional and behavioural problems. They had, as well, double the rates of alcohol and other drug use. This was a significantly higher percentage compared to children and young people in the mainstream population in West Australia.

Further findings indicate that:

> Seven-in-ten Indigenous children were living in families that had experienced three or more major life stress events (like a death in the family, serious illness, family breakdown, financial problems, or arrest) in the year before the survey, and one-in-five had experienced seven or more major stress events.[4]

This is just one of the obvious divisions in Australian society that has ongoing relevance for the spirit of some of the people in terms of experiences of connectedness, belonging and identity. Another, less obvious, division relates to religious difference.

### The religious divide: Historical factors

The hostilities between Catholics and Protestants in the old countries were transported to Australia at the beginning of the European settlement and Borus (1992) claims that, because of their concern about the influence of Irish priests and Irish sedition, the British authorities did not allow Catholics to practise their religion in the early years. This led to a strong sense of solidarity amongst the Irish whereby they clung to and promoted their 'Irishness' so that their links to their cultural identity remained stronger than those of other minorities. It is Borus's contention that this was because, to them, 'the law which sentenced them was an alien British Law, but it was also the result of a deliberate policy by the bishops in Australia to reinforce the feeling that Catholicism and Irishness were inseparable' (p. 120).

Hughes concurs with Borus and observes that the 'clannish' tendency of the Irish was sustained by a hatred for the British who, they felt, punished them for being Irish:

> In Australia, as in Ireland, each act of oppression contributed to a common fund of memory, fact might waver into legend, but the essential content did not change. By the 1880s, when the Protestant majority had all but sublimated the 'hated stain' of convictry, the Irish still kept the memory of the system alive.
>
> (Hughes, 2003, p. 195)

Certainly, the Irish Catholics were treated as a minority group in Australia and this segregation continued until the latter half of the twentieth century. In his history of Australia, Kenneally (2011) highlights the fact that there was a 'tendency within Catholic schools to emphasize Irish history and to distinguish Australianness from Britishness' (p. 23). Thus was born an Irish Australian identity, which is still in evidence in some circles of contemporary society. Kenneally supports Hughes's argument about the clannish feelings of the Irish when he points out that the constant mainstream prejudice which the Irish experienced 'cemented their Irish Catholics' attachment to each other' (ibid.), However, he also notes that they maintained a strong allegiance to their adopted country, Australia. Further, he alludes to the fact that in some centres of business, Irish Australians were discriminated against when seeking employment. Their reaction to this was for the Hibernian Association and the Knights of the Southern Cross to take over workplaces for their own kind. For instance, in the 1890s, Irish Catholic children in Melbourne would be told that 'members of the Holy Catholic and Apostolic Church had "taken over" the city's tramways and they could always get a job there' (p. 24).

It is of interest that Kenneally (2009) identifies a further religious divide between Catholics of English and of Irish descent; that is, one occurring between members belonging to a particular faith tradition so that tensions exist because of differences (p. 467). Evidence of these divisions amongst Australian Catholics may be observed in the present day as Australia has become a multicultural society. Certainly, it may be expected that divisiveness generated by ethnic and religious difference is bound to impact not only on the cohesiveness of the nation, but also on the spiritual wellbeing of individuals. I will revisit this issue later in the chapter; but first, I will examine the transformation of Australia from a monocultural and monoreligious society to one composed of much diversity.

### Early multiculturalism in Australia

During the twentieth century, the drive to populate the country led the Australian Government to articulate immigration policies to attract migrants from Britain and Europe and, in time, the White Australia Policy (as it was commonly called) was formulated. This was a clear political statement directed towards keeping Australia 'white'. Thus, Australia's approach to immigration from Federation until the second half of the twentieth century, in effect, excluded non-European immigration. The White Australia Policy, could not, however, withstand the attitudinal changes after World War II and the growing acknowledgement of Australia's responsibilities as a member of the international community. In 1966 the Liberal Country Party Government began dismantling the White Australia Policy by permitting the immigration of 'distinguished' non-Europeans (Public Affairs, Department of Immigration and Multicultural and Indigenous Affairs, 2005).

Until the 1970s, then, migrants to Australia were largely from European countries and government policies were intent on assimilation with a focus on encouraging people to adopt the Anglo-Australian culture that contributed to a sense of national identity. It was only in the 1970s that the Federal Government began to acknowledge the difficulties faced by new migrants whose culture and language made it difficult for them to assimilate into the dominant Anglo-European culture, and accepted the possibility that migrants could integrate successfully into Australian society without losing their own cultural identities. Multiculturalism became a key word in subsequent government policies and practices and funding became available for migrant groups, which helped them maintain their language and cultural heritage within the mainstream culture:

> While Australian multicultural policy has its roots in government responses to the post-settlement issues facing migrants, through the 1980s and 1990s policy was articulated more broadly as an element of Australia's nation building narratives. Today all Australian States and Territories have active policies and programs dealing with multiculturalism.
>
> (Koleth, 2010)[5]

Generally speaking, many new Australians through the 1970s, 1980s and 1990s experienced a genuine sense that they were part of a healthy and lively multicultural society. The feelings of belonging that resulted are likely to have promoted spiritual wellbeing for the individual. While Australian culture and identity were still dominated by Anglo-European perspectives in many sectors, they were also being shaped and expanded by a multitude of first and second generation cultural and religious identities that had originated in non-European regions.

As a country of migrants, Australia has always had new arrivals with new ideas, behaviours, languages and religions to add to the cultural mix. When he was Minister for Foreign Affairs in the 1990s, Senator Gareth Evans (in an address in Melbourne) rejected the notion of the 'melting pot'[6] to describe Australian multiculturalism. Instead, he recognised the vibrant nature of Australia's multiculturalism as 'rather that of the salad bowl – where the ingredients remain separately identifiable, but they mix totally harmoniously together' (Evans, 1995).[7]

For the first few decades of multiculturalism in Australia, then, there appeared to be a general feeling of enthusiasm and openness towards new arrivals; but by the first decade of this century, the shiny optimism of a cohesive society had become somewhat tarnished. In the past few years, prejudicial attitudes towards people who are religiously and culturally different have become more clearly evident, so that a society that prided itself on its friendly and welcoming disposition has discovered a subtle underlayer of tension and friction. This has had serious implications for the mental, emotional and spiritual wellbeing of many young Australians.

The problems associated with religious diversity, which create boundaries between different religious and cultural communities, may be further compounded by tensions when we find plural identities within particular religious communities. For instance, in an attempt to conduct some research into the religiosity and spirituality of young Australian Muslims who lived in a regional town, a colleague and I discovered that the community was composed of Muslims from different countries and cultures and who, therefore, did not connect easily with one another to form a united faith community. This is an issue that often goes unrecognised by people outside the faith group. It is a very real experience for those within the faith group, especially if their background proclaims them as being of a certain ethnic identity.

The Australian Catholic community is another faith group today wherein certain tensions linked to unity in identity may be found and which, therefore, impact on their spirituality in terms of belonging and connectedness. I would argue that, in Catholic circles, this is linked to a heritage of being a marginalised people.

### Multiculturalism and identity amongst Australian Catholics[8]

The intake of migrants from countries other than European ones has led to a variety of cultures that are now evident amongst Australian Catholics. Figures from the 2011 Census (Australian Bureau of Statistics, 2014) show that 25.3 per cent of the total Australian population, which numbered 21,507,719 people, indicated that they were Catholic. A further breakdown of the background of the Catholic population showed that:

- In 2011, nearly a quarter of Australia's Catholics were born overseas and about three-quarters of those were born in non-English-speaking countries.
- For the first time, Iraq and South Korea were included in the top twenty source countries for Australia's Catholics.[9]

In addition, the census data from 2011 provides a statistical and insightful overview of the multicultural nature of Australian Catholics today, and shows that Catholic cultures originate in thirty-seven different countries or regions. Importantly, the increase of Catholics in the 2011 Census was not about Australian born individuals but reflected the growth of migrants from Asia and the Middle East.[10] Equally important is that at one level, these are people who are identified as an integrated community precisely because they belong to the Catholic faith tradition. At another level, however, we find quite significant diversity in culture and language, since many of them come from non-English speaking countries and non-anglicised cultures. Consequently, we find a large variety of customs, practices and languages, not to mention the differences in the physical features and ethnicity of the members that comprise the Australian Catholic community in contemporary Australia. This is very different to the largely Anglo-Australian physicality that characterised Australian Catholics for most of the country's history since White Settlement. These visible differences have distinct implications when attempts are made to identify different members of the community as one and the same, and they impact on the sense of connectedness experienced by different members of the community. Thus, members of the faith group may experience a sense of loss and displacement within their own faith community but, often, associated tensions or frustrations will remain as undercurrents, rarely being aired or given attention. These factors do have implications for the spiritual wellbeing of both individual and community since they indicate division rather than union, and dislocation rather than belonging.

In other words, newcomers in the Australian Catholic community may experience a sense of belonging because they are part of a community in faith. However, they may also become more aware of a feeling that they don't quite belong, because they come from non-Anglo regions where their rituals and customs have led them to a different way of believing and expressing their faith tradition. In my forty years of working in Victoria's Catholic education system in Australia, I was offered many shared confidences from colleagues from European and non-European backgrounds, whose perceptions and experiences revealed some disquiet about 'them and us' situations because they felt that, for many of those in leadership, new arrivals did not appear to be perceived as 'one of us'. Certainly, the leadership in Catholic education today is still dominated by Anglo-Australians, suggesting that there is a tendency towards wearing the mantle of their forefathers, which was about seeking solidarity from within, thus resulting in outward expressions of exclusivity. I have collected much anecdotal evidence that would substantiate these claims and I believe anecdotal evidence can provide useful data since it is usually drawn from personal experience and transmitted in much the same way as the stories handed down in oral tradition. One such story that reflects the experiences and perceptions of many was offered to me by a colleague from an Italian-Australian background and who had grown up in Australia. She was someone who had spent many years teaching in secondary schools and who had recently completed doctoral studies. I was sitting next to her at a conference dinner when she recognised someone across the room and went to speak to them. When she came back to the table, she appeared to be upset for she muttered, 'If you are not Anglo-Australian, you have to work five times as hard to get anywhere in this system'. Perhaps she had just discovered that she had not got a position for which she had applied and that it had gone to an Anglo-Australian. I base my assumption on my knowledge and observations throughout my four decades of working in the system that such experiences have been the rule, rather than the exception, for many non-Anglo-Australians.

The situation is exacerbated because a significant number of the leaders in Australian Catholic education grew up in the 1950s and 1960s when Irish-Australian Catholics were still experiencing a sense of marginalisation. Thus, experiences of isolation and exclusion have been part of the life story of today's leaders in Catholic education. Many of them attended the parish primary schools, which served to distance them even further from the mainstream community. It is more than possible, as well, that the non-conscious learning of these leaders would reflect their experiences of growing up in an Australia influenced by government policies that intentionally sought to prevent non-white migrants from entering Australia, which undoubtedly promoted a level of racism based on a fear of difference in the community (see de Souza 2009 and 2010 for a more extensive discussion on non-conscious learning).

Furthermore, Catholic children were expected to support the Catholic missions where most activity were in Third World, non-European countries, so it is possible that, in the children's non-conscious minds, a sense of superiority was born because they were 'saving the pagan children' – most of whom were non-white. For most of us, non-conscious learning remains unrecognised and unacknowledged and, in the case of these leaders, their attitudes towards Catholics who not only have different cultural practices but who are also non-European and non-white can, quite often, be patronising. If attitudes and behaviour driven by such non-conscious learning are not addressed, they are bound to influence the dynamics and practices in the Catholic school system where, so often, the student and teaching population reflects the high levels of multiculturalism evident in Australian society today.

There are significant implications too, when educators who have little engagement with religiously diverse people attempt to teach about other religious cultures. For instance, Erricker (2010) identifies a problem that had occurred in Britain where 'the emerging teacher graduates did not reflect the new ethnic and religious population of England and Wales in their number, but often sought to represent them in the curriculum' (p. 6). Erricker also observes that there was 'always a tendency to understand the other in terms of your own cultural "grammar" and its conceptual base' (p. 50).

Similarly, in the Australian situation, it is possible that knowledge and understanding of other religions and cultures amongst some educators have been reduced to an understanding contextualised by a marginalised Anglo-Australian perspective, which may be based on a non-conscious assumption about the superiority of their own faith practices. Janet Helms's conceptualisation of cultural racism that:

> societal beliefs and customs that promote the assumption that the products of a given culture including the language and tradition of that culture are superior to those of other cultures. Cultural racism exists when there is widespread acceptance of stereotypes concerning different ethnic or racial groups.
>
> (Helms, 1993)[11]

I believe that the concept of *cultural* racism may be extended to include a concept of *religious* racism where an assumption about the superiority of one's own religious beliefs and practice leads to attitudes that marginalise other religions or, indeed, other cultural practices of the same religion. While this often happens between different religious groups, it is likely to be much more harrowing when it happens to an individual within their own faith community and impacts on their religious identity and sense of belonging.

Recently in Australia, the leaders in Catholic education developed a concept of a 'preferred' Catholic identity.[12] Within the context of the existing plural Catholic identities, the obvious questions are: Whose Catholic identity? Which Catholic identity? Moreover, the word 'preferred' is, itself, exclusionary. It reflects some superiority and implies a rejection of the 'Other'. The fact that the project was driven from an Anglo-European perspective does raise some questions for me about whether this endeavour is an attempt to colonise Catholic identity in Australia.

Bauman (2004) suggests that the creation of a 'national' identity is a feature of the twentieth century when the boundaries of countries were changing and it was used by governments and political leaders to promote the corresponding behaviours and attitudes that they desired in their citizens (p. 21). Understandably, religious leaders have used the concept of a religious identity to achieve much the same purpose – that is, to encourage an alignment with the particular teachings and behaviours that they wish to see amongst their adherents. And just as citizenship education may be one avenue through which political authorities can promote the particular identity they desire in their citizens, religious education can also be used to promote the desirable religious identity.

Again, anecdotal evidence suggests that this is what happened in Catholic schools in Australia in the 1940s and 1950s when, for instance, children of new Italian migrants were 'educated' to leave their 'Italian' ways of being Catholic at home and adopt an Anglo-Australian Catholic identity (de Souza, 2014b). Indeed, Rossiter (2013) argues that when an institution considers that it is failing to achieve its aims, it often becomes concerned about identity and suggests that this is, possibly, one reason why Catholic leadership in Australia has become so focused on maintaining a particular Catholic identity.

Whatever the motivations, the fact remains that there are multiple Catholic identities that have contributed to the culture of Australian Catholics today, who – while united in their adherence to Catholicism – are nonetheless visibly different through their cultural, historical, ethnic and regional heritage, so that their ways of being Catholic are distinctly diverse. Thus, focusing on one Catholic identity is suggestive of a lack of acceptance of the otherness of the Other and is more than likely to have a detrimental impact on the sense of identity and belonging of the children of that community and, in turn, on the cultural and spiritual wellbeing of the community.

### The growth of religious diversity

The cultural diversity that composes Australia today has been accompanied, not surprisingly, by religious diversity so that Australia is now a multi-religious society. Additionally, since 9/11, there have been many tensions for Australian Muslims which has raised significant problems related to social cohesion and the spiritual wellbeing of the wider community.

A quick overview of contemporary Australia, revealed through the 2011 Census,[13] finds that 26 per cent of Australians were born overseas. Among those who are Australian born, 20 per cent have one or both parents who were born overseas. There are 260 languages spoken and while Christianity may still be the dominant religion, there are many other active faith communities, with Buddhism and Hinduism being amongst the fastest growing belief systems in Australia. Indeed, contemporary Australian culture reflects a vast array of influences from many European and non-European countries alike. The essence of Australian society is the diversity generated by the multiplicity of cultures and histories of its people who appear to live peacefully and in harmony with one another. Therefore, Australia can be recognised, truly, as a migrant nation. Nonetheless, in order to get an accurate picture of Australian society we need to recognise too that, despite the celebration of diversity that marked the early years of Australia's multiculturalism, there was always another, more subtle, layer where intolerance, prejudice and a lack of acceptance were the experiences of new migrants.

As a multiracial society, there is a general perception that Australians have been remarkably hospitable towards migrants. While there have always been outbreaks of racial prejudice against the latest wave – whether Greeks, Italians, Yugoslavs, Turks or Vietnamese – the traditional Australian attitude towards migrants is that they have come here to become part of the Australian way of life and that, accordingly, they should be assimilated as quickly as possible (Mackay, 1993, p.155).

Today, as we have passed the first decade of the twenty-first century, various tensions continue to be apparent which revolve around inclusivity and exclusivity, belonging and displacement. In the 2011 Australian Human Rights Commission document, *Freedom of Religion and Belief in 21st Century Australia*, the authors noted the considerable growth of different religious cultures and traditions in Australia since World War II and concluded:

So, Australia is partly a Christian country, partly a multifaith country, and partly a secularist country. This can make speaking or generalising about religion in Australia complicated. As this report shows, many religious and spiritualist voices mingle with secularist and humanist voices, with little unanimity on issues.

(Bouma *et al.*, 2011, p. 4).

These significant changes to the structure and composition of the Australian population has led to the current tensions associated with religious and cultural differences. For instance, over these past few months, a minor political party, Rise Up Australia Party, has been holding rallies to reclaim Australia from Islam. This movement began 'with just a few Aussies who were sick of staying silent while Islam, through Multiculturalism, was slowly but surely taking away all of our rights and freedoms' but it had grown so that there were to be fifteen rallies in major cities and country towns.[14] These kinds of extremist views have become more common in everyday life as political correctness has lost its dominance – and they have implications for the mental, emotional and spiritual wellbeing of those who are being targeted by strident dominant voices from members of the mainstream community. Certainly, there is a growing concern for many about the visible evidence of discord generated by Islamophobia that is increasingly becoming part of everyday Australian life.

### The phenomenon of Islamophobia and the spread of racism

When attitudes and actions erupt to cause ripples across the surface of an otherwise relatively peaceful society, they point to certain undercurrents that should be identified and attended to. If ignored, they can potentially grow and pose subtle or serious threats to the everyday lives of many. This became evident when Australian-Lebanese youths clashed with other Australian youths in Cronulla, a beachside suburb in December 2005.[15] Given the healthy multiculturalism of Australia in the 1970s through to the 1990s, many young Muslims from the Middle East experienced tolerance and acceptance when they first arrived to settle with their families. The policies at that time not only enabled them to identify with their culture, but also to feel a sense of belonging to the mainstream community. With the occurrence of 9/11, suddenly and collectively, these young Muslims found themselves marginalised. This sense was captured by a young Lebanese-Australian who had been involved in the Cronulla riots:

I want to return to the harmony and tolerance of my childhood where I felt included, a valued member of society. I stand before you today as a proud Lebanese-Australian but in a very different Australia.

(Participant at a forum organised by the
Shire of Cronulla. Screened by Channel 7 on
*This Day Tonight*, 1 June 2006)

The experiences of this young man were shared by many in his community and they created not only anxiety and distress, but also bewilderment and loss since, in their perceptions, Australia was their home. More importantly, many Australian Muslims came from a range of different countries and have lived in Australia for many years so that there are second and third generations who have been born in Australia. Australia is, therefore, their home. The author Mohsin Hamid created a realistic version of this scenario in his novel, *The Reluctant Fundamentalist* (2007), where his protagonist suddenly loses his sense of belonging and his identity as a successful and valued member of a community, which leads him into previously unknown territory. Feelings of such loss were also captured by the opinions editor of a Melbourne daily newspaper, Sushi Das. Drawing on her own experiences, she was able to accurately describe the turmoil young people from different religious cultures experience when they are caught up in a clash of cultures between their parents' way of being and the more liberal culture of a Western democracy as a 'constant riot in the head'. She goes on to say:

> Lost and confused somewhere in between, their parents lose control of them and they fall into that dark place where they become susceptible to extreme messages, to a simplistic ideology that provides certainty, or to a cause that fills the spiritual void.
>
> (Das, *The Age*, 28 July 2005)

Growing up in Britain in the 1960s and 1970s, Das had experienced being marginalised with her Indian family and she recalls: 'I hated being Indian, and for good reason. I couldn't go anywhere or do anything without it getting in the way' (Das, 2012, p. 63). Thus, her comments on the identity crisis that many young migrants experience when they don't feel a sense of belonging in the country they think of as home are insightful. Such young people can no longer identify with the culture of their parents and equally, they don't feel completely at one with the mainstream culture because political events have served to make them a displaced people. It is quite likely that young Muslims in Australia and elsewhere, whose physical appearance locates them as people from the Middle East or, indeed, other young people who bear a physical resemblance to Middle Eastern visages, cannot go anywhere without their physical, religious and cultural differences getting in the way. We need to note that the emotions and spiritual wellbeing of these young Australian Muslims would probably mirror those of young people around the globe who have grown up between cultures; that is, the culture of their parents and the culture of the country they live in.

The crisis of identity that Das speaks of often leads to the emergence of multiple identities, especially amongst young people who may also be affected by and who respond to the influence of youth sub-cultures. Bauman's (2004) theory of 'liquid' identity, one that shifts and shapes in response to the plural contexts within which individuals live today, supports the argument that the pluralistic nature of contemporary societies is germane to the birth of multiple identities. Recent research studies have focused on the troublesome experiences of young people and the associated problems a society may face when multiple identities become part of the fabric of their existence. Erricker (2008), for instance, refers to plural identities of second generation young British people from Muslim communities: the cultural identity of their parents, their religious identity and their national identity, which was determined by the country of their birth. In particular, he notes the problems of having multiple identities following 9/11 when there was overt hostility towards British Muslims from other British. Equally, El-Haj *et al.* (2011) discuss the multiple ways of belonging that young Muslims experience in the US and which can lead to multiple identities. Speaking of a brother and sister from the same Palestinian family, they describe a scenario where these two young people were concerned with both the anti-war and the anti-occupation movements. Their cultural heritage meant that they felt a sense of belonging to other Palestinians, 'but, they did so while also "maintaining" – sometimes uncomfortably – their status as "Americans", and they consciously worked to challenge and reshape US culture and politics' (p. 31).

This discussion has referred to young people who are the second generation of particular ethnicities across Australia, Britain and the United States, and they appear to share similarities in terms of the anxiety and unease they experience in respect to having multiple identities. Depending on the social, economic and political climates in each of these countries, and the receptiveness of their hosts, people may either feel a sense of belonging or a sense of alienation. The former will lead to fruitful engagements and a blossoming of a healthy multicultural context as did happen in Australia at the end of the last century. However, the latter can lead to simmering tensions, unrest and disengagement – which has happened in Australia in the first decade of this century.

The security associated with belonging and being accepted invariably inculcates a sense of self/identity and place, which contributes to the spiritual wellbeing of an individual or community. When this is suddenly removed, it has a detrimental effect on the individual's self-assurance, self-confidence and, therefore, their spiritual wellbeing. When this extends to a group or community, the resulting sense of displacement can quite possibly generate a kind of 'mob' rage, resentment and hostility. On the other side, young people from the host nation who continue to hear disparaging and hostile comments about a particular group from their political leaders are likely to develop a collective fear and aversion towards such a group. A collision of both these groups is the eventual outcome, culminating in violence as what happened in the Cronulla riots in 2005. Rather unfortunately, while the problems may initially stem from religious difference, they spread to include cultural difference so that people from particular cultural backgrounds become targets of prejudice and racial abuse. In fact, the behaviour of the young people involved in the Cronulla riots reflects the claim made by Harris and Lieberman that:

A focus on how racism survives through social and political institutions would draw on the numerous advances that the social sciences have achieved in recent decades, illuminating how institutional forces shape personal decisions and identities and how the interactions of individuals with their surroundings systematically influence behavior.

(Harris & Lieberman, 2015, p. 17)

Furthermore, Appiah (2015) notes that the concept of race is a social construct rather than one generated by human biology. He argues that 'identities rooted in the reality or the fantasy of shared ancestry, in short, remain central in politics, both within and between nations' (p. 8). Nonetheless, he argues that most people around the world find 'the concept of socially constructed races difficult to accept because it seems so alien to their psychological instincts and life experiences' (p. 7).

What has become evident in the contemporary world is that a rise in prejudicial attitudes based on race appears to be one of the consequences of living in a society characterised by plurality and this can be intensified when politics are involved. The damage to the mental and spiritual wellbeing of an individual who experiences hostility because of their race is well described by Das:

Racism, in all its overt and insidious ways, has the capacity to sear its mark on a person. It doesn't always hurt so much when it's actually happening to you as a child – like pulling a plaster off your knee really fast. The pain comes in adulthood, when you look back at the wound and realize it's bigger and uglier than you thought. Delayed trauma seeps into your heart and hardens it ever so slightly. The feeling doesn't turn into pity. That's what other people feel. It doesn't even become despair. It is just a big solid lump that you carry around in your rucksack for the rest of your life. Your strength and stamina will determine how far you travel with it, how crooked your back becomes, how quirky your gait.

(Das, 2012, p. 63)

While there is always a significant number of people who reject racist attitudes and promote inclusion, empathy and compassion, there will always remain, in any society, a core of people who fear difference and who strive to defend their right to be exclusive and to project attitudes of non-acceptance of anyone who does not resemble themselves. George Brandis, the Attorney General and first law officer of Australia, indicated this when he proposed amendments to Clause 18C in the Racial Discrimination Act which was introduced in 1998. When challenged about his proposal in Parliament, Brandis retorted: 'People do have a right to be bigots you know. In a free country people do have rights to say things that other people find offensive or insulting or bigoted.'[16]

Generally speaking, the people who support such freedom are often white and privileged and they appear to lack certain levels of empathy with those who are not like them. Needless to say, Brandis's statement attracted a furore of arguments, particularly since a majority of Australians, from all walks of life, would not support such an attitude today. One response came from Waleed Aly, an academic and media personality, who claimed that the language did not have to be changed since it already allowed people to be bigots. He referred to Clause 18C of the Act, which states that it is unlawful to do something that is 'reasonably likely' to vilify or intimidate someone on the basis of race, and then posed the question: Who gets to decide whether something is intimidating or vilifying? He answers it by quoting from subsection (3) of the Act: whether something is 'reasonably likely' to vilify is 'to be determined by the standards of an ordinary reasonable member of the Australian community' and 'not by the standards of any particular group within the Australian community'. Aly interprets this to mean 'not by the standard of whatever racial minority is being vilified. Not the ordinary reasonable wog, gook or sand nigger; the ordinary reasonable Australian' (Aly, 2014).[17]

Further, Aly claims that it is only a white person who will be identified as the ordinary reasonable member of the Australian community as stated in the Act, because they are seen as having no particular race; as being racially neutral: 'Of course, only white people have the chance to be neutral because in our society only white is deemed normal; only whiteness is invisible' (ibid.).

To be sure, Aly's thoughts are shared by many Australians who have neither 'white skin' nor have been reared in the dominant Anglo-European culture. For instance, writing on tolerance, prejudice and fear, another Australian writer, Tsiolkas (2008), in discussing the violent clash between Lebanese and Anglo-Australian youths in Cronulla, suggested that there was little to distinguish him (as an Australian of Greek origin) from a Lebanese-Australian. Tsiolkas claimed that Australian nationalism 'reminds us that there are the true Aussies and then there are the boons, the wogs, the slope-heads, the refos, chinks and niggers' (p. 41). He was writing at the time when the then prime minister of Australia, John Howard, chose to create cultural and racial divisions by introducing the word 'unAustralian' into the public vocabulary, thereby quite overtly promoting 'them and us' attitudes between mainstream Australians and those who were different.

It is important to note that these issues of racism between people of different colour are prevalent in many countries other than Australia and, very often, religious difference becomes part of the equation. For instance, Britain with a much older history of multiculturalism has already identified issues that are now arising in Australia. Citing the Parekh Report on the future of multi-ethnic Britain set up by the Runnymede Trust 2000, which had a reference to 'this Christian land', Robert Jackson states:

> this equation of national and Christian identity, associating all other religious identities with difference and otherness, is a version of what Tariq Modood (1997) has called 'cultural racism' . . . Racism directed towards religious groups, or justified on religious grounds.
>
> (Jackson, 2005, p. 7)

It would seem that the perception of Christianity as the national religious identity in Britain, where all other religious identities are regarded as different or ethnic, may be aligned with Aly's comments that only 'white' people can be seen as racially neutral, while all others are identified by their race. More recently, the Australian journalist Peter Greste, who spent 400 days in an Egyptian prison, claimed that he was released because of his 'ethnicity', while the two other journalists who were jailed at the same time were not given the same freedom because one was Egyptian and the other was Egyptian-Canadian.[18] Clearly, Greste felt that being a white Australian was significant in him being released and sent home (Greste, 2015).

Racial prejudice is an issue that afflicts most countries with culturally and religiously diverse societies, since fear of difference is often a non-conscious human tendency that leads to prejudice and racism, which are generated by non-conscious learning (Myers, 2002; Wilson, 2002). As I have argued before (de Souza, 2012a), over the past few hundred years of human history, we have collectively perceived, at a conscious level, the disdain of white people towards the culture, intelligence, education and worldviews of non-whites. It is quite possible, then, at a collective non-conscious level, that this may have seared the human consciousness of the twentieth and twenty-first centuries so that, in general, white people may have unstated and unrecognised feelings of superiority towards their black/brown/yellow neighbours. Equally, non-white people may have non-conscious attitudes, in reverse if you like, towards white people and Western cultures which will affect the way they interpret particular situations and actions. This latter attitude may be evident in the search for a new *ummah* (Roy, 2004).

### The search for a new ummah

The combination of factors that have led to the rise in culturally and religiously diverse societies have also produced settings that are primed for an accompanying rise in prejudice and visibly expressed resentment. The birth of Islamophobia is just one outcome. Pratt (2015) discusses three attitudes that religious groups adopt, cognitively and behaviourally, in response to the context of religious diversity: inclusivism, exclusivism and pluralism. Each of these recognises the otherness of the Other but ranges from a level of acceptance to a level of rejection. Pratt argues that exclusivism is the most problematic since it leads to religious fundamentalism whereby the believers' attitude is that their religion is the only one that is right and true: 'All "others" indeed anything or anyone who opposes or contradicts the exclusivist, are necessarily denied and so devalued, even to the point of elimination' (p. 210).

Thus, Pratt identifies the problematic outcomes of exclusivist attitudes adopted by some religions where the otherness of the Other is not only rejected, but can lead to acts of decimation. Pratt's conclusion is that an extremist attitude which leads to fundamentalism, one expression of which is Islamophobia, may be seen as instrumental in provoking disaffected young Muslims in many Western countries to search for a community in which they feel a sense of belonging and connectedness. This search has led to the recurring dilemma that many countries are currently facing: the radicalisation of their young people.

The hostile and extreme attitudes young Muslims have experienced through the past decade must have had an impact on their non-conscious minds. While at the conscious level, many have begun to seek a community where they can experience a sense of belonging, it is possible that their non-conscious learning, in response to those earlier attitudes, has played a decisive role in their alienation from Western society. In a world besieged by media and technology, the internet has allowed them to reach out and identify with a global community of Muslims and, in recent months, many news items have focused on young Muslims heading to the Middle East to support ISIS activity. In fact, Chitwood (2014) claims that recruits from eighty-one countries have travelled to fight in Syria. As well, concerns are being voiced in the media by politicians and others about the brainwashing of young people through social media; and questions are being asked about measures that may be put in place to prevent these young people from being exploited by terrorist groups. However, little consideration has been given to the impact of their non-conscious learning in their early, vulnerable years. I will discuss non-conscious learning in more detail in Chapter 4.

The current situation of youth radicalisation is also, quite possibly, one outcome of the thesis offered by French Islamicist Olivier Roy, that the radicalism that is becoming evident in Islam is the result of the de-territorialisation of Islam:

> Democratisation goes along with religious freedom not with a curb on theological debate and various expressions of religiosity . . . This also occurs when there is no state to be fought for, and where Muslims are in a minority that is, moreover, divided and lacks cohesion. Islamisation in this case accompanies the privatisation of faith, the formation of closed religious communities, the construction of pseudo-ethnic or cultural minorities, and identification with Western forms of religiosity or with the choice of a new kind of radical violence as embodied by Al-Qaeda.
>
> (Roy, 2004, p. 5)

While Roy focuses on Muslims who had settled in Europe he also raises the same issue as Das (2005) about the differences between first and second generations of migrants. Speaking specifically of the generation gap amongst Muslims, Roy refers to the second generation, who were born and educated in Europe, as being different not only in culture and language, but also in social expectations. Moreover, Roy makes the point that there are significant discrepancies between the ways in which Islam has developed in the West and the forms and practices in the original cultures. He attributes this, partly, to the changing nature of migration where, in earlier times, people moved to improve their economic prospects and stability; whereas with globalisation, the ease of mobility has created a new pattern of migration. Thus, new settlers today are a well-educated 'floating and mobile' population who have contributed to the de-territorialisation of Islam in the West which has altered the production of Muslim discourse. Accordingly, resettled or uprooted Muslims tend to reassess and consider just what Islam might mean to them and, in response to the beliefs and practices of the non-Muslim societies in which they find themselves, they have reconstructed their Muslim identity by dissociating themselves from their original culture and, instead, have searched for a global identity:

> By global Muslim we mean either Muslims who settled permanently in non-Muslim countries (mainly in the West), or Muslims who try to distance themselves from a given Muslim culture and to stress their belonging to a universal *ummah*, whether in a purely quietist way or through political action.
>
> (Roy, 2004, p. 1)

Roy also discusses the impact of the greater freedom of speech that is available in the environments where these Muslims have resettled. Such freedom was not accessible in their traditional communities where the combination of authoritarian regimes and religious establishments dissuaded intellectual dissent. As a result, these new Muslim communities have adapted their way of being in the world so that they could fit more readily into Western culture and legal categories of identity:

> To sum up, we are witnessing an endeavour by many Muslim community leaders in the West, as well as reformist theologians, to express the difference between Islam and the West in terms compatible with and/or acceptable by other (a Western non-Muslim). This is the methodological use of the neo-ethnic perception of Muslims in the West, which by definition insists on the legitimacy of recognising differences. But it contradicts the very definition of Islam as a universal true religion.
>
> (Roy, 2004, p. 132)

Speaking of the series of terrorist attacks in Europe and America in the past decade, Francis Fukuyama supported Roy's theory that terrorism today is a direct product of the de-territorialisation of Islam which, in turn, has materialised as resettled Muslims responding and adapting to living in Western democracies and culture. He said: 'There is something about the situation of a Muslim, particularly in Western Europe that I believe has bred a particular form of Islamic radicalism' (Fukuyama, 2006).

Roy's thesis is that the de-territorialisation of Islam is responsible for the more radical, non-national, privatised and globalised forms that have become evident in the world today and that, despite their concern about the negative influences of Western culture on Islam and their opposition to Western values, Muslims in the West have embodied Western ways of being and have expressed their identity through Western models (Roy, 2004 p. 201). However, Chitwood (2014) is critical of this thesis and specifically argues that Roy uses the term neofundamentalism inaccurately when he discusses it as non-statist and de-nationalised. Chitwood contends that, by Roy's definition, ISIS would have all the characteristics of neo-fundamentalism, but points out that their aim is to establish an Islamic State, thereby tying themselves to a region and territory. Furthermore, Chitwood argues that Roy describes a post-Islamic world which ignores the current situation where Islamist regimes continue to operate and give shape to Islamic discourse around the world. Finally, Chitwood concedes that:

> The contemporary forces of deculturation, deterritorialization, and destabilization, specifically in regards to Islam's passage to the West and the westernization of the world at large, have rendered new theological, societal, ideological, and sociological realities yielding a new pedantic movement within Islam.
>
> (Chitwood, 2014)[19]

Roy's thesis certainly provides some interesting insights when pondering the current situation with young Muslims who have been affected by the growing divisiveness generated by racial and religious intolerance. However, we need to recognise that many Muslim Australians grew up with a sense of self and place in a migrant nation which was composed of others like themselves who had resettled in a new country. In general, most of them had made new lives for themselves, experienced a welcoming acceptance from their host communities, and felt comfortable calling Australia home. Consequently, they would not appear to be the de-territorialised people that Roy speaks of. Instead, they are a people who have experienced loss of what they once had: that is, a loss of their sense of belonging which impacts on their identity; a loss of their place as an accepted member in the community which further impacts on their sense of the country as their home. The enormity of such a loss is more likely to generate a sense of shock and dislocation, subsequently accompanied by a sense of grievance and injustice which can then provoke anger and aggression. Since identity and belonging are basic human needs and people may engage in violence to satisfy such needs (Gallimore, 2004, p. 72), these young Muslims can become susceptible to the advances of ISIS and other groups that promote themselves as purist global Islamic communities and that appear to be a powerful voice in Islamic discourse.

However, a different perspective was offered at a forum – *Countering the Radicalisation of Muslim Youths* – held on 8 April 2015 at the University of Western Sydney's Parramatta campus. Keysar Trad, a spokesperson for the Islamic community, presented the keynote speech and claimed that some responsibility for the radicalisation of young Muslims in Australia lies with the local mainstream and international media, which had created an industry out of Islamophobia, thereby adding to the sense of victimisation and alienation felt by Muslim youths. It was his belief that this is what was pushing them to the margins (Oriti, 2015). While Trad may have had some justification for his claim, given the complexities of the situation there are other aspects that should also be considered. By placing the blame elsewhere he did not acknowledge the seduction of the great expectations, favourably coloured by distance, promised by powerful political groups to young people feeling some levels of disenfranchisement. This is just one example of the difficulties that arise when there is a lack of empathy between different social and cultural groups so that one is unable to see the other's view. For instance, the divisiveness that is currently being experienced in mainstream society was revealed through the string of positive and negative responses to Trad's claims that were posted on the ABC website.[20] Such incidents make it vital that politicians and community leaders find collaborative ways to respond to the negativity that has impacted on the relationship young Western Muslims have with their host communities, so that they may promote a way of life where understanding of, listening to and respect for the Other is paramount. Wilson's (2005) discussion of the susceptibility of young people to the influence of violent gangs is pertinent here. He argues that humans generally desire peaceful lives with their families and communities wherein they can experience an elevation of social harmony and physical, emotional and spiritual wellbeing. However, in today's world, amidst the disruptions to family stability and the decline of influence of traditional communities, young people seek to assert their individuality and independence while, at the same time, they yearn to feel a sense of belonging:

> What specifically is missing from home, community, and schools that gang membership offers today's youths? Gangs offer real or imagined stability or continuity of relationships; a sense of belonging or community; an immediate extended family; a rigid hierarchical structure; strong, personal role models; power and a power base; and clearly defined benchmarks, milestones, or rites of passage.
>
> (Wilson, 2005, pp. 170–171)

The argument offered by Wilson may be applied to young disenfranchised Muslims who, in their search to belong, gravitate towards militant Islamic groups who hold out promises of an ideal Islamic life.

## Concluding thoughts

This chapter has looked at certain features that characterise contemporary Western societies which impact on the sense of belonging, identity and connectedness experienced by different members of the community. These features have to do with the problems pertaining to religious and cultural diversity as well as ethnicity or race, and the corresponding implications for inclusivity and social cohesion in society. All these factors have relevance for the mental, emotional and spiritual health of individuals and, therefore, their communities.

The subsequent discussions have noted the tensions that emerge as a result of migration. In particular, when religious groups, such as Catholic and Muslim young people who come from non-European backgrounds, attempt to preserve their religious identity, they may find itself at odds with the host culture. They may, then, develop multiple identities, which generates some significant questions: Which identity does the individual most identify with – the family's religious identity or the one that they have constructed through their education and learning experiences? How does this affect their identity constructs and sense of belonging within their family and their communities? And in a time of crisis, emotional or otherwise, which of these identities will be the most influential in determining behaviour?

For instance, one could argue that the response of young Muslims in joining ISIS has been generated by one of their multiple identities, a globalised Islamic identity. Certainly, it posits a significant question for governments, the wider society and the particular ethnic communities that are being affected in terms of how these problems may be addressed: What strategies need to be put in place and who is responsible for incorporating such strategies into programmes and practices into the wider community? A further consideration is the need to acknowledge non-conscious learning so that it may be identified and appropriate responses formulated.

An obvious avenue to counter these issues is through educational programmes, since the end target is children and young people. Schools are the containers in modern society that hold and train young people to become desirable citizens for future communities. Both students and their teachers need to be educated to rise above the fear generated through media reports about terrorism and to start learning more about and engage with the otherness of the Other. As Paul Gilbert points out in his thesis on developing more compassion in our lives, we feel positive if we experience things like friendships and gaining status (finding our place) in our communities, which give us a sense of connectedness to friends and family, but he adds:

> we can experience very negative emotions when these important aspects of our lives are blocked and we feel like outsiders, disconnected from family or friends, and/or feel as if we have been reduced to a lowly status and are inferior.
>
> (Gilbert, 2010, p. 31)

It is only through engagement that people may move on from mere tolerance through to acceptance and empathy. Understanding difference will help to remove the fear it often projects and it may, possibly, instill in us the feelings of compassion that Gilbert speaks of and which, he argues, actually make us feel happier and better about ourselves.

If young people from different backgrounds feel welcomed and accepted it should inspire in them a sense of belonging and provide them with a place within their communities. This should also provide them with the intimacy and security that is found amongst people who share beliefs and values, and it might just reduce their need to search for that distant, global community via the internet.

Communication through the internet can be misleading and often disguises any inherent problems that exist at the other end, which is something those young people who succumb to the seductive invitations offered by a virtual community won't discover until they are actually, physically, there – and when it may be too late for them to change their minds. The contemporary situation affecting many young Muslim people in Western countries and which, therefore, impacts on both the domestic and global community, certainly requires a proactive, whole-community response.

If the issues examined in this chapter are not to cast long shadows that could stretch over the next generation of children and young people, they must receive attention – and constructive strategies should be put in place which may eliminate them or, at least, reduce the impact of their potency. The following chapters will offer some ideas in relation to addressing and nurturing the spiritual dimension in education as one way forward in responding to this situation.

## Notes

1   Retrieved on 26 March 2015 from www.bbc.com/news/blogs-trending- 30479306.
2   The full report can be found on the Mission Australia website: www.missionaustralia. com.au/component/search/?searchword=mental%20health%20report& searchphrase=all (retrieved on 6 July 2015).
3   Mission Australia's Youth Survey is the nation's largest online annual 'temperature check' of teenagers aged between 15 and 19. For more information see: www.missionaustralia.com.au/what-we-do-to-help-new/young-people/under standing-young-people/annual-youth-survey (retrieved on 22 January 2015).
4   Retrieved on 13 February 2015 from www.healthinfonet.ecu.edu.au/health-facts/health-faqs/sewb.
5   Retrieved on 31 March 2015 from www.aph.gov.au/About_Parliament/ Parliamentary_Departments/Parliamentary_Library/pubs/rp/rp1011/11rp06.
6   This was a description applied to American multiculturalism whereby different cultures and ethnicities were 'melted' down and fused into the creation of a new common identity.
7   Retrieved on 13 February 2015 from www.foreignminister.gov.au/speeches/ 1995/multi.html.
8   I have discussed this elsewhere. See de Souza, M. (2014b). Religious identity and plurality in Australia: Inclusions, exclusions and tensions. *Journal for the Study of Religion*, South Africa, *27*(1), pp. 210–233.
9   Data taken from Australian Catholic Bishops Conference (ACBC) Pastoral Research Office E-news Bulletin, 10 August 2012.
10   Presented by Professor Des Cahill at an Interfaith Workshop, Brahma Kumaris Retreat, Frankston South, Victoria, 17–18 May 2014.
11   Retrieved on 16 May 2014 from www.health-psych.org/Cultural.cfm.
12   See www.schoolidentity.net/ (retrieved on 7 January 2014).
13   Retrieved on 28 March 2015 from the Australian Bureau of Statistics 2011 Census Data, www.abs.gov.au/census.
14   Retrieved on 26 March 2014 from riseupaustraliaparty.com/.

15  More details of this occurrence may be viewed online at www.sbs.com.au/cronullariots/documentary.

16  Retrieved on 30 March 2014 from www.abc.net.au/news/2014-03-24/brandis-defends-right-to-be-a-bigot/5341552.

17  Retrieved on 14 April 2014 from www.theage.com.au/comment/brandis-race-hate-laws-are-whiter-than-white-20140327-35lv7.html#ixzz2xbNuPmu5.

18  Retrieved on 26 March 2015 from www.abc.net.au/news/2015-03-26/national-press-club-peter-greste/6350778.

19  Retrieved on 31 March 2015 from www.academia.edu/8873410/REVIEW_and_COMMENTARY_Globalized_Islam_the_Search_for_a_New_Ummah_by_Olivier_Roy.

20  These responses may be found on the ABC website: www.abc.net.au/news/2015-04-09/muslim-forum-told-australia-alot-learn-understand-radicalisation/6379384.

# Chapter 4

# Connectedness and *connectedness*

## Spirituality and the shadow

The discussion in the previous chapters have focused on spirituality as an innate human trait that is implicit in the relational dimension of Being. It promotes the wellbeing of individuals by providing them with a sense of identity and belonging and is an essential element in their lifelong search for meaning and purpose. In other words, we search and reach out for something beyond ourselves precisely because we are spiritual beings. Given this conceptual foundation in our discussion on spirituality, it stands to reason that spirituality requires serious consideration if we desire to increase the opportunities for our children and young people to grow into healthy, happy, inclusive and productive adults who will continue to contribute to the welfare and prosperity of their communities. I have examined findings from neuroscience which suggest that individuals are programmed to be empathetic so that, in the right environment, children should develop their spiritual natures, expressed by their deep connectedness to the Other. Alongside this, I have explored various factors in contemporary life which enhance or hinder experiences of connectedness which, respectively, nurture or impede spiritual growth. I will now turn my attention to yet another dimension of spirituality, one that is not often talked about in relation to children and young people: the darkness that accompanies humans on their life journeys.

This chapter, then, will begin by drawing on understandings about the human shadow and its effect on personality, attitude and behaviour. I will extend this discussion to explore experiences of connectedness which do not nurture or enhance an individual's wellbeing. Instead, those experiences which are more likely to impede an individual's progress towards human flourishing, and which can lead to disease, disorder and/or disconnection, are identified as elements that comprise the dark side of spirituality.

Early in 2011, I presented a paper at a spirituality conference in Prague and during the course of my talk I explained how my early research, triggered by Hay and Nye's (1998) concept of relational consciousness, had clearly pointed to relationality as being the essence of spirituality (de Souza 2003a; de Souza, Cartwright & McGilp 2004). I also spoke of my research which had indicated that spirituality was an innate human trait and that it was not confined to the religious dimensions of human life or, indeed, restricted to an understanding that it reflects a relationship with God (de Souza 2009). Finally, I described the concept of the relational/spiritual continuum to which my findings had pointed.[1] I further emphasised my conclusions that, at one end of the relational continuum, the individual Self is separate from everything that is Other – that is, one is clearly recognised as an individual being[2] – and that movement along the continuum reflects greater degrees of connectedness so that, logically and inevitably, the end point is a place where the individual experiences union with the Other, the Self becomes part of the Whole, which comprises the Other, and the individual enters the realm of Ultimate Unity.[3]

At the end of my presentation, one of the delegates rejected the notion that the essence of spirituality was human relationality or connectedness. She proceeded to tell me a story about a young woman she had known who had been deeply connected to her partner so that she lived her life according to his beliefs and expectations. However, this young woman had been unhappy and unfulfilled in her personal search and, in the end, the relationship had ended badly. Thus, this delegate was adamant that the notion of spirituality as connectedness was quite flawed. As often happens, this challenge generated more questions for me and prompted me to look further, thereby extending my own thinking. In revisiting and updating my literature review, I realised that most of the research, both mine and others', and the subsequent discussions in which I had participated had talked up spirituality as a positive human trait. In fact, it seemed that the aforementioned delegate also had this perception of spirituality as something positive. On reflection, we may note that the words usually associated with spirituality are positive expressions of human experience and certainly, the positive role of spirituality in promoting human wellbeing has been well documented (see de Souza *et al.*, 2009). We also find that research in different cultures and regions have indicated that nurturing spirituality is an important factor in promoting a sense of identity and belonging in the individual, leading to individual and community wellbeing.[4]

However, the challenge in Prague made me rethink the whole research situation and I had to acknowledge that, while addressing the shadow in human wellbeing was a distinct area of study in psychology, many of us who were examining spirituality from other disciplines and perspectives had, in fact, neglected the other side of spirituality: the darkness and shadow that are so much part of human life. In particular, we need to explore its implications for the lives and education of children and young people, which form the focus for this chapter.[5]

## Light – the positive side of spirituality

As we have shown, the role of spirituality in human life has received widespread attention across many regions and cultures. Professionals and researchers from a multitude of disciplines have been investigating spirituality as a positive element of the human condition. We continue, as well, to find through contemporary research and literature that the concept of connectedness pertaining to human spirituality remains a subject for discussion, which provides it with some credibility. Ervin Laszlo's contention offers further affirmation:

> Until the last decade or two, scientists and science-minded people considered the feeling of human and human–nature interconnection mere delusion. Then the evidence started to come in. A fresh look at our connections in the framework of the new sciences – quantum physics above all – *began to indicate that the 'oneness' people sometimes experience is not delusory* and that the explanation of it is not beyond the ken of the sciences. As quanta, and entire atoms and molecules, can be instantly connected across space and time, so living organisms, especially the complex and supersensitive brain and nervous system of evolved organisms, can be instantly connected with other organisms, with nature, and with the cosmos as a whole. This is vitally important, for admitting the intuition of connections to our everyday consciousness can inspire the solidarity we so urgently need to live on this planet – to live in harmony with each other and with nature.
>
> (Laszlo, 2008, p. 3; note the italics are mine)

More importantly, if the concept is translated into practice with applications for the everyday, we need to recognise that it requires that *the individuals live their lives with an awareness of their connectedness to everything other than Self.* In other words, one must live one's life recognising that one is a relational Being. It is this understanding that led me to describe the relational continuum because as one's awareness of one's relationality grows, one continues to reach yet another level of consciousness[6] which involves an expanding awareness. On reaching the absolute height and breadth of such awareness, one is led *past the point of relationality*, where Self becomes submerged in the Other – a place of No-Self.[7]

In general, the type of connectedness that is experienced along this continuum (or along one's life journey), which has been recognised as the positive side of spirituality, is the side that nurtures wellbeing and provides meaning for one's life experiences. I realise that it is this aspect of spirituality, the light side, which has been the motivating factor in my research, and the focus of many others, over the past few decades. We have concentrated on the connections between spirituality, education, health and wellbeing to help our children flourish and achieve their potential. Therefore, we have studied and identified those elements that are beneficial in helping children become whole people; however, this of course this does not constitute the complete picture.

What is needed now, to balance current studies, is the recognition that there is always *the other side* to any single thing. If any single thing is to be seen as a whole, we have to turn it around or inside out to examine the other side. In order for anything to be identified as positive, there has to be a negative. Without the negative how do we know what is positive? Logically then, there must be both positive and negative aspects of spirituality: those that illuminate our lives and fill us with hope, wonder and empathy; and those that drop us into darkness and reduce us to being only a part of ourselves. If we seek to enhance our wellbeing and enrich our everyday lives, as well as address those things that obstruct us in our quest for meaning and purpose, we need a holistic picture of spirituality. We need to recognise and detect the many different elements that constitute the experiences and expressions of our connectedness to the Other. This includes those that are positive and negative, good and evil, as well as those that take us into the light-filled parts of our lives in the world or which encourage us into the shadows.

## Darkness – the shadow side of spirituality

It is not surprising that Jung's theory of the human shadow has been foundational for many of the writings on this topic and it is probably a good place to start. Peter O'Connor offers the following interpretation of Jung's ideas on the shadow:

> The shadow is the inferior part of the personality, the sum of all personal and collective psychic elements which, because of their incompatibility with the chosen conscious attitude, are denied expression in conscious life and therefore coalesce into a relatively autonomous splinter personality with contrary tendencies in the unconscious mind. This shadow systematically behaves in a compensatory (that is, balancing) manner in relation to consciously held attitudes, views etc. Hence its effect on our everyday conscious life can be both positive as well as negative.
>
> (O'Connor, 1996 p. 46)

Tacey (2006) writes that Jung's life and work reveal his preoccupation with the dark side of humanity; he felt that people should not neglect their dark sides but, instead, they need to enter it and discover what lies within. The process would help them achieve balance in their lives. It is Tacey's understanding that Jung felt that people in Western culture had remained in the 'light' for too long and avoided the darkness and that 'the more an individual or group strives for light, the longer and darker is the shadow that is cast' (p. 55). In other words, they would rediscover a hidden part or parts of their personality without which they would not achieve wholeness. Thus, the shadow or the less desirable elements actually complement the positive and socially acceptable traits in a personality, and discovering the dark side is essential in the process of an individual attaining a sense of wholeness.

If we accept this, there appears to be some logic to the notion that identifying and accessing the darkness may be needed to balance the light side of spirituality and that the dark side has a distinct contribution to make to spiritual wellbeing. This has been one of the themes found in the writings of contemporary scholars (Bly, 1988; Collins, 2007; Earl, 2001; Finnegan, 2008; Gilbert, 2010; Hillman, 1996; Palmer, 2000; and Tacey, 2006 among others) who have argued that, in order to be whole, individuals must recognise, accept and, perhaps, embrace the shadow side of their lives. Indeed, Tacey (2006) asserts that some Jungian scholars believe the 'gold' in the shadow that consciousness rejects is often the stuff that injects into life its highest value.

Another claim from Tacey that is quite relevant to contemporary times is that when cultures emphasise the light and ignore the shadow, they end up as 'pallid, empty, bloodless, superficial, routine, devoid of adventure – but also . . . unprepared for onslaughts of pure evil' (p. 56). Thus, if the shadow continues to be ignored, it can lead to outbursts of irrationality, anger and hostility which, at a national level, can result in war, terrorism and violence. Tacey further explains that the unconscious mind may introduce a rather different dimension to the way one perceives or experiences the world, so that 'we have to view darkness with greater respect, and learn to appreciate not only its capacity for destruction, but its capacity for vitality, growth and transformation' (p. 61).

Fordham (1953), whose introduction to Jung's work includes a foreword by Jung himself, says that we develop a persona which enables us to live in and engage with the world. We develop an attitude, either as an extrovert or an introvert, and a function – both of which compose our persona. Hence, we will develop the function that we are most gifted with, whether it is thinking or intuition, feeling or sensation, but this is balanced by the expectations of society and education which require us to behave in a certain way. In succumbing to the social pressures, then, various parts of our personality are repressed. We haven't actually lost these parts but they have become submerged deep in our non-conscious minds.

O'Connor (1996) describes the persona as the mask or masks we don, through which we relate to the outside world and through which the world sees us (p. 60). O'Connor believes that while a mask is 'a necessary and vital piece of social equipment useful for social lubrication, the task of being is to strive to complete ourselves; that is to bring into the light of consciousness, *all* of who we are' (italics were in the original text). Citing Kierkegaard, he adds 'to hide behind a mask is to condemn oneself to a life of "half obscurity"' (p. 61).

A further perspective on living a life of half obscurity is offered by Bly (1988). Speaking from within a Western cultural framework, he claims that children, from their earliest days, are socialised into a form of dualistic thinking, where the light and dark sides of their personalities are split and polarised:

> When we were one or two years old we had what we might visualize as a 360-degree personality. Energy radiated out from all parts of our body and all parts of our psyche. A child running is a living globe of energy . . . but one day we noticed our parents didn't like certain parts of that ball. They said things like: 'Can't you be still?' Or 'It isn't nice to try and kill your brother.' Behind us we have an invisible bag, and the part of us our parents don't like, we, to keep our parents' love, put in the bag. By the time we go to school our bag is quite large. Then our teachers have their say: 'Good children don't get angry over such little things.' So we take our anger and put it in the bag. By the time my brother and I were twelve in Madison, Minnesota we were known as 'the nice Bly boys'. Our bags were already a mile long.
>
> (Bly, 1988, p. 17).

Following this line of thought, Bly maintains that out of that 360-degree ball of energy, individuals at twenty will end up with about a slice of what they started with and then may spend the rest of their life trying to recover what has been non-consciously put in the bag. If the substance in the bag is ignored, Bly claims, it will take on a personality of its own – often with damaging results: 'Every part of our personality that we do not love will become hostile to us' (p. 20).

Furthermore, Bly (n.d.) concurs with Jung's view when he comments on the determined efforts of people in the West to avoid facing up to their shadow, personally or collectively. He suggests that many people who suffer grief or trauma deal with the experience by repressing it rather than confronting it; and he alludes to the subsequent fallout in later years when, for instance, relationships may break down because of unresolved conflicts that have been residing in the non-conscious mind and comprise the personal shadow. Another example he uses is the trauma suffered by war veterans that was never effectively resolved because of the rather ineffectual rehabilitation they received in the post-war years. He refers to Martin Pratchel's identification of 'unmetabolized grief' which he suggests may be recognised as another component of both the personal and collective shadow (Bly, n.d., p. 9).

Moving to another perspective, Finnegan (2008) uses the metaphor of 'dangerous memory' to discuss a spirituality which cannot forget the horrific acts that make up our history. A spirituality that acknowledges dangerous memory learns how to stand alongside victims of tyranny and social inequality. Dangerous memory can lead to expressions of spirituality that take away a degree of comfort and security from the individual precisely because it requires integrity and courage to stand up for what is right. Therefore, perhaps, it may lead an individual to finding him or herself standing alone. While Finnegan is referring to adults, we need to remember that children also have 'dangerous memories'. This has been illustrated in the appalling cases of child abuse that have come to light in the past few years, some of which have been described in detail by witnesses interviewed by the Royal Commission into Institutional Responses to Child Sexual Abuse in Australia, established in 2013.[8] The extensive damage that has been done to so many children in care and elsewhere is, indeed, a very dark stain on our consciousness today, especially when we hear of the cover-up by those who could have done something to make a difference in those young lives. Further instances of children's 'dangerous memories' may be linked to the treatment of refugee children in detention in Australia.[9] The large number of people who have worked tirelessly to bring these issues into the public arena so that some action is taken are expressions of spirituality, which are not always comfortable or attractive to the individual, and reflect Finnegan's 'dangerous memory'.[10] Taking a deliberate action that leads to isolation or which puts oneself outside the mainstream may feel like walking on the dark side, since a foundational element in being human is the desire to belong and live in congenial and affirming relationships with the Other. Individuals who put their own interests aside to act in the best interests of others can find that their reaching out has led to dark experiences, including distress, fear, loneliness and indescribable horror, all of which are a direct result of actions reflecting the connectedness they experience to the Other.

## Children and the shadow

Drawing on some of these perspectives on the human shadow, we can recognise that children in their early years often demonstrate personality characteristics of acquisitive, possessive and aggressive behaviour which are natural to them. Zweig and Abrams (1991) claim that the development of the individual shadow is a natural process in every young child. Thus, children learn to 'identify with ideal personality characteristics such as politeness and generosity, which are reinforced in their environments and at the same time they bury in the shadow those qualities that don't fit the self-image they are creating' (p. xvi). As adults, we have long learned that particular kinds of behaviour are unacceptable in society and we, therefore, pass this learning about the desirability to conform onto our children so that they resort to hiding or removing unattractive tendencies. An interesting idea developed by Zweig and Abrams is that the components that make up the shadow may be culturally derived:

> The shadow acts like a psychic immune system, defining what is self and what is not-self. For different people, in different families and cultures, what falls into ego and what falls into shadow can vary. For instance, some permit anger or aggression to be expressed; most do not. Some permit sexuality, vulnerability, or strong emotions; many do not. Some permit financial ambition or artistic expression, or intellectual development, while some do not.
>
> (Zweig & Abrams, 1991, p. xvii)

Indeed, we may extend this understanding to recognise that the components of the shadow may also be gender specific. Thus, when girls and boys are encouraged to hide those parts of themselves that do not fit the socially constructed feminine or masculine moulds, young people who do not conform to the accepted patterns are bound to have their shadow composed of the mental, emotional and psychological issues and anguish that can be associated with sexual orientation and gender identity. The restrictions on their lives, the impact on their sense of belonging and the mental and emotional distress that can become a part of their daily lives have been well documented for several years (for example, Brown, 2002; Rosenstreich, 2013).[11] Rosenstreich, for instance, found that GLBTI (gay, lesbian, bisexual, transgender and intersex) people had the highest rate of suicidality of any population in Australia (2013, p. 3); while Brown's (2002) research highlights a further problem for young people when they 'come out' because their families often have difficulty accepting them. This has an immediate consequence for their sense of belonging and identity which, in turn, impacts on their spiritual wellbeing.

Certainly, all the instincts and abilities that are rejected by the individual in their attempt to define 'what is self and what is not-self' are relegated to the shadow to become the hidden power of the dark side of human nature (Zweig & Abrams, 1991, p. xvii). Parents, educators and other professionals often don't concern themselves that these hidden traits that reside in the child's unconscious mind and remain part of the child. Over time, as the shadow is unheeded, it becomes more powerful and, remaining out of sight of the conscious mind, it becomes instrumental in the display of particular attitudes and behaviours of the adolescent or adult that the child has become. As well, when conditions are favourable for the emergence of these hidden traits, individuals may find themselves exploding in completely unexpected and unpalatable actions, driven by their non-conscious mind.

A further reference that is pertinent here is from Berryman (2008), who speaks of the problems when children ask questions or seek stories about evil. Their own pain and suffering make them realise that evil is real, but adults usually have limited language in order to answer their questions. Berryman makes the point that children can 'juggle awful reality and hopeful questions to fashion new ways to understand and cope with evil' (p. 67). However, he cautions parents and educators to be alert to the language they use when they speak of evil and concludes: 'To help children look for that better ending, however, we must be on our guard against the evasions of evil that is built into our language' (ibid.). Berryman argues that because our language in Western culture is fairly restricted when applied to difficult and emotional situations, adults generally become evasive when they answer children's questions about pain and suffering. This is usually because they are uncomfortable and not always equipped to deal with such questions. When children find that the answers do not really address the issue they are asking about, they are left with 'why' questions that have no answers and which serve to reinforce their pain and suffering. Further, it is possible that the experiences of pain and suffering which are not addressed or resolved in childhood can disappear into the shadow hanging over the child, to become part of the non-conscious story which accompanies them into adulthood.

It is Zweig and Abrams' (1991) contention that children are introduced to shadow issues through the fairy tales they are told which depict the war between good and evil, fairy godmothers and wicked witches. However, they claim that censorship in Western culture tries to 'throttle the voice of darkness' because it fails to understand the urgent need for the child to become acquainted with the darkness. Thus, in their efforts to protect the young, fairy tales are rewritten with happy endings and 'in the end, the young are left unprepared to meet the evil they will encounter' (p. xx1).

In Jung's view, the shadow is the primitive, uncontrolled and animal part of ourselves; the inferior being in ourselves, the one who wants to do all the things that we do not allow ourselves to do and who is everything that we are not. This is our personal shadow (Fordham, 1953, p. 49). However, the shadow is also something more than the personal non-conscious; it remains personal when it concerns our own weaknesses and failings, but it is also common to all humanity. In this guise it may be seen as a collective phenomenon, and the collective shadow may be characterised by irrationality (O'Connor, 1996, p. 54), or expressed in collective acts of prejudice, hatred and mob riots (Fordham, 1953,

p. 51) or, in contemporary times, as corporate greed, ethnic cleansing, war and acts of terrorism, among other things.

Abrams (1998) discusses how the shadow begins in the earliest years of a child when they begin to develop their concept of 'I' and become aware that they are separate from the Other. This construction of Self relates to the Theory of Mind which was discussed in Chapter 2. Abrams suggests that when children begin to recognise their individual selves between the first and second years, the social construct of the Self begins in response to the expectations of the people with whom the child interacts – siblings, parents and other significant adults. The process leads to the child displaying those aspects of their personality which draws a positive response from those around them and which reinforces a particular notion of what and who a 'good' child is. As a result, 'shadow-making runs parallel to ego development. What doesn't fit our developing ego-ideal – our idealized sense of self, individualistically reinforced by family and culture – becomes shadow' (p. xv).

From a New Age therapeutic stance, Ford (1998) points to the problematic nature of repressing parts of ourselves in childhood as Abrams discusses. She refers to a holographic model of the universe, which emphasises the connection between the inner and outer world and reflects the understanding that 'we, as individual beings, are not isolated and random' (p. 4) and argues that many are too frightened to look beyond the light to the shadow of our deepest selves. We spend so much time hiding those faces of ourselves that reflect the unacceptable aspects of ourselves (p. 10), so that we no longer remember who we really are (p. 5). Ford claims that it is only when we integrate all of ourselves, when we take the time to discover our whole Self, that we find happiness and fulfilment. Moreover, she believes that for this to occur we need to confront and embrace our darkness; we cannot live in the beauty of our highest Self without knowing the dark side, which is the gatekeeper to true freedom (p. 12). In other words, in order to be whole, we have to embrace *all* of ourselves, the positive and the negative, the good and the bad (p. 13). Without knowing all of ourselves and developing a sense of wholeness, our mental, emotional and spiritual wellbeing is affected. We lay ourselves open to assault from the shadows we have repressed, which may erupt without warning to destroy our sense of self, our peace of mind and our ability to become the people we hope to be. These different views do point to the importance of getting to know our shadow, that dark presence in our lives, and learning to be comfortable with it.

## Confronting the shadow – some concerns

Further perspectives and discussions on the shadow do highlight the problems in dealing with it. Collins (2007), whose research draws from OCCUPATION THERAPY, refers to the complexity of engaging one's spirituality because it includes the chance that one will encounter the darkness within. Entering the darkness is a scary experience and one that should be undertaken only with professional guidance – or it could further intensify any anxieties experienced by the individual, thus hindering them in their search for meaning and their ability to live a balanced life.

Collins agrees with the Jungian notion that the 'concept of shadow is an important feature of any authentic exploration of the self . . . since the shadow represents all of the rejected or unexplored feelings and inner tensions that fuel
projections' (p. 89). He emphasises that there is a need for reflection on the
relationship between spirituality and shadow. In addition, Collins points to the
need for an increased awareness and the development of safe parameters when
exploring this relationship in therapeutic practice.

From a clinical psychological stance, O'Connor (1996) claims that dealing
with and coming to terms with one's shadow is the work of a lifetime and, perhaps, a first step is to recognise how we project our shadow onto someone else –
whether this is someone we detest intensely or, at the other extreme, someone
we fervently idealise (p. 58). But O'Connor claims that the process of confronting the shadow and attempting to withdraw projections can be a challenging and
miserable experience:

> Confronting it (the shadow) in some people brings on feelings of insuffer-
> able guilt, powerful feelings of having wasted one's life, of having lived a life
> of self-deception. So in some it creates a feeling of hopelessness, in others a
> feeling of panic, and in yet others a feeling of impossibility.
>
> (O'Connor, 1996, p. 58)

By drawing on his professional work and experience with adults, O'Connor's
words highlight why it is vital that we nurture the spiritual wellbeing of children
and young people in education to ensure that they will grow up learning about
and embracing their shadow. Teaching them to explore the shadow early in their
lives will encourage them to live with both the lightness and darkness of their
personalities, so that they experience themselves as cohesive beings, complete in
their wholeness. In today's world where cultural tendencies tend to promote the
positive over the negative, addressing this aspect in education is necessary before
the shadow becomes a destructive force which may obstruct the flourishing of
children in their adult years.

One further offering on the projection of the shadow, which has implications for teachers and other leaders in education, has been articulated by Palmer
(2000). His assertion is that someone in leadership (for instance, a classroom
teacher within the confines of the classroom) has the power to project either light
or shadow onto a part of the world where they dwell and therefore, on the people
who are their co-dwellers. It is in the hands of a leader to create the ethos within
the spaces where others live and this can result in 'an ethos as light-filled as heaven
or as shadowy as hell' (p. 78). Further, he contends that 'a *good* leader is intensely
aware of the interplay of inner shadow and light, lest the act of leadership do
more harm than good' (ibid.) and he reminds us that if we ignore our shadows,
we sustain a delusion that 'our efforts are always well intended, our power always
benign, and the problem is always in those difficult people whom we are trying to
lead' (p. 79). Given the distance between the views and attitudes of many political

and religious leaders and those held by young people today, Palmer's words are cautionary. Indeed, they have special significance for times when decisions are made that impact on the jobs and careers, lifestyles, health and spiritual wellbeing of children and young people.

Drawing on the arguments offered by these writers, it would seem that recognition of the shadow is vital if an individual is to develop as a whole person. Just concentrating on the positive features of one's personality merely transfers the less desirable characteristics into the shadow that resides in the non-conscious mind.[12] If ignored, the non-conscious mind will, in time, start to project elements of the shadow so that it impacts, usually adversely, on the individual's life in some shape or form. These, then, are some of the elements of the human shadow that have implications for understanding the dark side of spirituality. However, there is a further aspect that requires attention and it is the situation when experiences of connectedness impede growth and wellbeing and prevents the individual from blossoming into the person they are meant to be. This, I believe, is the kind of connectedness that the delegate at Prague spoke of and it is, clearly, a negative experience, specifically because it has the potential to lead to disconnectedness from one's inner Self. Losing sight of the potential of one's true Being will, ultimately, disconnect the Self from the Other.

Some of the words that may be associated with feelings of disconnectedness are: alienation, disenfranchised, fragmented, disenchanted, unhappiness, discontent, disillusioned, prejudice and racism, frustration, envy, feelings of loss and being lost, anxiety, fear, guilt, alone with no one to talk to/confide in, boredom and apathy. Each of these words reflects a state of Being where the nurturing of the individual's spiritual Self is being impeded; and often, this will impact on the subsequent flourishing and progress of the individual. It is imperative, then, that teachers and parents find ways to promote the sense of belonging, Self/identity and place for children and young people to experience, which will help to connect them to their individual selves and to their communities. Moreover, some may need encouragement to dream and imagine, as well as to reach out for self-transcendence and the mystery beyond their physical existence.

We can see from these various theories and points of view that it is important for children and young people to be provided with the skills and strategies that will allow them to access their inner selves and to become reacquainted with those parts of the Self that they have hidden away. They should, as well, learn to embrace these hidden parts so that they can feel good about themselves and learn to love themselves as whole people. This, unfortunately, is an area that has received little attention in educational programmes so that the shadow side of children's personalities has been quite neglected.

## The neglect of the shadow in education

About a decade ago, when spiritual education was first being discussed and debated in Britain, Earl (2001) was critical of a tendency to focus on the light side of spirituality. She argued that people assumed that spirituality was a positive experience that allowed a person to transcend the dreariness of their reality; but they failed to acknowledge the difficulties inherent in the process. Moreover, they concentrated on spiritual elements of 'awe, wonder and mystery but not with the difficulties of holding these together with degradation, despair and destructiveness – or even the ordinariness of most of our lives most of the time' (p. 277).

It was Earl's contention that although there was a general acknowledgement of the existence of the shadow side of spirituality, this did not translate into educational practice or into related academic writing. Thus, teachers were not guided or encouraged to address their own shadow, which usually meant that they lacked either skills or confidence to help children address theirs. Certainly, it is easier and more comfortable for individuals to ignore their shadow since delving into such things can lead them into challenging and disturbing arenas. Earl drew on Jung to discuss this less positive side of one's personality and argued that while individuals tend not to own up to their own shadows, they end up projecting them onto others. Thus, they go into denial and reject that part of themselves which agitates them and with which they have difficulty coping.

Earl's criticism that there has been a lack of recognition of the shadow in education is a valid one. In a culture that encourages living in the light and neglecting the shadow as identified by Jung and others discussed earlier, I am reminded of assessment practices in education in the 1980s and 1990s in Australia. There was an acknowledgement that many children who were not gifted in literacy and numeracy skills were disadvantaged in an education system where success was determined by excellence in these areas. As a result, many children were destined to experience failure repeatedly, so something was needed to be done. A series of six ministerial papers were released by Victoria's Minister for Education in 1985, of which the sixth was focused on curriculum development and planning and the words 'access' and 'success' were included. These words, then, became a motivating factor for educators to find ways to enable all children to have access to success in their learning programmes. Many schools began to adopt different ways of assessment that removed experiences of failure amongst their students. This was my experience in a new secondary school, as it entered its fifth year, where I had arrived to take up the senior leadership position in curriculum. I discovered that the assessment practices for the previous four years, Years 7 to 10, had been without any form of grading. Instead, students were given descriptive comments which, if they had been carefully constructed with identification of the strengths and weaknesses inherent in the work and suggestions for improvement, would have been effective. However, this had not apparently been the case as I discovered when I began teaching a Year 11 English class. Year 11 meant that the students had to be prepared for the external examination at the end of Year 12, when they were competing against the rest of the state. Hence, graded assessment had to be introduced and I remember the shock and disbelief from some of the 17-year-old students in my English class when they received a 'C' grade for an essay along with a long paragraph detailing the strengths and what else needed to be done to improve it. The descriptive comments that they were used to had led to an artificial situation where students had a rather elevated expectation of their own ability, since failure had not been part of the system in their first four years. On receiving the first marked essays, some of them came to question why they had not received an 'A' grade. I believe that it was only after several weeks, when they started noticing that their own writing was beginning to improve, that they began to realise the difference between one grade and another.

The point of this story is related to Earl's comments about the reluctance to allow students to face the shadow in education. In trying to avoid a situation where students experience failure, an atmosphere of unrealistic and inflated ideas of one's proficiency had been created and it was unlikely to do the students any favours when they entered the adult world where the individual's chance to experience success is dependent on so many other factors such as competition, political expedience and connections to influential people. Students need to face up to the fact that there are some areas where their ability or skills may not be good enough and that their talents lie in other directions where they can excel. However, the education system, geared as it is to weighting some subjects over others, does not allow a well-rounded picture of the child to emerge. Rather, it fails to recognise the many human gifts and qualities that complement one another and which provide an essential basis for any community to function well. A variety of human capabilities are needed to create an enriching and cohesive society so that all members can feel empowered, precisely because they have a specific place and role in contributing to the wellbeing of their people. Indeed, an aspect of helping children feel connected to themselves and to others in the world around them is to acknowledge and value all their gifts. As a result, this should foster feelings of being a valued member of the community just for being who they really are. In addition, the knowledge that they have something worthwhile to contribute to communal life promotes their sense of belonging.

An educational system that implements such an approach will, potentially, foster spiritual wellbeing in their young, raising their awareness of their connectedness to the Other, and thereby assuring them of their identity and place within their social group. A sense of belonging and identity, as we have seen, will promote the wellbeing of the individual and, surely, this is a desirable goal in the current climate where so many of our young are displaying physical and mental health problems.[13] On just one of the websites dealing with such problems, that of *headspace National Youth Mental Health Foundation* (which is funded by the Australian Government Department of Health under the Youth Mental Health Initiative Program), we are confronted with statistics that indicate the high incidents of mental health and alcoholic and substance abuse problems involving our young people. For instance, 75 per cent of mental health problems emerge before the age of 25 and up to 50 per cent of substance use problems are preceded by mental health issues in young people. Corresponding issues are the links between high suicide rates amongst young adults and untreated mental health problems.[14]

These figures should be alarming for all parents, educators and other professionals who work with children and young people. If we accept that unresolved problems from early childhood do become part of the shadow that impacts on the child in later life, we may see the rise in statistics related to mental health issues as one of the outcomes in a society that has discouraged confrontations with the human shadow. Certainly, it is an issue that requires further research leading to a proactive response involving innovative strategies that will help to renew the current education charter.

## The impact of a materialistic and consumeristic culture

One factor that appears to prompt disconnectedness – and therefore support the emergence of the shadow – is living in the materialistic culture of today. This could be because the attractions and distractions of a consumeristic society soothe and manipulate the physical Self and therefore are too hard to resist. Or it could be that the busyness of life allows people to avoid delving into the depths of their Being where shadows may lurk; thus, they can avoid the discomfort and/or fear associated with such an activity. As Zweig and Abrams (1991) assert, while we may be somewhat aware of an inner need to grapple with our inner concerns, this can be overridden by outer concerns, such as the need to work long hours, distractions by other people or antidepressant drugs. All these things serve to dampen our feelings of despair and allow us to retain a distance from the dark side of our psyche.

One cause for the busyness of life and longer working hours could be attributed to the impact of globalisation, as people who network across the globe build different time zones into their daily lives whereby their times for rest and relaxation are reduced. Another impact of globalisation is examined by Elliott and Lemert (2006), who discuss the notion that a new individualism has emerged as a result of globalisation. In their study, Elliott and Lemert observe that in the affluent globally networked cities of the West where 'the lures and seduction of individualism' reign supreme, people are avoiding interpersonal intrusions in their ceaseless search for self-fulfilment (p. 3). They further claim that 'the culture of individualism has come to represent not only personal freedom but the essential shape of the social fabric itself' (ibid.). The authors argue that modern societies are both enabling and constraining, so that individual identities develop in response to the high powered urban and economic pressures to become 'egoistic, calculating and blasé' and lead people to 'seek reassurance of their independence and power in an overwhelmingly indifferent and impersonal world' (p. 56).

More importantly, Elliott and Lemert allude to other studies which suggest that social changes have led to a greater disconnection of the individual from family, community and the social system itself (p. 63). Nonetheless, they conclude that culture does not reduce people to a one-dimensional life; rather, they suggest a more optimistic picture of men, women and also many children all over the world 'who see and feel the self within, accept it for what it is, and use its aggressions and drives for attachment to others with whom they remake themselves and what corners of the worlds they can' (p. 196).

Thus, Elliott and Lemert actually echo the interpretation of individualisation offered by James Moffett many years ago, when he said:

> The *nature* of individualization has also been evolving, some stages of which are selfish and narcissistic, attained by the majority now, further stages of which, attained by a leading minority, are empathic and compassionate. The latter seem to return to the original group solidarity, but there is a world of difference between the primal herd feeling, which is unconscious and incapable of personal thought or action, and the expanded consciousness of the individual who has parlayed self-cultivation into transcendence.
>
> (Moffett, 1994, p. 10)

It would seem that, in some ways, an individualistic way of being in the contemporary world has translated into a distancing of the Self from civic involvement, including voluntary work, so that there is less interest in involving oneself in working for the Other. However, there is some hope that the processes of individualisation as described by Moffett and identified by Elliott and Lemert will reach a point where communal life becomes important again, where individuals will be able to confront the narcissistic, egoistic aspects of their shadow and move forward to forge deeper connections to the Other. These new relationships are ones in which they can cultivate a sense of belonging while retaining their individualism. The relationship may, in fact, be stronger because individuals are more grounded, and present themselves as whole people who have come to terms with and embraced their shadow. As a result, their vulnerabilities no longer make them prey to the next good idea, the latest product in the marketplace or a desire to present an image to the world that is untrue to who they really are. This is the hoped-for height of the maturation of individualisation. Thus, it is a goal we can work towards when nurturing our children and young people in combatting the pressures of contemporary life.

Hyde's (2008) identification of two factors that tend to inhibit children's spirituality in terms of their interaction and connections with one another (see Chapter 1) is pertinent to the discussion here. The first is 'material pursuits' (p. 144), which demonstrates the socialisation of children into forming connections to the superficial elements in life and, perhaps, placing a value on things above relationships. The second is 'trivialising' (p. 149), which suggests that even in primary school, various influences, whether social, family or community, have taught or encouraged children to avoid confrontation with the things about themselves that make them uncomfortable. It is easier to become distracted by the latest fad, gadget, fashion, movie and so on; and, as Bly (1988) described, the bags they carry behind them would, in all probability, get bigger and heavier. This is an important factor, one that requires a considered response in education where both the positive and the negative aspects of contemporary living are identified and utilised for the benefit of children and young people.

A further factor that seems to encourage people to live at the surface of their lives is the incredible pace of contemporary life. Paul Gilbert describes the situation in Britain after World War II as one where policies focused on the welfare of people and communities – but the emphasis today is on maintaining a 'competitive edge':

> There is a depressing shift away from welfare-focused and 'quality of life' politics towards the business model, which is focused on shareholders' dividends and 'efficiencies', often at the expense of quality and a concern with human welfare.
>
> (Gilbert, 2010, p.10)

Certainly, what Gilbert describes is pertinent to many other countries, particularly those which share the trappings of a Western culture similar to that of Britain. Following his line of reasoning, Gilbert refers to findings of the World Health Organization which reveal that 'depression will be the second-most burdensome disorder on Earth by 2020 and other mental health problems will be in the top ten' (ibid.).

Addressing one's shadow requires time and stillness without diversion and it brings with it fear, anxiety and other uncomfortable feelings. It is not surprising, then, that many people may prefer to avoid the tension generated by such conflicting experiences by becoming immersed in the busy lifestyle on offer and persuading themselves that success in the material world is what will make them happy. That parents may pass such perceptions onto their children may be evidenced by the busy lifestyles of so many children today. Their days and weeks are made up of schedules that compose most of their waking hours: from school through sport, gym, ballet, martial arts, music lessons, supervised play and so on. Their free time is taken up with activities associated with technological and communication devices that promote 'distant connectedness' (de Souza, 2009; 2012b) or being 'alone together' (Turkle, 2011). Such experiences of connectedness are different to the nurturing connectedness that encourages growth and flourishing amongst children as a result of positive engagement and interactions with other human beings.

Yet another example of the dark side of spirituality is when the relational dimension of an individual's life becomes distorted – that is, when connectedness to something other than Self becomes obsessive. The obsession could be a focus on another person, on an unrealistic goal, on poor self-esteem or a lack of acceptance of Self and so on. This creates a situation where disillusion, disappointment and/or despair may set in so that individuals may become victims of their own relational selves with consequences for their spiritual blossoming. Once again, if attempts are made to balance the child's learning and life experiences, and also to prompt realistic and accurate self-assessment and self-acceptance, there is a chance that children may develop a wide array of interests and outlets for their energies where they feel competent, content and, indeed, happy and peaceful. These experiences may assist in moving them away from obsessive behaviour.

Finally, another feature that is particularly pertinent in the pluralistic context of today's world is the fear of the otherness of the Other. Often, this further illustrates the socialisation process referred to earlier and, until this fear is brought to light and a person acknowledges its residence within the dark shades of his or her non-conscious mind, it remains out of sight but continues to project its negativity onto the Other. Therefore, the role of the non-conscious mind in impeding experiences of connectedness is something that needs to be factored in when exploring human spirituality.

## The non-conscious mind: Where the shadow resides

I have written extensively on the role of the non-conscious mind in promoting prejudices and racism (de Souza 2008, 2009 and 2010) and, in the context of what we have been discussing in this book, I would like to revisit some of those ideas. There have been quite a few writings exploring the role of the non-conscious mind in how people learn through perception, which involves the instant processing of information by the non-conscious mind and the more delayed information processing by the conscious mind (see Gladwell, 2005; Hillman, 1996; Hogarth, 2001; and Myers, 2002 among others). In addition, Klein (2003) speaks of how intuitive decision-making is generated by the non-conscious mind as a result of extensive experiences, which has led to a huge amount of information being absorbed through non-conscious perceptions and stored outside our conscious minds. One of the books that most influenced my own thinking around this topic, because of its relevance to the concept of spirituality as connectedness and how this may be expressed in multicultural societies, is by the social psychologist Timothy Wilson (2002). I had been reading the literature on intuition, which informs the approach to learning that I was developing (and which I will discuss in Chapter 5), when I came across Wilson's book *Strangers to Ourselves: Discovering the Adaptive Unconscious*. The title intrigued me and I found the content illuminating, especially in relation to the notion of how the human person forms prejudices.

When we live in a world immersed in cultural and religious diversity and which, in turn, is besieged by prejudices generated by a lack of knowledge and understanding about the stranger in our midst – the different Other – we need to learn about how and why people develop prejudicial attitudes. We need to discover, as well, ways in which we can combat and address such mindsets. Certainly, the prejudices that are formed early in life, often at a non-conscious level because of what we have seen and/or heard, become components of our shadow. They remain hidden away in that bag over our shoulders as described by Bly (1988), erupting when the conditions become conducive for their re-appearance.

Some of the tensions and conflict in Australia and in many other societies today, it would appear, are driven by misunderstandings and misconceptions which reflect attitudes and behaviours displayed by particular groups towards those that are perceived as 'them' and not 'us'. It is important to remember that this feature is not restricted to just one or two groups that compose the multi-cultural fabric in society, but are reflected in the attitudes of all groups who may define themselves by their ethnicity, thereby recognising their difference from the Other. When a society is experiencing a peaceful and optimistic phase, and when the economic situation is good so that unemployment levels are low, these attitudes remain out of sight but, as has happened since 9/11, they have mate-rialised in, sometimes, horror-filled and unspeakable actions committed by one group towards another that is different. Examples are the recent terror attacks or threats of terror, race-related riots, ethnic cleansing and other forms of cultural and religious conflict in Australia and many other countries.

Wilson (2002) contends that an essential part of our personality and way of being in the world is to be able to respond to experiences and events in 'quick, habitual ways'. This means that we have psychologically developed a healthy defence system to ward off any threats to our person in 'reasonable and adaptive ways'. Rather significantly, this all happens outside our conscious minds (p. 22) so that we remain unaware of these processes taking place. Wilson uses the term 'adaptive unconscious' to identify the fact that non-conscious thinking is an evolu-tionary adaptation. It is the capability that we have developed 'to size up our envi-ronments, disambiguate them, interpret them, and imitate behaviour quickly and non-consciously' (p. 23) – which then places us in an advantageous position over others. Wilson describes two ways in which the mind processes information – conscious and non-conscious – and these relate to two ways of learning, explicit and implicit (p. 25). More importantly, through implicit learning, which is the function of the adaptive unconscious, we can absorb complex information at much greater speed and detail than our conscious minds (p. 26). In the pro-cess, when our senses are being bombarded with information, we engage a non-conscious filter called 'selective attention' (p. 28) which determines what part of the information needs to be sent to the conscious mind; the rest disappears into and is retained by the non-conscious mind (ibid.). However, even though this information is out of our awareness, it still influences our attitudes and behaviour:

> The adaptive unconscious is thus more than just a gatekeeper, deciding what information to admit to consciousness. It is also a spin doctor that interprets information outside of awareness. One of the most important judgements we make is about the motives, intention, and dispositions of other people, and it is to our advantage to make these judgements quickly.
>
> (Wilson, 2002, p. 31)

Yet another facet of the adaptive unconscious is its ability to decide what informa-tion to select, how to interpret and evaluate it and which goal to set in motion

(p. 35); and these decisions are motivated by the individual's desire to perceive and create a world that promotes and maintains their sense of wellbeing. 'We are masterly spin doctors, rationalizers, and justifiers of threatening information' (p. 38), and Wilson recognises that this process can lead to conflict within the individual because:

> the need to be accurate and the desire to feel good about ourselves is one of the major battlegrounds of the self, and how this battle is waged and how it is won are central determinants of who we are and how we feel about ourselves.
> (Wilson, 2002, p. 39)

Wilson acknowledges that the solution to the conflict within the individual is not always obvious, especially if the aim is to remain healthy and well-adjusted. The answer lies in individuals not losing touch with reality and ensuring that they have an honest knowledge of their own abilities to engage in self-improvement (p. 40).

If we take Wilson's thesis on board, there are several factors that we can identify which have implications for the specific problems related to cultural and religious diversity that we have witnessed over this past decade. For instance, if we consider the amount of air space given, in the early years following 9/11, to politicians' rhetoric on the war against terror – including the most graphic images of war and victims of war – the implicit message was that the perpetrators of the terror attacks were Muslims. Little was done to distinguish the fact that not all Muslims are terrorists. The impact of this kind of media presentation on young children constantly exposed to such messages and images is that they are usually relegated to the non-conscious mind. Because of the dominance of the media in today's world and the overabundance of negative issues, in time these earlier impressions become buried under the more current communications. However, when the time is ripe, they will still have the power to determine actions and responses to particular situations.

If we move on to consider the radicalisation of young Australian Muslims, as discussed in an earlier chapter, we may begin by perceiving it as a very large shadow hanging over the Muslim community. As well, within the context of Wilson's arguments about the role of the non-conscious mind on the development of racist and prejudicial attitude, we may get a glimmer of understanding about some of the motivations of young Muslims in joining extreme groups. These young people, after all, were exposed to censorious news items about – and hostile attitudes towards – Muslims during their most vulnerable years. If this has become part of their shadow – that is, the understandings and attitudes hidden deep inside Bly's (1988) bag – it could mean that the shadow continues to project its fear and negativity on these young people, thereby making them susceptible to online seduction and becoming perfect targets for organisations who are determined to whip up a frenzy of fundamentalism as a strategy to extend their membership. This is possibly because, at some dark level, these young people believe there is something wrong with them as a consequence of all those early messages which they absorbed. It is easier, then, for them to project this darkness onto Westerners who become the source of evil, the ones who are destroying Islam and, therefore, them. This, of course, is just one interpretation of why so many young Muslims in Australia and elsewhere have become passionate and motivated to join ISIS and groups that are similarly oriented, and they astound us with their declared hatred of the West. This hatred may be part of the Self story these young people have created because, as Wilson (2002) states, the Self story promotes and maintains their sense of wellbeing and helps them feel good about themselves.

Children regularly hear or see attitudes indicating a lack of acceptance of minority groups or, given the increased episodes of male perpetrated violence against women,[15] promoting domestic violence.[16] At the non-conscious level, then, they develop negative attitudes about aspects of male and female relationships or towards different ethnic and minority groups, which are prejudicial, and while they learn that these attitudes are not acceptable in a society that prides itself on its egalitarianism, or where the order of the day is about being politically correct, the attitudes remain hidden. They grow up believing that they are inclusive and accepting people, and this is the way they present themselves to the world at a conscious level. It is only when anything happens that upsets their equilibrium, whether it is something serious like a threat to their security or fear of physical assault, or some minor incident that irritates them, they are provoked into speech, attitudes and/or behaviour that are driven by their non-conscious mind. The negativity or prejudice that is reflected in their subsequent actions will correspond to the seriousness of the situation that angered or made them fearful in the first place.

These issues that I have explored reflect Wilson's argument, based on his research in social psychology, which suggests that a person can be both prejudiced and non-prejudiced (2002, p. 189). He concludes that:

> The adaptive unconscious might have learned to respond in prejudiced way, on the basis of thousands of exposures to racist views in the media or exposure to role models such as one's parents. Some people learn to reject such attitudes at a conscious level, and egalitarian views become a central part of their self-stories. They will act on their conscious, non-prejudiced views when they are monitoring and controlling their behaviour, but will act on the more racist disposition of their adaptive unconscious when they are not monitoring or cannot control their actions.
>
> (Wilson, 2002, p. 190)

Wilson's theory that prejudicial and biased attitudes are often controlled by elements outside our conscious awareness has been supported by extensive research. Bargh, Chen and Burrows (1996) conducted three experiments to determine if social behaviour is capable of automatic activation – that is, it is preconscious and not dependent on the individual's conscious intentions. They concluded that 'social behaviour is like any other psychological reaction to any social situation, capable of occurring in the absence of conscious involvement or intervention' (p. 242) and that this has implications for stereotype confirmations and empathic reactions.

Hogarth, (2001) also identifies two systems by which we learn and take action: the *tacit* system, where all processes occur tacitly or automatically (that is, largely without use of conscious attention); and the second is the *deliberate* system, which encompasses all processes that require effort (that is, attention and deliberation) (p. 21). Through passive observation, people acquire distinct feelings and attitudes which can lead to automatic prejudicial attitudes towards particular social, cultural and/or ethnic groups (p. 48). Hogarth acknowledges that once individuals are made aware of their prejudices, they are able to combat any possible negative reactions. However, he also recognises that just knowing that they have inappropriate views does not automatically render these opinions powerless. He concedes 'it is probably impossible to suppress some stereotypes that emerge from the operation of the *tacit* system. However, it is possible to learn to use the deliberate system to avoid acting on tacit prejudice' (p. 49).

Another proponent of the dual attitude system is Myers (2002), who discusses the automatic or *implicit* attitude towards someone or something, which differs from the consciously controlled, *explicit* attitude. He says that our likes and dislikes or, indeed, our preferences and prejudices are drawn from both our non-conscious and our conscious minds:

> From childhood, for example, we may retain a habitual, automatic fear or dislike of people for whom we now verbalize respect and appreciation. Although explicit attitudes may change with relative ease . . . implicit attitudes, like old habits, change more slowly.
>
> (Myers, 2002, p. 35)

To sum up this discussion, we can understand the two ways in which individuals process information: one is at the conscious level and it takes more time; while the second occurs in a flash at the non-conscious level and remains beyond the cognisance of the individual. It is the latter that has relevance for the human shadow, the dark side of spirituality, since it can generate negative actions and behaviour to the detriment of the individual and those they may encounter. This is revealed through experiences of connectedness or relationships which do not enhance the individual's life but, instead, actually obstruct the flourishing and spiritual wellbeing of the individual. They can, as well, lead to forms of alienation or marginalisation from the community to which the individual belongs. Alternatively, it may lead to a disconnectedness from the Self, the inner person, so that the individual feels adrift and unable to ground themselves in a communal belief system that may be essential for their spiritual nurturing. Such experiences are likely to lead to mental distress and other health issues, all of which have, in fact, become symptomatic in the contemporary world.

Certainly, the signs suggest that we need to find ways to address issues that are affecting the spiritual wellbeing of our children and young people. Expert assistance needs to be employed to help them confront their shadow and rediscover those parts of themselves that they have hidden away. It would assist them to become whole again and connected to their communities. They may also begin to appreciate that plural ways of being in the world are not something to be feared; rather, they may find that developing a deeper connectedness to the Other can override diversity and strengthen connections – which enlivens and promotes wellness in themselves and their communities.

## Balancing the light and darkness

The ideas highlighted here clearly indicate that the ongoing suppression of our shadow side has the potential to lead us down a path towards neuroses and other health problems, including serious mental illness which, ultimately, affects our spiritual wellbeing. If we are to live out our lives as whole people, we must embrace both the light and dark sides of our personalities. In other words, if we are to prosper as whole human beings and develop our potential to be the people we are meant to be, we must find a way to live in a creative tension between our gifts and our limitations. Indeed, if we subscribe to the idea that human flourishing depends on learning to live productively with the light and dark sides of our person, there are some important considerations for educational practice.

For many years there has been a distinct move amongst curriculum writers and practitioners to create programmes where every child has access to success. One of the problems associated with this intention is that it has been introduced into an education system which, for the most part, is one that has been generated by and was responsive to the European context and culture of the nineteenth century. Despite a wealth of literature that has identified the problems of such a system in responding to the needs of students and the expectations of parents and societies in today's world,[17] most curriculum reviews (and these occur every few years) merely introduce changes that patch up the old system rather than completely overhauling it. Thus, we have a system that answers to the calls of politicians, the corporate world and industry and the concept of economic rationalisation. Further, the general public who are highly influenced by what they read in the media – which, in turn, reflects the powerful and influential voices in society (usually related to financial incentives and rewards) – are raucous in their demands on the system. Consequently, the real and more valid concerns and voices of those at the coalface – the teachers, parents and children – often get lost in the clamour of political and social rhetoric. For two or more decades now, there has been a huge focus on literacy and numeracy to the detriment of other subjects, such as the arts, the social sciences and physical education, all of which are required for children to develop as whole people. This is one result of the rather conservative views that dominate education reform today, so that any notion of providing a holistic curriculum continues to be compromised by a focus on developing knowledge and skills for the workplace.

If we return to the goal that all children will have access to success in the system as it currently exists, it has to mean that the only way it can work is if children are given misleading ideas about their abilities – as indicated in the anecdotal evidence offered earlier. After all, to succeed in a system that focuses on particular areas of learning and particular knowledge and skills means that some students will never be the best they can be in such areas. They may have other abilities and skills, for instance, innate wisdom in how to deal with people, or creative and imaginative skills in the arts or in technical subjects, or intuitive thinking that leads them to the heart of a problem – all of which are essential for a society or a community to function effectively and smoothly. Nonetheless, these other attributes that students possess are not given the same value in contemporary education, which is geared towards testing and exams. Instead, various manipulative practices and strategies are introduced which will allow all children to achieve success despite their lack of ability in the areas that have been designated as the important ones. It is my belief that, as long as there continue to be children whose gifts and abilities come down on the side of the less valued subjects, they will continue to experience rejection of the very elements that make them who they are and which, in response to these external pressures, they may be tempted to consign to their shadow. Not surprisingly, such experiences for children in their vulnerable, growing years can lead to self-rejection. In other words, their spiritual lives in terms of their growth to wholeness become constrained.

A corresponding problem is the underlying message in education and the media that has led many children to believe they can be and do anything they want. This is the result of rejecting the dark and living in the light. Certainly, the media's exploitation of children by creating images of beautiful people, beautiful places and so on – all designed to lead to false hopes and unrealised expectations – has been well documented (Mercer 2008; Turpin 2008). As Bishop Urwin succinctly puts it: 'This self-image has been imposed on them by the false shepherds of a secular and materialistic culture.'[18] In a real world, these expectations and prospects are, of course, unrealistic for most; and when children or young people realise these untruths and arrive at a conclusion that they have been misled and that they have set their sights on something quite out of their reach, it can lead to adverse consequences. It is no wonder so many children today escape into a virtual world where they are able to live out this belief that they can be and do anything; but it is not the answer for, at some stage, they have to return to and live in the real world and learn to face up to their real selves.

We need to help children realise that none of us are nice people all the time. We have our good and bad days, our good and bad times; the times when we may love the world and the times when we hate the world and everyone in it. This is being human in all of our wholeness and, in all these experiences, we remain spiritual beings. More importantly, we need to teach children to become more discerning. Until value is placed on the variation and spread of human gifts and children are led to recognise that their individual gifts are as important as others, precisely because they complement the gifts of others, the flourishing of the child will continue to be hindered and the shadow will prevail. Again, to quote Bishop Urwin, 'one cannot be glorious by making the other inglorious'.[19]

## Concluding thoughts

One way to address this issue is in education. For instance, an area of study within the wider curriculum could be incorporated which focuses on learning about and engaging with the different belief systems and worldviews that have emerged through human history, especially those that are evident in their own communities. It is only through learning about and engagement with the Other that fear and distrust may be removed, thereby leading the individual to understanding and acceptance, empathy and compassion.

What is important, here, is the recognition of the need and subsequent action to create reflective times and spaces where children and teachers are able to reflect on and encounter those aspects of their personality that they have learnt to accept as negative. It is only by facing up to that which we fear, or which provokes in us a sense of unease, that we may realise it is much less significant than we had made it out to be; the tiger's growl becomes a kitten's purr and the threat of the unknown becomes safe because it is familiar. As John Keane (2012) remarked: 'Feelings can change or shift when we attend to them in a certain way. Attending to feelings can reveal wisdom or a gift.'

Certainly, one strategy would be to introduce children to various disciplines, skills and strategies which will enable them to become discerning and help them find a balance in their lives between the positive and negative experiences generated by their relational lives. The aim would be to enhance their sense of self, place, meaning and purpose and provide them with a sense of wholeness. This would include finding ways to overcome any obsessive behaviour which may impact on their health and wellbeing; for instance, obsessive eating disorders which impact on their physical and mental lives.

The main topics that I have focused on in this chapter, I believe, are some of the most neglected elements in education today. Most education systems in Western cultures have reduced and/or ignored the need for time and spaces that are conducive to allowing children to get to know and accept their inner selves, to encounter the light and darkness, and to become familiar with these elements that are the very fibre of their Being. By helping them to acknowledge and respond positively to these parts of themselves and helping them to learn how to keep them in balance, they will be better enabled to deal with the shadows and bring them into the light, thereby moving forward on the path to human flourishing, wholeness and Ultimate Unity.

Finally, I would like to refer to Palmer's (2000) statement as an appropriate way to sum up this discussion: 'To embrace weakness, liability, and darkness as part of who I am gives that part less sway over me, because all it ever wanted was to be acknowledged as a part of my whole self' (p. 71). Thus, by bringing these less desirable traits out into the light, much of their potency may be removed and we may find a way to maintain a healthy balance between the light and shadow sides of our spirituality.

## Notes

1  See Chapter 1 for a detailed discussion of the spirituality/relational continuum.
2  As discussed in Chapter 2, this is based on the understanding that babies are born into this world as deeply connected souls/individuals. It is in the months after birth and later, in the early years of childhood, when children have been socialised into becoming individuals who are distinctly separate from all others.
3  It is important to note here that this understanding of spirituality extends beyond Hay and Nye's (1998) concept of relational consciousness. Rather, the relational continuum discussed here points to a movement along this continuum towards a place/space where the boundaries that create separateness or individual identities become less distinct, until the individual arrives at a point where the boundaries cease to exist and all becomes one. This also implies that a consciousness level is reached where the individual is able to experience transcendence, where body, heart and mind become one and unity becomes the essence of lived experience. Such an understanding of unity is discussed widely in the literature but only a selection of writings have been used here to substantiate this perspective.
4  A Google search using the words 'spirituality and wellbeing', for instance, reveals 2,310,000 related websites that include conferences, journals, seminars, organisations and so on (down from 3,280,000 in September 2012). A corresponding search using the terms 'spirituality and health' provides 94,100,000 results (up from 82,500,000 in September 2012). And a search for 'spirituality and wellness' provides 15,300,000 hits (accessed 27 April 2015).
5  Much of the content of this chapter first appeared in my article: de Souza, M. (2012b). Connectedness and *connectedness*: The dark side of spirituality–implications for education. *International Journal of Children's Spirituality*, *17*(3), pp. 291–304.
6  While 'consciousness' has become an area of intense study in recent decades – and there are still many different understandings of it – I use it here as the 'mind': that human thing for which, as yet, there appears to be no physical evidence. However, for a further discussion, see Laszlo's (2008) chapter on consciousness in his book *Quantum Shift in the Global Brain: How the New Scientific Reality can Change Us and Our World*, pp. 122–126.
7  I acknowledge that some Christian perspectives, and perhaps others, do not recognise this notion that the individual Self can become one with the Other. They, instead, subscribe to the notion of duality, where God is always separate from the human person. However, with the understanding of Ultimate Unity – where Self becomes submerged in the Whole and reaches a place of No-Self – the ego or sense of a separate Self disappears and duality becomes unity. I also believe that in a contemporary world where a plurality of beliefs exist, these alternative perspectives have emerged as viable and complementary understandings of the human condition – and they cannot be ignored if we are serious in our search for meaning and in our understanding of the Other.

8  See the website www.childabuseroyalcommission.gov.au/ for more information.

9  There have been many news items about this situation in Australia but the following is an official website that has been investigating the issue: www.humanrights.
gov.au/our-work/asylum-seekers-and-refugees/national-inquiry-children-
immigration-detention-2014.

10  The Australian Border Force Act that came into law on 1 July 2015, which has
placed restrictions on professionals speaking out on their experiences from working in detention camps, is an interesting and relevant topic for this discussion, as
it demonstrates clearly the quite frightening, isolating and detrimental outcomes
that are intended for those who speak out. For one comment about the Act see
Andrew Hamilton's (2015) article in *Eureka Street* which may be accessed online
at: eurekastreet.com.au/article.aspx?aeid=45107#.VZxozu8VirR.

11  See suicidepreventionaust.org/wp-content/uploads/2012/01/SPA-GayLesbian-
PositionStatement.pdf for a position paper on suicide and self-harm within GLBTI
communities that highlights the higher incidences of suicide amongst GLBTI
young people.

12  See Tacey's (2006) discussion of Jung's theory of the human shadow in *How to
Read Jung*, pp. 53–55.

13  The rise in the number of young people who are displaying symptoms of mental
health problems has led to a corresponding rise in the number of government and
community initiatives that are dealing with them (a Google search for 'mental
health statistics for Australian teenagers' revealed 8,670,000 hits). For instance,
headspace is one initiative (funded by the Federal Government) and Youth Central
(funded by the Victoria Government) is another which address physical and mental
health issues. Both these organisations are focused on young people.

14  Retrieved on 29 April 2015 from www.headspace.org.au/about-headspace/what-
we-do/why-headspace.

15  See www.womensagenda.com.au/talking-about/top-stories/two-women-are-now-
killed-by-domestic-violence-every-week-the-time-for-discussion-is-over-it-s-
time-to-act/201502185319#.VULU9O-Jipo, where the headline reads: 'Two
women are now killed by domestic violence every week. The time for discussion
is over. It's time to act.' The reporter, Lucia Osborne-Crowley, goes on to state:
'As of this week, 13 Australian women have reportedly been killed as a result of
domestic violence in the first seven weeks of 2015. That's almost two women per
week' (retrieved on 5 May 2015).

16  For instance, see the website theconversation.com/out-of-the-shadows-the-rise-
of-domestic-violence-in-australia-29280, which provides recent statistics (retrieved
on 5 May 2015).

17  See my 2011 article in the *Journal of Religious Education*, 59(1): Promoting interspiritual education in the classroom: Exploring the perennial philosophy as a useful strategy to encourage freedom of religious practice and belief, where I have
some discussion on this.

18  Bishop Lindsay Urwin, Administrator of the Shrine of Our Lady of Walsingham,
in a presentation to delegates at the 12th International Conference for Children's
Spirituality, 2012.

19  Ibid.

# Chapter 5

# A holistic approach

## An integration of cognitive, affective, spiritual and multisensory learning

Schools play a vital role in promoting the intellectual, physical, social, emotional, moral, spiritual and aesthetic development and wellbeing of young Australians, and in ensuring the nation's ongoing economic prosperity and social cohesion.

(www.curriculum.edu.au/verve/_resources/national_declaration_on_the_educational_goals_for_young_australians.pdf)[1]

The Australian Curriculum . . . sets out, through content descriptions and achievement standards, what students should be taught and achieve, as they progress through school. It is the base for future learning, growth and active participation in the Australian community.

(www.australiancurriculum.edu.au/)[2]

The two quotes that I have employed to begin this chapter are both from recent Australian Government curriculum documents. The first is from the opening lines of the document known as the *Melbourne Declaration on Educational Goals for Young Australians* released in 2009. This is a document that follows a meeting of the combined State and Federal Education ministers every ten years and is a vision statement outlining the goals for the following ten years. Of interest is one particular aspect of the *Melbourne Declaration* in that it identifies 'spiritual' development along with the other, usually recognised, elements that compose the human person such as physical, mental, social, emotional, moral and so on. Spirituality in education is an area that has rarely been included in core curriculum documents in Australia and where it may have received passing reference, it has usually been in relation to religious, moral and personal development education (Lovat, 2010; Rossiter, 2014). One noteworthy exception is the specific identification of spirituality in the Early Years Learning Framework for Australia that was introduced in 2009. However, not enough preparation appears to have been undertaken to reach a clear understanding of what spirituality may mean in education so that, for many practitioners, addressing spirituality has not always led to successful application in practice; and as Bone (2014) acknowledges, despite the policy change, spirituality is still a marginalised area (p. 125). This reflects the situation in many Western countries where networks of people are striving to identify the role of spirituality in education, but the ambiguous nature of spirituality has meant that it is a difficult concept to capture and inject into current education programmes (for instance, see Watson, de Souza & Trousdale, 2014). The issue is a focus of this chapter.

The second excerpt is taken from the Australian Curriculum, Assessment and Reporting Authority (ACARA) website as an introduction to the current Australian Curriculum. This initiative represents a significant stage in the history of Australian education because it is the first time that a national curriculum has gone past the conceptual stages to practical implementation across all states in Australia. The curriculum statement is more specific to the structure, content and other pedagogical aspects related to the learning programmes that are offered in the schools. The learning areas are the traditional subject areas that have been part of Australian curricula for the past thirty years, such as English, maths, science, history, humanities and social sciences, the arts, technologies and languages. However, the inclusion of a section on general capabilities and cross curriculum priorities were more innovative in the way they were intended to be applied. Seven general capabilities were identified: literacy, numeracy, information and communication technology capability, critical and creative thinking, personal and social capability, ethical understanding and intercultural understanding. The three cross curriculum priorities also focused on Aboriginal and Torres Strait Islander histories and cultures, Asia, and Australia's engagement with Asia, and sustainability.[3]

Probably the least innovative part of the curriculum is the way in which the subjects are weighted. Here we find a return to an emphasis on the traditional subjects like English language, maths and the sciences. In addition, the current documents contain words such as standards, knowledge, assessment and reporting practices – all of which suggest a revisitation of the past rather than a visionary outlook for the future. Furthermore, there is an explicit expectation that this new curriculum will prepare students to participate in their future communities and contribute to the economic prosperity of the nation. In other words, the underlying aim of traditional curricula remains: to prepare students for the workforce, as indicated by the reference to 'economic prosperity'. A particular omission is the lack of recognition of the multi-faith texture of contemporary Australian society which has created a need for students to understand the multiple belief systems and worldviews that are evident in everyday life. Therefore, despite much deliberation and consultation throughout the planning and implementation stages, we find that the Australian Curriculum does not reflect the kind of transformation we actually need to meet the challenges of the twenty-first century. As Claxton (2008) observes, the point of school is to help young people develop the capacities they need in order to thrive – the ability to have the confidence to talk to strangers, to try things out, to handle tricky situations, to stand up for themselves, to ask for help, to think new thoughts – which is every young person's basic educational entitlement. However, Claxton claims that they are not getting it (p. vi) and this issue becomes another focal point for this chapter.

## The problems implicit in a system that calls for constant curriculum renewal

It is appropriate to refer to these two government sponsored educational initiatives to begin this chapter since they are reflective of the ongoing action that has been undertaken in curriculum renewal and revisions over the past thirty or more years. Each renewal is accompanied by a huge expenditure of the tax-payer's dollars, and the arrival of each new curriculum brings an anticipation that it will be innovative and forward looking. Moreover, the implications are that it will overcome the shortcomings in the existing programmes. However, the fact that we have continued to have, over the past several years, expensive rewrites of existing curricula clearly points to some lack of vision and inefficiency in providing solutions to the identifiable problems in education today.

Too often, children and young people experience limited success in the current education system which undermines and erodes their sense of self and wellbeing. Thus, for some, school experience not only means failure in achievement but it can also prevent them from attaining a sense of confidence and trust in their own individual gifts and capabilities. Too many students have found that they do not fit comfortably into an education system that is founded on philosophical understandings and societal expectations of a world that lies in the past.

For the most part, Western education is based on a system that was generated by and responsive to both the European Renaissance and the Industrial Revolution. The aim was to prepare children to be workers in industry, so particular subjects and abilities were weighted favourably over others. However, today, industrialisation and manufacturing have been overtaken by the rapid pace of developments in communications and technology. While these changes have had some impact on educational practices through the use of computers and other social media so that, at some levels, classrooms may have a different physical set-up from traditional classrooms of the past, the differences are fairly superficial. The changed social, political, global and technological contexts of the contemporary world have not yet had a significant impact on the philosophical and structural underpinnings of the education system. Thus, many school programmes and timetable structures still resemble those of a bygone era with more attention given to literacy and numeracy related subjects, while others that promote interpersonal and intrapersonal learning might be squeezed into the weekly timetable or left off altogether. The fact that the new curricula have a relatively limited lifespan before there appears to be a need for yet another review is evidence that we are just patching up a flawed system through which the needs of many of today's students and parents continue to fall through. The frequency of the reviews are a clear indication of the urgent need to find ways to transform education today and to move forward towards a system that is more wholesome and relevant to the times. Tobin Hart describes transformation in education as:

a movement towards increasing wholeness that simultaneously pushes toward diversity and uniqueness, becoming more uniquely who we are, and towards unity, recognizing how much we have in common with the universe and even recognition that we are the universe. In this way self-actualization and self-transcendence do not contradict one another; instead they form part of the same process.

(Hart, 2001, p. 150)

Hart argues that education needs to move from information to transformation. He firmly asserts that today's schooling is about 'adaptation to the status quo' so that we produce students who will 'fit in and fill our expectations of them in the workplace' (ibid.). Such a system produces mediocrity and inhibits the individual from experiencing transcendence. Transformation, on the other hand, 'emphasizes liberation, fluidity and flexibility' leading to a process of creation, regeneration and freedom so that individuals are able to 'actualize their ever expanding potential by transcending current self-structure' (ibid.).

Along with Hart, there have been many significant ideas from educators, philosophers and theorists over the past several years, which have provided illuminating insights about how education can be transformed. For the purposes of this chapter, a small selection of some notable individuals and the relevance of their ideas will be examined. The aim is to establish some common elements that inform a holistic learning approach and which address the spiritual dimension in education.

For instance, one particular problem identified by many is that education systems are top heavy. They are policy driven and responsive to factors that are more about societal and economic pressures and workplace demands (for instance, Claxton, 2008; Robinson, 2001). In response to this situation, the thesis offered in this chapter is that the goal of education should be more than preparing a child for the workplace. It should:

- be multidimensional and involve a process that allows each child to draw on his/her individual gifts, abilities and resources, whatever they are, so as to reach his/her potential to become a well-rounded, whole person;
- equip each child to engage positively with the world and its diversity in all aspects of his/her life as each of them experiences it;
- develop innate strengths and capabilities that will empower each child to make effective and beneficial contributions to the wellbeing of future communities which, in turn, will promote his/her own sense of self, place and wellbeing.

This chapter, then, intends to examine the current situation and, subsequently, offer some reasons as to why and how approaches to education that incorporate the spiritual dimension of the student's life may offer a holistic and positive model of education for this century, when the world has become contextualised by both positive and negative influences of plurality, globalisation and a technologically driven changing workplace.

## A selection of some pertinent theoretical and philosophical perspectives

Given the commonality and recurrence of problems associated with the way schools and curriculum programmes are organised, there has been a stream of educators who have called for radical changes to curriculum structures as opposed to the application of the 'Band-Aid' approach that currently exists. Others have identified different inadequacies of the present systems and have outlined ideas that they believe would be more suitable for addressing the issues and requirements that characterise the new century. Generally, the elements that are identified as deficient are associated with a system that espouses the scientific, dualist, objectivist and reductionist mindset of a past era; one which, therefore, compartmentalises learning, focuses on competition and assessment, and gives weight to some gifts and skills over others, thus dehumanising some students and creating divisive elements within the class and school community. Consequently, the call for change is usually about transforming the teaching and learning processes as well as redesigning the learning environments to reflect more clearly the paradigm shifts that have emerged in recent years.

As one of the more visionary educators today, Ken Robinson (2001) describes the situation well when he notes that 'academic ability has been conflated with intelligence'. How this plays out, then, is a system built on 'testing, examinations, selection procedures, teacher education and research' (p. 7). Robinson claims that our educational institutions are structured on the assumption that there are only two types of people in the world, academic and non-academic, which leads to the rather discriminating attitude that labels them: 'The able and the less able' (ibid.). In a later book, Robinson with Aronica (2009, p. 21), expound this theory by identifying three key features that indicate the inappropriateness of the current education system for the world we live in. First, there is a preoccupation with certain sorts of academic ability, for instance, skills in literacy and numeracy and some kinds of critical analysis and reasoning. Second, there exists a hierarchy of subjects, with maths, the sciences and languages leading from the top, the humanities in the middle and the arts languishing at the bottom. The third feature is the emphasis and reliance on standardised testing (p. 13). These three features have been derived from the political and economic interests of earlier times when specific knowledge and skills were required to fulfil jobs in the industrial world. Robinson and Aronica argue that this system provides a very narrow view of intelligence and capacity and it overvalues particular talents and abilities (ibid.). Thus, in many schools, there are reduced opportunities for children to engage in arts programmes which are seen as fringe subjects; and in this way, education 'systematically drains the creativity out of our children' leaving them unimaginative and uninspired (p. 16). Hart goes further when he says:

> Overemphasis on information acquisition has inadvertently worked against higher-order intellectual skills as well as the development of character, dimensions that create, shape, evaluate, and use information. Ultimately the result is a constriction of human consciousness.
>
> (Hart, 2001, p. 5)

Hart insists that when we mistakenly place so much emphasis on the role of information in education we betray our lack of understanding of the capacity of human nature. Citing Gopak, Sealts and Whitehead, Hart claims that we end up with an education system that is not just mediocre, it is 'dangerous, it results in "arrested growth" and it even threatens "soul murder"' (ibid.).

While both Robinson and Hart are describing the Western system of education, we need to note that its spread, operation and influence has stretched across many Western and Eastern countries over the past century as a result of colonialism. Accordingly, the problems identified here are common to many countries across the world today.

One educator, Ivan Illich (1970), proposed such radical changes to develop new learning environments that they seemed quite unattainable for his time. His notion of 'de-schooling society' argued for the devolution of schools into networks of learning communities where individuals could group together with other like-minded individuals to focus on their specific needs and concerns and bounce ideas off each other in their passage to further learning. Illich maintained that when an education system institutionalises its values, it 'leads inevitably to physical pollution, social polarization and psychological impotence' (p. 9). Hence, the lack of attention and care given to individual needs in such a system can lead to alienation and, in real terms, impacts on the right of every child to be recognised and enabled according to their own specific needs and inherent talents. Illich's solution – that we break out of the rigidity and conformity that characterise schools to embrace a more liberating, learning environment – was, possibly, too extreme for the world of the 1970s. However, in the rapidly paced technological world of the twenty-first century, where there is the possibility to create networks of online learning communities who are linked because of their specific passions and interests, Illich's vision does not seem to be quite so revolutionary.

Another view, which also had implications for the rights of the child, was contained in Freire's (1970) argument. He examined the use of an education system as an instrument employed by the rich and powerful to cultivate a culture of silence and restrict any advancement of the poor, thereby ensuring that social and class divisions were maintained. He described it as a 'banking model' which led to domination, and he argued for an education system that would transmit freedom.

Both Illich and Freire recognised the rigid educational framework of the 1970s, derived from the values of an old-world class system that determined the curriculum and pedagogical content and structures on offer. Accordingly, little attention was being given to the rights of children to an education that empowered them to discover their individual potential and become active contributors to and creators of a society that benefitted themselves and all others. To sum up, the respective visions offered by these two perceptive educators revealed alternative systems where the strengths lay in the nurturing of individual qualities and aptitudes, and in opening doors to further horizons, thereby liberating children and young people to experience new realms.

Approximately two decades later, bell hooks (1994) moved the argument further by introducing another dimension: the concept of educating the soul of the student with the aim of freeing them from the social, cultural and political constraints that dominate their life. Thus, hooks echoed the notion that education should promote the practice of freedom where anyone could learn, where care for the soul of the student is paramount; and she felt that students should be taught to 'transgress' against racial, sexual and class boundaries in order to be free. This was a far cry from educational systems that encouraged children to conform to set patterns of thinking, attitudes and behaviour, and which promoted the standardisation of learning and assessment as a preparation for work.

The dimension in education that hooks had touched on moved away from objectifying students as pawns in the educational game towards paying attention to the actual person that composed the child. This notion of care as a particular focus in education was also a feature of Noddings' (1992) writings. She discussed extensively the problems associated with the restrictive organisation, structure and curriculum practices and processes in schools of the 1990s and highlighted the harmful side effects on children's self-worth and wellbeing. She proposed an alternative model for schooling, one where education was organised around centres of caring – 'care for self, care for intimate others, care for associates and distance others, for non-human life, for human-made environment of objects and instruments, and for ideas' (p. 47).

Jack Miller (2000) has been a long-time advocate of addressing the soul in education, which recognises and gives priority to the inner life. Here, again, we find a transfer from the focus on the attainment of test scores in specific work-targeted subjects, towards the child as a whole person. Such a curriculum will seek a balance and connection between the child's inner and outer lives. As we have shown, schools traditionally reflect the culture within which they are located, so when Western culture continues to ignore the inner life, the education system reflects these values and also neglects the child's inner life (p. 49). Miller cites early research by Jerome Singer in 1976 that found connections between the development of the inner life and behaviour, and that the risks of an undeveloped imagination included delinquency, violence, over-eating and the use of dangerous drugs (ibid.). Thus, one of the key elements in Miller's philosophy is that attention is given to the inner life of the child and appropriate learning experiences should be incorporated into the curriculum which will achieve this. Some of the activities Miller suggests are forms of meditation, relaxation exercises, story-telling, creative writing, connecting subject matter with a student's inner life, achieving goals, skill development (e.g. sporting, interpersonal skills) and a focus on changing attitudes. He notes, as well, the importance of using the arts as an integrating factor to teach across the curriculum – for instance, dream booklets/journals and autobiographical writing and earth education – which promotes a sense of space.

Miller, hooks and Noddings are concerned with the problems inherent in an education system that neglects to address the individualistic features which are found in any group of students and which compose both their inner and outer lives. Their thinking is reflected in Thomas Merton's concept of the spirituality of education, where 'the activation and development of our inner capacity to understand and live fully as our real selves is the central concern' (see Del Prete, 2002, p. 165).

Around the same time another educator, Moffett (1994), spoke of spiritual education as one which focused on personal growth and individualisation. Thus, his thinking mirrored aspects of both hooks's concept of education for freedom and Noddings's centres of caring. We can also find an echo of Freire when Moffett claims that when students' learning programmes and processes are determined by external authorities, the students become passive learners and stop thinking for themselves:

> Homogenizing a populace through a cookie-cutter curriculum at once nul-
> lifies the diversity that ensures collective survival and thwarts the individuali-
> zation on which self-realization depends. Thus, it works equally against the
> social and the personal, the practical and the spiritual.
>
> (Moffett, 1994, p. 6)

Moffett offers an illuminating understanding of spiritualising education. He says it is intended to include everyone because:

> It brings to our daily efforts to improve our life in this world a sorely needed
> focus on being good for one another because we're not just thinking of
> ourselves. It energizes these efforts with a life force common to everything
> but working through each of us in a particular way characteristic of our indi-
> viduality. It validates the inner life of thought and feeling and the sense of
> personal being in the face of depersonalization and a preoccupation with
> physical things. It calls us back from surfaces to essences, to whatever may be
> at the bottom of things or beyond our immediate kin and ken. It invites us
> to seek commonalities beneath common-places, for the sake of mind as well
> as morality. It's a toast to wits with spirit.
>
> (Moffett, 1994, p. 19)

However, in the current system, when the aim is that all students will achieve particular outcomes in particular subjects – regardless of where their own talents and interests lie – it can have a stultifying impact on the dynamics of the learn-ing environment which affects both the whole group and the individual. This is symptomatic of education that is driven by testing and assessment. For instance, as I was planning and writing this chapter, a news item reminded me that school children in Australia were undertaking their NAPLAN (National Assessment Program – Literacy and Numeracy) tests. These tests are administered to children in Years 3, 5, 7 and 9.[4] Therefore, children as young as seven are being subjected to these tests which ignore the multidimensional nature of the child, since they are restricted to measuring knowledge and skills specific to only a couple of areas that compose the child's all-round intelligence and ability. Each year there have been news reports on the practice of some schools who, expecting that some of their students will not experience success in the tests, advise their students to stay at home on the day.[5] Unfortunately, this practice is not always generated by concern for the individual child. Rather, in a highly charged competitive climate where schools are under enormous pressure to attract students and maintain or increase their numbers, the current practice of ranking schools is often linked to the results of their NAPLAN testing.

Of course, effective teachers always strive to find ways to overcome these problems so that they can address the individual needs of their students, but the system usually works against them. One example of teachers' concern for their students shone through in the most recent NAPLAN testing period in 2015, as evidenced by the report, 'NAPLAN: Queensland school's letter of affirmation to students facing test goes viral'. It presented excerpts from a letter sent out by three teachers in one school which reminded their students that the test did not assess the special and unique things about them, such as 'you love to sing, are good at drawing or can teach others how to use a computer program', or that 'you have improved on something you once found difficult. They can't tell you that you brighten up your teacher's day. They can't tell how amazingly special you are'.[6]

While these efforts reflect the caring and compassion that are essential qualities of an effective teacher, they cannot remove the deeper and broader impact of a child having to sit these tests. Indeed, the pressure on children when they undertake these tests are reflected in the high stress levels which have been identified in them (Bagshaw, 2015).[7] It is more than likely that the children's test experiences will have far-reaching effects on them as they progress through school, especially if their gifts and aptitudes fall into areas outside literacy and numeracy.

Stress amongst school children, as has been widely acknowledged, is a serious issue for many young people. In one of his recent publications, Claxton (2008) devoted the first chapter to this topic. With ample references to substantiate his claims, he concluded that stress in children had reached epidemic proportions (pp. 1–15) and one of the stress inducing factors was school. Speaking about the British school system, Claxton further asserted that the 'UK Government's concern with standards and accountability have led to teenagers being tested virtually to destruction' (p. 9). As he points out, the message throughout their school lives is that success is about achieving enough tertiary entrance points to get into university and 'by that yardstick, three out of every four young adults are going to fail' (ibid.). Moreover, Claxton believes that schools fail to teach their students the 'habits and qualities of mind' that will provide them with the confidence they need in order to meet the demands imposed on them by a system fixated on testing and assessment (pp. 9 and 10). Finally, he makes the vital point that 'the stress of school is aggravated for many because they cannot see the relevance of much of what they are learning at school'. Citing a report from the Work Foundation, he observes: 'Schools are seen by young people as failing to equip them with the ability to learn for life, rather than for exams' (p. 11).

While Claxton is speaking specifically about the British school system, we need to remember that Australia, as well as other countries, has much in common with the British system and, certainly, testing at different levels of schooling is a dominant factor in many countries. Stress happens when the demands made on children and young people outstrip their inner resources and ability to cope. This leads to feelings of inadequacy, anxiety and being out of control. Such experiences, then, can lead to withdrawal, denial, blaming, escapism and displacement activities, as well as self-harm and depression (Claxton, 2008, p. 12). The increase of mental health issues is a serious problem that affects many young people in Australia and elsewhere, as noted in earlier chapters, and we can now identify their experiences in school as one of the contributory factors. This makes it all the more important that something is done to alleviate the stress that young people experience – and working for the transformation of education is just one possible avenue where action can be taken to achieve these ends.

There is a unifying premise that underlies the writings and propositions of the theorists discussed earlier as well as the attitudes of the concerned teachers referred to above. It is about focusing on children as individuals who carry within them a breadth of human characteristics and dispositions, all of which are vital to the functioning of any community. If we accept this premise, we begin to realise the limitations of the current system in its attempts to educate the whole child. This is made even more challenging in a world that is characterised by a rapid pace of change in science and technology, so that we have no real understanding what future employment markets will look like (Robinson, 2001). Some jobs as we know them today will disappear as their relevance for a new world diminishes and they will be replaced by work places of which we currently have little conception. This should be a matter of concern when one of the dominant aims in education is to equip children to enable them to live well in their future lives, one aspect of which will be for them to flourish in their future careers.

These factors are clearly indicative that what is needed goes beyond patching up our existing system. Instead, we need to – creatively and imaginatively – effect a transformation which will empower the students of today to create worlds of self-fulfilment, promise, hope and the flourishing of all for tomorrow. Moreover, as discussed extensively in earlier chapters, the focus on nurturing the inner life has significance for all children and young people. Accordingly, it should be given particular attention in the learning situation and, as such, it should be a specific consideration in the planning of educational programmes today.

## Intelligences and the role they have in the learning process

Traditionally, many learning programmes have been generated by a particular assumption about intelligence and this assumption has led to the overuse of intelligence quotient (IQ) tests. IQ tests tend to focus on abstract reasoning and literacy and numeracy skills, but we know that to be successful and well-adjusted in real life requires a whole variety of attributes (Lucas & Claxton, 2010). When I was first developing an integrated learning approach that incorporated different concepts of intelligence, I examined ideas from different theorists (de Souza, 2001); I now offer a brief overview of how intelligence has been traditionally mapped and applied in conventional learning systems, as well as newer under-standings that have emerged. I will then examine how new understandings of intelligence can inform the development of a learning approach that addresses the whole child as a rational, emotional and spiritual being.

To begin with, tests to measure rational and logical intelligence were devised in the early 1900s (Binet 1905, revised by Terman at Stanford University 1916)[8] and they measured processes – such as memory, attention, comprehension, discrimi-nation and reasoning – and linked these to the age of a child. Further, Terman introduced the notion of an IQ which expressed the child's level of performance in these tests. Learning and assessment in Western education throughout the twentieth century were drawn from this concept of intelligence, so that perfor-mance in particular areas – such as language and logic, skills such as verbal and mathematical, and processes such as comprehension, reasoning and memory – were measured to determine a person's intelligence.

It was in the 1980s before any significant changes were made to this practice. It began with Gardner (1983; 1993) who rejected both this unitary view of intel-ligence and the concept of IQ. He proposed a case for the plurality of the intel-lect. He described intelligence as the 'ability to solve problems or fashion products that are of consequence in a particular cultural setting or community' (1993, p. 15). Accordingly, individuals would identify a particular goal they wished to achieve and they would follow up by developing strategies within and relevant to their cultural setting to obtain that goal. Using this theory, Gardner identi-fied eight intelligences – linguistic, musical, mathematical, spatial, kinaesthetic, interpersonal, intrapersonal and naturalistic – but firmly resisted the suggestion that there was a spiritual intelligence. Instead, he referred to a possible ninth intelligence which he called existential. Gardner's theory of multiple intelligences was well received and widely adopted by educators because it provided them with the means whereby they could identify different abilities and skills amongst their students who were previously neglected or remained unacknowledged in traditional practice.

A different perspective was proposed by Sternberg (1985) who also rejected the notion that a person's intelligence could be measured with IQ testing. He proposed a triarchic theory of human intelligence. One was analytical intelligence, which was the traditional understanding of rational intelligence reflected in the ability to solve problems and complete IQ tests. Another form of intelligence was creative intelligence, which allowed a person to be innovative in devising new situations or finding inventive solutions. The third was practical intelligence, which helped a person deal with the challenges of everyday living. Sternberg, by recognising a creative form, moved the concept of intelligence forward.

More recently, Lucas and Claxton (2010) present a different perspective on multiple intelligences by identifying 'new ways of being smart'. They suggest that there are eight different dimensions of intelligence which are needed if individuals are to manoeuvre their way through the contemporary world. Most significantly, they assert that intelligence is not something that is fixed from the time we are born. Instead, human intelligence can be grown and developed. The eight dimensions indicate their thinking of the holistic, seamless nature of intelligence and include practical, intuitive, strategic, social and ethical dimensions. Thus, rather than speak of multiple intelligences, Lucas and Claxton prefer to talk of different dimensions and highlight the fact that some dimensions are valued more than others in the current education system. Consequently, they emphasise the need for attitudes to be changed so that recognition is given to the complementary nature of these different dimensions which, when they work together, grow a smarter child.

Robinson with Aronica (2009) discuss an additional perspective and identify three main features of intelligence which are essential for creativity to happen when people are in the 'Element'. They firmly believe that being in the Element leads people to experience things that change their lives, gives them direction and purpose and impacts on them in a way nothing else has ever done (p. 8). The first feature is the extraordinary diversity of intelligence (p. 46). Robinson and Aronica claim that this is one of the fundamental underpinnings of the Element (p. 49). The second feature is that intelligence is dynamic; thus, it is through intense interaction between different parts of the brain that new connections are forged and true breakthrough occurs (ibid.). Finally, they claim intelligence is individual and distinctive, so that every person's intelligence is as unique as a fingerprint (p. 50). Implicit in Robinson and Aronica's description of the three features is the role of the non-conscious mind. The idea that creativity requires intense interaction between different parts of the brain implies that much of this working happens outside the conscious mind. Thus, the bridging across disparate knowledge and information that resides in the non-conscious mind leads to creativity and, indeed, intuitions, as discussed in Chapter 4; and this will be discussed again later in this chapter.

There are many other theories and interpretations on human intelligence, but I would now like to identify three broad facets that compose a well-rounded human intelligence. I find these three dimensions of human intelligence quite significant and essential for a holistic learning process and they inform the concept of a learning approach that I developed which, I believe, is notably appropriate for the twenty-first century.

The first, which we cannot ignore, is the traditional form of intelligence – rational intelligence – and it is linked to intellectual or cognitive learning. However, there are two others which provide an illuminating understanding of the child as a whole person. These are emotional intelligence, which is linked to affective learning; and spiritual intelligence which, I suggest, is linked to intuitive, creative and imaginative learning. I have already examined different perspectives of rational intelligence so I will look at theories of emotional intelligence next.

Goleman (1996) popularised the concept of emotional intelligence and drew on previous research, such as that by Salovey and Mayer (1990), to support his stance. Salovey and Mayer were the first to propose a theory that described a different category of intelligence: emotional intelligence (see also Salovey, 1998; and Mayer, Salovey & Caruso, 2000). Mayer *et al.*, psychologists from Yale and New Hampshire Universities, were the first to propose a theory that described a different category of intelligence – emotional intelligence. They defined emotional intelligence as the ability to process emotional information, involving perception, assimilation, understanding and management of emotion. In other words, it has the capacity to carry out abstract reasoning which, for them, is the first hallmark of intelligence.

Goleman maintains that intellectual and emotional intelligences are not opposing competencies but are separate ones. Immediate emotional responses are something the rational mind cannot control and they are perceived to be a response of the 'heart', not the 'head'. However, the mind can trigger an emotional response through its thoughts and such responses can be controlled – that is, thinking precedes feeling but these take longer (by seconds or minutes) to unfold (1996, p. 293). Using their rational minds, individuals are able to make logical connections between causes and effects, but their emotional minds work indiscriminately so that connections are made between things that have similar striking features. The logic of the emotional mind is associative, whereby it takes elements that symbolise a reality or it triggers a memory of it, to be the same as that reality. Goleman maintains that this is why similes, metaphors and images speak directly to the emotional mind, as do the arts – novels, film poetry, song, theatre and opera. To him, the great spiritual teachers, like Buddha and Jesus, touched their disciples' hearts by speaking in the language of emotion, teaching in parables, fables and stories: 'Indeed, religious symbol and ritual makes little sense from the rational point of view; it is couched in the vernacular of the heart' (p. 294). Ultimately, Goleman is pointing out that emotional intelligence is a basic requirement for an effective use of our rational intelligence – that is, our feelings play an important role in our thought processes.

Finally, a third facet of intelligence, spiritual intelligence, is proposed by Emmons (2000), amongst others. Emmons identifies five features of spiritual intelligence, which include the capacity for transcendence and to reach higher states of consciousness as well as to have an understanding of the sacred in the everyday. Emmons also identifies spiritual behaviour such as showing forgiveness, expressing gratitude, being humble and displaying compassion.

A further case for spiritual intelligence (or spiritual quotient, SQ) is also proposed by Zohar and Marshall (2000). They claim that spiritual intelligence is utilised to address and solve problems of meaning and value, and it helps individuals place their lives and actions in a wider, richer, meaning-giving context (pp. 3–4). According to them, this is the intelligence that allows an individual to assess that one course of action or one life path is more meaningful than another. Moreover, Zohar and Marshall argue that SQ is essential for the effective functioning of both IQ and emotional quotient (EQ):

> Neither IQ nor EQ, separately or in combination, is enough to explain the full complexity of human intelligence nor the vast richness of the human soul and imagination . . . SQ allows human beings to be creative, to change the rules and to alter situations. It allows us to play with the boundaries, playing an 'infinite game'. SQ gives us our ability to discriminate. It gives us our moral sense, an ability to temper rigid rules with understanding and compassion and an equal ability to see when compassion and understanding have their limits. We use SQ to wrestle with questions of good and evil and to envision unrealized possibilities – to dream, to aspire, to raise ourselves out of the mud.
>
> (Zohar & Marshall, 2000, p. 5)

This process of spiritual intelligence 'unifies, integrates and has the potential to transform material arising from the other two processes. It facilitates a dialogue between reason and emotion, between mind and body. It provides a fulcrum for growth and transformation. It provides the self with an active, unifying, meaning-giving centre' (p. 7). Amongst the characteristics that Zohar and Marshall identify are a heightened self-awareness and an inclination to seek answers to the big questions; a capacity to face up to and grow through pain and suffering; being holistic and visionary; the reluctance to cause harm; the ability to be flexible and defy convention; and finally, the capacity to be a 'servant leader', that is, being able to bring a higher vision and value to others and showing them how to use it (pp. 15–16).

Certainly, the features offered by Emmons and Zohar and Marshall and others – for instance, Smetar (2000) and Buzan (2001) – do suggest another dimension of intelligence which is not completely captured by theories of rational and emotional intelligence. As a result, they offer compelling reasons for a consideration that there may, indeed, be a spiritual dimension to human intelligence, especially in light of the understanding that spirituality is an innate feature of being human. My own thinking is that the concept of these three dimensions of intelligence reflect the multidimensional nature of education and they do provide a useful framework for a holistic approach to learning and teaching. As such, they should be given some consideration in developing a foundational basis for curriculum development.

## The multidimensional nature of education

A starting point would be to begin by recognising that the child is a multidimensional being: an individual with a rational mind that thinks, an emotional mind that feels and a spiritual mind that intuits, imagines, wonders and creates. And this multidimensional mind is encased in the physical body which allows the individual child to engage, mediate and interact with the world around them through their perceptions and senses. Thus, if we accept that the child is a rational, emotional and spiritual individual, we need to question why education has traditionally only catered for the first of these qualities in core programmes. As a general rule, the additional extracurricular activities are often designated as the ones that will address other dimensions such as emotional and spiritual. Some of these are clearly recognised as nurturing spirituality, such as reflection days or retreats, usually because of their historical links to religious practices. However, others such as music/drama and sports days also promote connectedness, group and self-esteem and positive values relating to belonging and place; but these aspects have not always been clearly identified as spiritual traits. The idea that we may try to capture more than cognitive ways of knowing to produce knowledge and skills becomes buried in the tedium of mind-numbing and uninspiring learning activities that fill the greater part of the school day. The aim for children to be constantly exposed to learning environments that recognise the role of their feelings, or that stimulate their thinking beyond comprehension and memorising facts, is too often relegated to the idealist's basket. Ventures into areas of wonderment, imagination, compassion, feelings of liberation and self-transcendence and finally, a holistic approach to problem solving, are usually perceived as generally unobtainable in the current system, requiring too much time, expense and resources. This is not to say that there are schools all over the country that have overcome the restrictions of the current system so that the approach to education is more multidimensional and innovative, thereby providing children with opportunities to develop holistically. Unfortunately, these examples tend to be the exception rather than the rule. And yet, ordinary, everyday classrooms can be enlivened by thinking outside the regular framework so that children enjoy their learning, find relevance in what they are doing, cooperate and respect one another, and maintain a happy and hopeful outlook in the process.

Most educators will be able to recall those inspired moments in their classrooms when everything seems to come together. There is a highly charged buzz as students become completely involved in the content and activities, bouncing thoughts off one another to arrive at innovative and original ideas, strategies and/or solutions. Student characteristics that could be described at such moments include interest, passion and enthusiasm, concentration, absorption and immersion – resulting in insightful, creative, enterprising and exciting initiatives or outcomes. Csikzentmihalyi discusses these moments as optimal experiences. He uses the term 'flow' to identify a concept which captures that moment or moments when the individual's mind and body are so involved in an activity that nothing else seems to matter. Achievement of the outcome, then, is dependent upon the individual's own ability and creativity:

> The optimal state of inner experience is one in which there is *order in consciousness*. This happens when psychic energy – or attention – is invested in realistic goals, and when skills match the opportunities for action.
>
> (Csikzentmihalyi, 1992, 2002, p. 6)

Csikzentmihalyi continues to explain that if a person seriously pursues a particular goal it requires deep concentration and absorption so that other thoughts, worries, anxieties and so on are forgotten. Instead, the whole being is focused on the achievement of the goal for its own sake whereby, consciousness becomes 'harmoniously ordered' (ibid.).

Robinson and Aronica's (2009) discussion of the 'Element' appears to reflect Csikzentmihalyi's concept of 'flow'. They claim that when we find our passion for something, it changes everything. The Element is 'the place where the things you love to do and the things that you are good at come together' (p. 8). Robinson and Aronica argue that the components of the Element are universal but it manifests itself differently in every person. They believe that all people have wonderful natural abilities but they lose touch with much of these talents the more time they spend in the world, especially the world of education (p. xi). The authors' words are reminiscent of the discussion we had in the previous chapter on the shadow. In this case, they believe that certain talents that are not valued, or are considered as unimportant or unessential in education circles, are rejected by the individual and so become lost to them.

Csikzentmihalyi, Robinson and Aronica appear to be discussing the potential of the individual which, if the conditions are just right, can blossom into something special and noteworthy, bringing happiness, satisfaction and contentment. Such experiences, in turn, promote feelings of self-worth and wellbeing. However, if people are not given the opportunity to connect with their true talents, 'they don't know what they're really capable of achieving. In that sense they don't know who they really are' (Robinson with Aronica, 2009, p. xi). Robinson and Aronica actually identify something of the human shadow here and, as shown earlier, individuals remain stunted, angry and unfulfilled when their shadow becomes too much to carry. The authors attribute some of this to the current education system; they argue that 'our best hope for the future is to develop a new paradigm of human capacity to meet a new era of human existence' (p. xiii).

To illustrate the points I am attempting to make here I would like to draw on my own professional experience as a classroom practitioner in music education. Traditionally, music was, and still is, seen as a subject that only special people can do or excel at. Common perceptions are that an individual has to be especially gifted in order to perform music. Music has a whole new language that has to be learnt and not everyone has the capacity to learn it. Usually, it is expected that most children have some capacity to draw, paint and engage successfully in other art activities, which are an integral part of early childhood and primary education. However, other than singing and basic rhythmic activities which may be included in general education programmes for children, music is not necessarily treated in the same way as other art and craft subjects. Indeed, many adults will recall being told, when they were children, that they couldn't sing in tune or they couldn't sing at all! Of course, this notion that music education is only meant for the especially talented child has been challenged by the philosophies and practices of music educators such as Dr Shinichi Suzuki, Carl Orff, Zoltán

Kodály and others. Nevertheless, in my early career experiences as a classroom music teacher in Australian high schools (state schools), it was the traditional view that I encountered. I would like to revisit that time and explain how I responded to the challenges that confronted me every day to show how I developed a multidimensional approach to teaching classroom music.

When I began teaching in the high school system in the early 1970s, music was about the most challenging subject to teach, alongside subjects like French or German. Students generally thoroughly disliked classroom music and found it completely irrelevant to their lives. In fact, while music was a big part of the lives of most teenagers, they perceived music and school music to be two vastly unrelated things. The curriculum in those days was centrally prescribed and was based on the music appreciation classes from twenty or more years earlier. A regular experience I had was for my students to arrive, fling themselves into their seats with the moan 'Why do I have to do music? It's not going to get me a job'. Inexperienced as I was, I felt they had a valid point. Teaching them about Bach, Beethoven or Mozart or chanting rhythms such 'ta ta-te ta ta' had little to with their lives. Their ears, attuned as they were to the popular music of the day, were completely unacclimatised to listening to recordings of classical music which reached them as a fog of sound, completely impenetrable. They had no means or strategies that enabled them to glimpse anything meaningful through this blanket of alien vibrations. Like others, I confronted the problem by trying, where I could, to connect the music content to their lives, so I would use popular songs to teach a theoretical concept or a TV jingle which was based on a melody from the classical repertoire. In this way, I achieved an uneasy truce in terms of classroom discipline and slowly, very slowly, made some progress in their music education.

Now, fast forward to the early 1980s. Music keyboard laboratories were a very new inclusion in schools, usually only found in the private schools which could afford them. I was in a newly developing school, but was fortunate enough to have a principal who believed in the work I was doing in the music classroom. Therefore, he provided some funding to the music department to set up a Yamaha music keyboard laboratory. The labs were designed by Yamaha to be a sound source, which could be effectively implemented in promoting basic musical skills amongst students. Using strategies from a range of music education programmes, such as Suzuki, Kodály, Orff and Yamaha, as well as John Paynter's creative, experimental music-making approach, I started developing a music programme that was used as part of the core curriculum for Years 7 and 8 and as elective programmes for Years 9 and 10. Finally, I wrote a Master of Education thesis that discussed the implementation and evaluation of the Year 7 curriculum I had developed. By then, I was achieving some success, so that many of my students would enter the classroom with the question, 'What are we going to do today?' – thereby displaying their enthusiasm and readiness to 'do' music. I certainly felt that my music classes had come a long way from those early days. In fact, the classroom music, which was focused on active music playing and experimentation as well as the listening and historical aspects, stimulated enough interest for the students to want to be involved in the extracurricular activities. I also ensured that the students had opportunities to perform to an audience, whether it was work that came out of the classroom programme or was part of the extracurricular programme. Thus, music learning was not done in isolation; it became shared learning across classroom and school.

From this background and context I would now like to recount a particular incident:

*It was a cold, wet, gale-blasted winter's day in the second week of a new term. The timetable had been changed that week so that my Year 9 elective music class had been shifted from period 4 to period 3 and I forgot about the change. So, at the start of period 4 I was making my way down the hill to the corner of the grounds where the music room had been built, and remembered with some horror, the timetable change as I noted my students walking back up the hill towards me. There was a real buzz about them and as they passed, they greeted me with 'Hi' and 'Bye'. It transpired that they had got a key from the visiting instrumental teacher next door to let themselves into the music room. My immediate response on hearing this was panic and the question: What state would the music room would be in? The students had been taught to respect the instruments, including the drum set, electric guitars and bass guitars that hung off the wall, as well as all the speaker systems and, of course, the keyboards. As a result, nothing was ever locked away and students had easy access to everything. I expected that their correct behaviour around the instruments could have evaporated when they found themselves unsupervised in the room.*

*I was wondering how on earth I was going to explain any damage to the principal when one girl stepped out of the line. I shall call her Jenny.[9] I can still see her face in my mind's eye, aglow and with eyes shining. She said, 'That was the best lesson.' I anxiously queried, 'What did you all do?' She instantly understood my concern because she reassured me, 'It's fine, we just got the key and Mary[10] set up the teacher's keyboard, and we all put on our headphones and practised. And in the last five minutes, we took our headphones off and Mary set up the rhythms like you do and we all played together.' She then joined the line and went on her way.*

*On reaching the room, I noticed one stool out of place and, except for the rather heavy atmosphere that lingers in a closed room that has been full of twenty teenagers on a cold day, there was no other evidence that the class had been in the room. They had treated the room with respect and left it as they had found it.*

I often tell this story to my university students when I teach a unit on learning. I had been teaching the Year 9 students about triads, chords and chord relationships, and applied this learning to the playing of a 12-bar blues progression. Students had already had a couple of lessons to practise the chords. If a student needed help, they invariably took their headphones off and spoke quietly to their neighbour. They only called on me if the neighbour could not help. In other words, there was ongoing support and cooperation between all students, regardless of how much previous learning they may have had or how musically gifted they were. Jenny, unlike some of the others, had no previous musical background so her playing had involved a rather plodding, laborious movement of chords. I suspect, from her demeanour that day, that Jenny had finally achieved a smooth transition of chords so that she was able to keep up with the rest of the group when they had their 'jam' at the end. The jam that I always included at the end of the lesson was accompanied by the built-in rhythm section on the teacher's keyboard and aimed to help the students realise what the end product would sound like when everyone played their parts. Those students who were more gifted and experienced would improvise, as did I, so that we usually achieved a pretty good sound. It didn't matter that some students were only playing the basic chords; their individual contribution was combined with all others and became an indistinguishable part of the whole. As a result, every student was able to own the music being performed – each could claim a part in its creation. Also, connections were formed between student and student, student and music, student and instrument, student and the act of creating and appreciating and, of course, student and teacher. I usually end the story by saying to my student-teachers, 'Of all the music lessons she had, that is the lesson that Jenny is going to remember, and I wasn't even there!'

It was many years later that I was able to identify the successful elements of those music classes. I had, without even realising it, actually created an optimal learning environment which engaged and nurtured the emotional and spiritual dimensions of learning. Students were eager and motivated to be in the music classroom: they were learning at their own pace; they were inspired and achieved a sense of satisfaction in their own learning; they were happy to share their knowledge and skills with one another; they respected and appreciated the gifts of one another; and, in the end, they contributed their individual learning to make a wondrous whole. Moreover, these aspects enhanced the cognitive learning that I had set out to teach – an understanding of triads, chords and chord relationships. Thus, the complementary roles of cognitive, affective and spiritual learning were an intrinsic part of the process.

I believe it was my experiences in those music, drama and English classrooms that prompted my identification of the multidimensional nature of learning. The combination of formal and informal learning situations which accompanied these subjects released a level of freedom that fostered experimental and adventurous learning, particularly as the restrictions imposed by an examination system are not of as much significance in the more creative subjects like drama and music. As a result, I was constantly amazed by the students who, through their experiences of working together and respecting others' voices, were usually able to unite into a community of learners where individual gifts were shared without hesitation for the benefit of the group, so that individuality and communality became seamlessly integrated. In fact, individuality was recognised as an essential component of the collective.

## The complementarity of intellectual, emotional and spiritual dimensions in learning

It is not surprising that my classroom teaching experience was a motivating factor for my subsequent research into the role of different intelligences and different ways of learning. I had, for too long, worked in an educational context that gave credence to the understanding that the human person is an intellectual being who has the ability to think, but which neglected the feeling and intuiting elements that compose the whole person. In an age when we recognise that the role of the emotions and spirituality have significance in the thoughts and behaviour of the individual[11] and, at the same time, we have extensive knowledge and understanding of the learning process[12] of how the brain works,[13] there is surely a need to move from a learning approach which emphasises cognitive learning and recognises that effective learning requires cognitive, affective *and* spiritual elements to work in complementary roles.

Accordingly, I have proposed a framework based on the concept of the three intelligences, intellectual, emotional and spiritual. The corresponding processes work in complementary roles: perceiving/sensing, thinking/feeling, intuiting/imagining/creating and/or problem solving. The interaction and integration therein involves multisensory learning and has the potential to lead to depth learning that is transformational. I have discussed this approach more extensively elsewhere (see de Souza, 2004; 2005; 2012a) but will provide an overview here.

The foundational basis for recognising the interactive nature of the processes identified above is drawn from Jung's theory that humans experience phenomena in four ways (O'Connor, 1996). They first perceive the facts through their senses. This generates thoughts as the facts are pieced together in a logical structure with the interplay of the conscious and non-conscious mind. The thinking triggers feelings which spring from memories stored beyond the conscious mind and which may relate to previous experiences and/or factors that may be closely or distantly associated with the event. This can lead the individual to 'gut' responses or intuitions and value judgements and views. Finally, the combined action leads the individual to look beyond the existing facts to other possibilities, creations and so on. This latter process is the intuition at work (p. 75).

The interplay of these processes is an integral part of the learning process and they enable individuals to become acquainted with their inner and outer worlds. As a result, the holistic nature of the learning makes it more meaningful. If the learning is balanced between these different processes, we move past the existing frameworks that give unequal emphasis to cognitive, affective and spiritual learning. The additional elements – intuitive, imaginative and creative aspects of learning – operate at a non-conscious level where new thoughts and feelings, which have been provoked by new perceptions or sensations, become absorbed through a 'rumination' process (Claxton, 2000, p. 40) into previously accumulated perceptions and thoughts that are stored deep within the non-conscious mind. Thus, non-conscious processes such as intuition and imagination become the connecting factor between new and old learning, and raise the potential for learning to address the relational aspects of a student's life, that is, the spiritual dimension. Subsequently, new learnings evolve from this merging, which may translate into changed attitudes and/or behaviour; thus, learning that is transformational is an interplay and integration of these different elements – perceiving, thinking, feeling, intuiting, imagining and creating. Without such integration, it is possible that learning will remain superficial – that is, 'surface' learning.

A further aspect to consider is that this holistic approach engages students at different levels. Cognitive-based learning tends to focus on knowledge acquisition garnered from different media outlets; this can result in passive learning. The problems associated with passive learning have been identified by educators like Moffett (1994) and Robinson (2001) and these have been compounded by the use of new technology, where different sized screens have become an increased source of education and entertainment for young people. As a result, there is a generation of children who have accumulated hours of television viewing and internet surfing. Accordingly, they have amassed a huge amount of information which they may be able to recall, but which they are unable to act on. This is precisely because although the part of the brain that receives and memorises information may have become well-developed through their activities, the brain has failed to make the appropriate connections that enable a person to interpret and act on the information they have received.

Zull describes clearly how an imbalance in the learning process can occur. He points to three components in the process that leads to transformative learning: *sensing*, *integrating*, and *motor*,

> which means moving . . . These three functions of the cortex are not an accident. They do the key things that are essential for all nervous systems. They sense the environment, add up (or integrate) what they sense, and generate appropriate movements or actions.
>
> (Zull, 2002, p. 15)

I have discussed Zull's thesis elsewhere (see de Souza, 2009; 2011), where he describes the integration as the process where the individual's senses act as the interface through which a number of signals are picked up from the external environment. When they reach the brain, they combine to form a pattern which is recognisable as the sum of the individual parts. That is, the individual parts merge to form something more meaningful: 'In the human brain these meanings are then integrated in new ways that become ideas, thoughts, and plans. At their most basic, these integrated meanings become plans for action' (Zull, 2002, p. 16).

Zull further aligns the movement from perception to action to the physical shape of the brain, where the integrative part lies between the sensory cortex and the motor brain (pp. 31–46). Thus, when signals are transferred from the outside world or from the individual's own body (sensory input) to the sensory cortex in the brain, they move through the integrative part of the brain, which is situated close to the sensory part, and then move through to the integrative part of the brain, which is close to the motor brain. This is then detected by the whole sensory brain so that the output of the brain becomes new sensory input. Thus, new learning and action is generated, which in turn generates more new learning and action.

Zull asserts that these changes happen at the same point in time, 'a juncture defined by the structure of the brain itself . . . this juncture is the fulcrum on which information is leveraged into understanding' (p. 34). The structure of the brain has two parts: one for receiving, remembering and integrating information from external sources; and the other for acting, modifying, creating and controlling. With passive learning, it is only the first part of this structure that is activated, so the learning becomes imbalanced. In other words, Zull's analysis provides physical evidence of the integration of learning from perception to action.

The integrative action discussed by Zull is indispensable to the multisensory learning approach I have proposed. The approach recognises that while students' learning is based on what they consciously perceive through their senses, their initial response may be at the intellectual level (thinking – generating and furthering knowledge acquisition) or the emotional level (generating feelings that influence subsequent thinking and actions). These responses will then lead to an integration of the two, so that thoughts and feelings work together to produce a deeper level of knowledge and engagement. However, if the learning is to go beyond the surface, it must touch the 'soul' of the student; it must reach that core where the learning becomes transformed by an inner response which may, and should, lead to outward expressions of changed thinking and behaviour. It is at this level that intuiting, imagining and/or creating become additional aspects of the integrated learning process, so that the learner's response becomes transformed without them consciously knowing exactly how or why the change has occurred. The motion then is perpetual, moving from initial perceptions at the surface, through thoughts and feelings that merge with previous learning and instincts at the centre, before returning to the surface in transformed knowledge and expressions which affect future perceptions; and so the process begins again.

I would like to illustrate how this process works. I had been presenting a paper on this topic at a symposium some years ago and I had decided to engage the participants in the process as a prelude to presenting my research. It was April which, in Australia, means that teaching topics related to Anzac Day are often used in school classrooms and, as it was a time when Australia was involved with the War in Iraq, I decided to use war as a topic. I had some war music playing in the background, which included a lot of sombre drum rolls, as people entered the room and the slide on the screen had a shaded red background to the words 'Shades of War' in bold black print. Once people were seated, I turned the music off and explained that I was going to take them through a process before I would talk about it. I returned to the music and set up a slide show which consisted of related war images, poetry, quotes and so on. The audience appeared to be completely engrossed as there was a stillness in the room. When it was over, I asked for their immediate responses, which stimulated some discussion and which then gave me the lead into my presentation about the approach that involved the complementarity of the cognitive, affective and spiritual dimensions of learning. There was a lot of thoughtful questions but, towards the end, one young man challenged me: 'I had a brother who died in the war, and I feel that by putting us through this process, you have completely manipulated me. What have you got to say to that?' The young man was obviously upset and hurting, so I responded with a general comment about how most educators actually do manipulate learning environments if they want their students to get from A to B and C. However, what I really felt had happened was that as soon as the young man saw the word 'war' and then watched the images with the selected music impacting on his non-conscious mind, his emotions and feelings were activated. All his subsequent thoughts were coloured by his feelings, leading to his angry question to me. It is quite likely that he did not 'hear' much of the discussion that had been going on or, if he did, it would have been through a mist triggered by his grief. His learning experience, then, would have been very different from that of other participants whose responses to war were also negative, but were not affected by personal tragedy. The incident confirmed for me that we must attend to the multisensory nature of learning as well as the interplay of the cognitive, emotional and spiritual dimensions of intelligence that impact on individual learning.

What is important to remember is that there are many responses to topics when they are introduced into a classroom. Some will be thoughts that spin away into inspired ideas leading to other topics, but others will be feelings which will be determined by the individual's previous associations with the topic. For instance, a discussion on families and family celebrations can either provoke positive or negative feelings in different individuals, depending on what their family life is or has been. The point is that if negative feelings are evoked, they will affect further learning, most often, in a negative way. Children's concentration may become less focused as they drift into unpleasant memories and so on. Thus, at all times, teachers need to be aware of and alert to the fact that children will respond to topics and discussions cognitively, affectively and spiritually – and each of these responses will be different. Time needs to be factored in for children to allow the new learning to integrate with earlier learning; and strategies need to be devised which will allow children time to reflect on the 'how and why' of their feelings as part of the process. By understanding the elements that shape their learning and responses, the student will be better placed to manage their emotions and feelings and, perhaps, affirm their own sense of connectedness and wellbeing.

## Concluding thoughts

As I have written elsewhere (de Souza, 2005), if cognitive learning continues to dominate classroom practice and if affective learning outcomes remain 'tokenistic', it is possible that children may achieve the complex cognitive skills desired so that they produce the 'right' answers; but this does not guarantee that the learning has reached a depth level which has the potential to be transformative. By articulating learning outcomes to address cognitive, affective and spiritual aspects, and then planning appropriate learning activities, there is a greater probability that the learning can become a transformative experience which helps the child connect to previous learning, to their inner thoughts and to the Other in their school community. Learning, then, has the potential to have a more lasting impact, something that the children may be able to revisit throughout their lives; and the learning experiences should provide those moments that both teachers and students remember as enjoyable and meaningful.

One of the drawbacks with using this approach is that, in the current outcomes-based system and with the prescribed subjects in the curriculum, classroom practitioners may feel unequal to the task of articulating and assessing affective and spiritual learning outcomes. My own students were taught to use the stem 'By the end of the lesson the student will have opportunities to:' – which made it clear that opportunities would be planned for the learning outcome to be accomplished, although there was no assumption that the learning would take place within that particular class. This is different from the statement and intention of cognitive learning outcomes which expect the learning to be achieved within that lesson. Sometimes, learning may occur outside the conscious mind and the individual may only discover it at a later point in their life when something triggers the early learning so that it is retrieved from the non-conscious mind.

My students were also advised to consider the learning they hoped to achieve amongst their own students to determine if it related to feelings such as a show of excitement, enthusiasm, participation and so on; or if it related to something deeper that indicated some change in the student like a demonstration of care, kindness and compassion, wonder and awe, or something so deeply felt that it led to obviously changed attitudes and behaviour, such as empathy and inclusion. Unlike the achievement of cognitive learning outcomes that are reported on, different strategies can be put in place for affective and spiritual learning to be observed. For instance, specific learning behaviours associated with affective and spiritual learning may be identified and recorded during a lesson or a series of lessons. As well, students can be encouraged to reflect on their own learning in relation to the affective and spiritual learning outcomes, keep a journal or fill in self-evaluation sheets and so on. These ways of recording affective and spiritual learning are different to the reporting of knowledge acquisition, which states clearly that knowledge and skills have been gained, or which indicate a performance level at which the achievement of knowledge and skills has been reached. By adding observations and/or self-evaluations into the process, a much more holistic learning and assessment programme is effected and, additionally, connections are made between the different dimensions of learning – cognitive, affective and spiritual.

A further problem that confronts teachers who use this approach is the challenge to find innovative and stimulating multisensory resources and activities which will seriously engage and challenge their students. However, I believe the enrichment of the learning that can happen with this approach should provide the motivation to continue. More activities that draw on the inner Self and involve creativity, imagination, story-telling, reflection and contemplation, stillness and silence should be explored and trialled to evaluate their effectiveness in addressing the three dimensions. Daily timetables and classroom structures can be designed to promote communication, connectedness and an integration of learning across different subject areas. These are all ways in which this learning approach can be implemented effectively.

If educators recognise their students as intuitive beings and develop learning programmes and environments that provide space and time for an integrative learning approach – where the interplay of cognitive, affective and spiritual learning is enabled – they will be creating the potential for today's students to become balanced, insightful, inclusive and concerned citizens for tomorrow's world. Surely, this is the goal of every educator.

The next chapter will examine one additional feature that has relevance for the education of children and young people today. It is about addressing the plural nature of contemporary society to enhance relationships and connectedness between people of different cultural backgrounds and belief systems. Accordingly, it will explore interspirituality as an educational theme for the twenty-first century.

## Notes

1  Retrieved on 26 May 2015.
2  As above.
3  Retrieved on 26 May 2015 from www.australiancurriculum.edu.au/english/curriculum/f-10?layout=1.
4  See the NAPLAN website for further details: www.nap.edu.au/.
5  For instance, see ABC News: www.abc.net.au/news/2015-05-12/qld-schools-letter-offering-naplan-support-goes-viral/6463644 (12 May 2015).
6  Ibid.
7  Retrieved on 13 May 2015 from www.smh.com.au/national/naplan-parents-and-teachers-urged-to-calm-students-down-20150511-gguetta.html.
8  From Becker (2003), History of the Stanford-Binet intelligence scales: Content and psychometrics. Retrieved on 22 October 2015 from www.assess.nelson.com/pdf/sb5-asb1.pdf.
9  Pseudonym used.
10 Pseudonym used.
11 For instance: Kessler (2000); Goleman (1996); Mayer and Salovey (1997); Mayer, Salovey and Caruso (2000); Pearce (1977; 1985, 2003); and Zohar and Marshall (2000).
12 For instance: Csikzentmihalyi (1992, 2002); Claxton (1998; 2005); Del Prete (2002); Gardner (1983; 1993; 1999); Gardner, Kornhaber and Wake (1996); Lucas and Claxton (2010); Miller (2000); Robinson (2001); Robinson with Aronica (2009); and Wilber (2001).
13 For instance: Newberg, D'Aquili and Rause (2001); Pearce (2002); Persinger (1996); and Ramachandran and Blakeslee (1998).

# Chapter 6

# To the future

## The implications of an emerging interspiritual age

The context and content in earlier chapters and the subsequent discussions were varied and, in some ways, disparate. However, the one thing they have in common are features of the contemporary world that contextualise the lives of children and young people and which therefore have implications for education. The focus of this chapter is on yet another element which has significance in the contemporary world and its far-reaching impact on children and young people. This is the situation where religion – which had through the twentieth century resided on the fringes of society – has emerged to reclaim some prominence in political, social and cultural spheres. Indeed, a recognition of this factor has, in recent years, led to the assertion that we have moved into a post-secular climate (see, for instance, Habermas, 2008; Habermas *et al.*, 2011; King, 2009).

The attention being given to religion today could be attributed to the fact that religious diversity has become a distinguishing characteristic of contemporary societies in many parts of the world; and the need for people to understand one another has given rise to a wide range of intercultural, interfaith and interreligious activities at all levels in society, from governing bodies to grassroots citizenry. However, in light of the observations and arguments that have been part of my research journey over the past twenty years, and which I have revisited in this collection of writings, my focus is about the spiritual dimension of religion. Therefore, in this chapter, I would like to explore the rather visionary concept that we are moving into an *interspiritual* age (Griffiths, 1989; 1994; His Holiness the Dalai Lama, 2010; Johnson & Ord, 2012; Teasdale, 1999; 2003) and examine the implications for education.

## Religion and religious diversity in a secular world

While I have taken care to establish spirituality as a separate entity from religion, I have also recognised that the two are closely connected. Traditionally, there has been a perception that spirituality emerged from and found its identity in religion. However, I subscribe to the argument that religion is a human construct which has been generated by the human person's spiritual nature. Thus, the search for something more that is triggered by the individual's innate spirituality has, over human history, led to gatherings and the formation of communities inspired and driven by a vision of mystical union or oneness, which was given different forms and different names.[1] In time, these communities of faith slowly organised and became institutionalised into religion. This has been the process for the past few thousand years and, for hundreds of years, these religions served to unite people, providing them with meaning and purpose and a way by which to live. However, many have become driven by their obsession with doctrines and regulations and, in the process, appear to have lost sight of the original vision which inspired them in the first place.

The end result has been the drift away from traditional religions, because many adherents not only fail to realise the original vision within the tradition – so that it no longer has relevance to or meaning in their everyday lives – but have also been hurt or damaged by rules and regulations that have distorted the original vision. As Teasdale (1999) remarks: 'Religions are valuable carriers of the tradition within a community, but they must not be allowed to choke out the breath of spirit, which breathes where it will' (p. 11).

Indeed, the large movements of people 'out' of religion and 'into' an individual spiritual search, which became a distinct trend in the latter half of the twentieth century, could be attributed to a certain fossilisation of some institutional religions. While it may have been an exhilarating and liberating experience for many, as they threw off the shackles of a belief system that had ceased to have significance and meaning in their lives, the seeds of another challenge were sown. This is what we are witnessing today. Many young people – as a result of the culture of relativism that has crept into society, following the loss of power and influence of organised religion and other traditional institutions – have been left ungrounded. They lack the intergenerational experience of belonging to a community founded on a shared wisdom tradition which provides a lens through which one may understand or explain the happenings in one's life. When young people are unable to draw on the history and accumulated wisdom of a community because the deep connectedness which membership of that community brings is no longer available to them, they may find themselves adrift in a culture of 'anything goes' that infiltrates their lives.

As we have identified in earlier chapters, belonging and identity are essential elements in an individual's self-understanding, self-esteem and wellbeing. However, when multiple identities construct an individual's sense of self, each identity rests on a set of beliefs and values. In order to function and engage with the Other in their everyday lives, a young person must negotiate between these different identities and ways of being. The fact that they must swing from one to another, perhaps several times in a day or a week, does raise the potential that the accompanying beliefs and values retain a quality of relativity in order to make it easier for the individual to move from one to another. This is different to an individual who has been reared in a belief system that has grown up and been continually reinforced within a community, one which has been founded on years of tradition and wisdom and is identified by its particularity. In the latter situation, the beliefs and values are grounded into the core of one's Being. If, in a relativistic climate, beliefs and values retain a degree of superficiality, it would not be too difficult for young people to accept and adopt others to replace them, always depending on their mental and emotional states and the situations they find themselves in. This is one reason why, in a climate of threat and terror, many young people who are disillusioned or suffering from an identity crisis will respond to online propaganda that offers them the opportunity to belong to a community founded on particular religious ideals. Without being sufficiently grounded in any particular faith community or tradition, they have little knowledge or support against the onslaught of misinformation and the manipulative marketing of a cause. This is just one feature of Australian and other Western societies today, where many children may not be affiliated to a particular religious tradition; neither do they learn about other religions and their role in human society.

To be sure, discussions about religion have dominated the media and politics over the first decade of the twenty-first century. This attention has been driven by both the positive aspects of religious diversity, leading to interreligious and interfaith dialogue, and the negative combinations of religion and terror, based on particular interpretations of and attitudes to different religious traditions. Religious diversity cannot be ignored since, through the twentieth century, it has slowly become a distinguishing characteristic of many countries. Rabindranath Tagore recognised this in the years following World War I when he observed:

> The races of mankind will never again be able to go back to their citadels of high-walled exclusiveness. They are today exposed to one another, physically and intellectually. The shells, which have so long given them full security within their individual encounters, have been broken and by no artificial process can they be mended again. So we have to accept this fact, even though we have not yet fully adapted our minds to this changed environment of publicity, even though through it we may have to run all the risks entailed by the wider expansion of life's freedom.
>
> (Tagore, 1931, pp. 141–142)

However, religious diversity has also generated elements of unrest, fear of the Other and, most recently, the threat of terrorism. As the His Holiness the Dalai Lama acknowledges:

> For many religious people, accepting the legitimacy of other faith traditions poses a serious challenge. To accept that other religions are legitimate may seem to compromise the integrity of one's own faith, since it entails the admission of different but efficacious spiritual paths . . . Yet without the emergence of a genuine spirit of religious pluralism, there is no hope for the development of harmony based on true interreligious understanding.
>
> (His Holiness the Dalai Lama, 2010, pp. 145 and 146)

More importantly, his contention is that genuine interreligious dialogue and understanding should not be contingent upon pushing the view about the ultimate oneness of all religions, since such an approach is problematic for most adherents of other religions:

> True understanding of the 'other' must proceed from a genuine recognition of and respect for the other's reality. It must proceed from a state of mind where the urge to reduce the other into one's own framework is no longer the dominant mode of thinking.
> (His Holiness the Dalai Lama, 2010, p. 148).

Speaking from the discipline of religious education, Andrew Wright recognises a similar situation when he discusses the confrontation posed by the Other to an individual's self-understanding and identity:

> Since the Other is irreducible to the sameness of my treasured world-view, my experience of alterity and difference brings about a disruption that challenges me to look beyond myself towards a wealth of new horizons.
> (Wright, 2007, p. 70)

Certainly, there has been an abundance of writings, conferences and other gatherings, as well as organisations and community groups, that have focused on interreligious and interfaith relations and activities.[2] Nonetheless, religious diversity has also brought about the rise in religious fundamentalism. Pratt's (2015) discussion in reference to Islamophobia and the rise in radicalised Muslim young people clearly identifies the problems associated with exclusivism which provoke religious fundamentalism.[3] In their efforts to create specific identities for their followers, religious leaders have continued to create cultural and social divisions by putting boundaries around their own followers to encourage them to see the Other as different. In other words, it is aspects of rigid religious doctrines and practices that are at the core of much of the divisiveness observed and experienced in today's world which threatens social cohesion and wellbeing. The spiritual dimension of religion, however, transcends difference, thereby raising the potential for the emergence and recognition of a Universal Consciousness (Griffiths, 1989; 1994; Johnson & Ord, 2012; Teasdale, 1999; 2003; Wilber, 2001). If there is recognition, acknowledgement and emphasis placed on the esoteric dimensions of religion – which highlight the similarities and the notion of unity rather than the exoteric aspects, which concentrate on the differences – there is a greater potential that we will be able to address and ease the contemporary problems linked to cultural and religious diversity. To this end, we need to transform our notions of interreligious and interfaith dialogue to incorporate a concept of interspirituality.

The term 'interspirituality' was used by Wayne Teasdale when he discussed a vision of a universal spirituality in the world's religions. He asserted that:

The real religion of humankind can be said to be spirituality itself, because mystical spirituality is the origin of all the world religions. If this is so, and I believe it is, we might also say that *interspirituality* – the sharing of ultimate experiences across traditions – is the religion of the third millennium.

(Teasdale, 1999, p. 26; emphasis in the original text)

Teasdale felt that interspirituality could provide the foundation to prepare the way for a more enlightened culture. Like His Holiness the Dalai Lama and Wright, Teasdale did not argue for the elimination of different religions in order to replace them with a 'homogenous superspirituality' (ibid.). Rather, he felt that developing interspirituality could be:

a world-changing force which was made up by the openness of people who have a viable spiritual life, coupled with their determination, capacity, and commitment to the inner search across traditions.

(Teasdale, 1999, p. 26)

In more recent discussions on interspirituality, Johnson and Ord (2012) suggest that at the core of Teasdale's vision is the conviction that a universal unity consciousness lay at the heart of all inner exploration (p. 20). Teasdale felt that the concept of unity consciousness or nondualism found across all spiritual traditions could be a 'great globalizer, bringing to a culmination the world's millennia of spiritual journeying' (ibid.). Furthermore, Johnson and Ord identify an alignment between the search for unity consciousness and the growth of globalisation; that is, the awareness of the world as an interconnected place because, they claim, the non-dual view of reality has pervaded several areas of human pursuit in the contemporary world, for instance, quantum mechanics and string theory in the new physics, various areas of cognitive psychology, as well as the core unitive mystic experience described in all the world's Great Wisdom Traditions (p. 23). They argue that it is important to recognise the connection between these two entities, unity consciousness and globalisation, because it may best serve a 'global integrative age' (ibid.):

Interspirituality is the natural discussion among human beings about what we are experiencing. In academic terms, it's the intersubjective discussion among us all about who we are, why we are here, and where we are going. In the context of religion, interspirituality is the common heritage of humankind's spiritual wisdom and the sharing of wisdom resources across traditions. In terms of developing human consciousness, interspirituality is the movement of all these discussions toward the experience of profound interconnectedness, unity consciousness, and oneness.

(Johnson & Ord, 2012, p. 9)

Part of their motivation for interspiritual rather than interreligious dialogue is that religion is about right belief, which tends to 'value creed over deed', while spirituality is about right being, which values deed over creed (p. 33).

Teasdale's (1999) study of the interdependence between and among different religions does support Johnson and Ord's arguments. Teasdale identifies interdependence as an 'inescapable fact of our contemporary world' since it has significant implications for international commerce, cultural exchange and scientific collaboration: 'The more the bonds of interconnectedness define the shape and scope of the future, the less likely they will be ruptured' (p. 5). He goes further to establish a spiritual interdependence between different religions and how they influence one another:

> This interdependence is more subtle, though the actual impact of traditions on each other is clearly discernible in history, particularly where cultural contiguity exists . . . Endless studies demonstrate the impact of earlier, lesser-known traditions and myths on the development and doctrines of the historical faiths.
>
> (Teasdale, 1999, p. 6)

Ultimately, Teasdale believed that the twenty-first century would herald in the dawning of a 'new consciousness which was a radically fresh approach to our life as the human family in a fragile world' and which would transcend 'past religious cultures of fragmentation and isolation' (p. 4). This would comprise an interspiritual age entirely appropriate for a global, plural world.

While the term interspirituality came into use at the turn of the century, the element intrinsic to it and from which it derives its essence has been around for centuries. It is about the spiritual vision of a Universal Consciousness that is foundational to every religion (Griffiths, 1989). Griffiths points to the fact that all religious truth comes from an original experience – that of seer, the prophet, the saint (p. 268) – but emphasises that the truth is then interpreted in the light of rational, conceptual thought within particular cultural frameworks. Thus, while the truth springs from the one source, its interpretation and application is dependent on the rational mind of the individual who experiences it as well as the cultural setting that determines the way the individual thinks. This is how and why expressions of the original vision may differ from one another – but we need to remember that they originate from a unified source:

> In each religion, as we have seen, the point is reached when the cosmic Lord is acknowledged. But now the next stage is to go beyond that and to realize that in and through the cosmic Person the whole of this universe, physical and psychological, is being reintegrated into its source. When we come to the Supreme, everything returns to unity. Everything comes out of that original unity, exploding into a universe and evolving through all these forms that we see.
>
> (Griffiths, 1989, p. 269)

Much earlier, Aldous Huxley began his thesis on the perennial philosophy with the words:

Philosophia perennis . . . the metaphysic that recognizes a divine Reality substantial to the world of things and lives and minds; the psychology that finds in the soul something similar to, or even identical with, divine Reality; the ethic that places man's [*sic*] final end in the knowledge of the immanent and transcendent Ground of all being – the thing immemorial and universal.

(Huxley, 1945, p. 9)

Huxley claimed that the perennial philosophy may be found in the beliefs and lore of tribal people in every region of the world as well as in the highly developed forms of the world's great religions and that it was first written about more than twenty-five centuries ago. Thus the concept of a common element in all religions is not new.[4] Huxley asserted that there are two ways to Ultimate Reality: in and through the soul, and in and through the world. He also doubted that the ultimate goal could be reached by following any one of these two paths to the exclusion of the Other. The way forward was that 'which leads to the divine Ground simultaneously in the perceiver and in that which is perceived' (p. 83).

Oldmeadow (2010), who is well published in the field of the perennial philosophy, acknowledges that there has always been some exchange of ideas and influences between the great religious cultures, but stresses that today 'we are living in unprecedented times where different religious traditions are everywhere impinging on each other' (p. vii). Oldmeadow concurs with Smith (1976) when he refers to the past when each civilisation exhibited a spiritual homogeneity undisturbed by religious pluralism (ibid.) so that the interrelationship or interdependence between religions was of little concern. However, today we live in a 'smaller world' (p. viii) so that it is impossible to ignore the presence of different religious cultures and traditions that are beginning to impact on our lives, at both the individual and collective level:

The interrelationships of the religions today is an issue which has taken on a new immediacy in the cyclical conditions in which we live, especially for those concerned with fostering a harmonious world community. Furthermore, in an age of rampant secularism and scepticism the need for some kind of interreligious solidarity makes itself ever more acutely felt.

(Oldmeadow, 2010, p. viii)

This idea of a common vision of reality in all religious traditions has been examined extensively in the past, but it has become much more significant in the contemporary world which is characterised by religious diversity. Huston Smith (1976) suggested that in earlier times, people remained cocooned in their different cultures and belief systems so they were largely self-contained. However, in today's multicultural and multi-religious societies, a level of interdependence between religions has become more apparent and 'one finds a remarkable unity underlying the surface differences' (p. v). Smith points out that outwardly, collective cultural and religious outlooks may differ but inwardly, 'it is as if an "invisible geometry" has everywhere been working to shape them to a single truth' (ibid.).

What we may elicit from the arguments and ideas offered by the selection of scholars and writers I have drawn on is the recognition that social constructs that are dominated by religious plurality are a completely new phenomenon in the history of humankind – and they are here to stay. As a result, we are witnessing quite specific problems associated with religious diversity which can be attributed largely to complete ignorance and misunderstanding of the religious Other. As Oldmeadow says:

> The resolution of the peculiar tensions and antagonisms arising out of our new global circumstances, and the fulfilment of its inherent spiritual possibilities, is one of the most momentous tasks facing all those concerned with the spiritual welfare of humankind.
>
> (Oldmeadow, 2010, p. viii)

Jack Miller (2006), whose research and practice has influenced and energised the field of holistic learning for most of the past three decades, discusses the idea of 'Timeless Learning', which is generated by the wisdom contained in various spiritual traditions. Miller alludes to the perennial philosophy and believes that aspects of this philosophy can be identified 'within the mystical thread of most religions and spiritual psychologies' (p. 15). While there are, indeed, many critics who reject the use of the term 'perennial philosophy' in relation to education, I agree with Miller's response when he says: 'I think it is possible to have a relaxed universalism using the term "perennial" but bringing a stronger awareness and respect for pluralistic approaches to spirituality and spiritual practices' (p. 16). Miller identifies the following traits of the philosophy which are relevant to education:

> There is an interconnectedness of reality and a mysterious unity in the universe;
>
> There is an intimate connection between the individual's inner self, or soul, and this mysterious unity;
>
> Knowledge of this mysterious unity can be developed through various contemplative practices;
>
> Values are derived from seeing and realizing the interconnectedness of reality;
>
> The realization can lead to social activity designed to counter injustice and human suffering.
>
> (Miller, 2006, p. 16)

Thus, for Miller, education should be informed by the wisdom of the great spiritual traditions where there is a recognition of an underlying unity between all things. The interconnectedness that reflects this underlying unity should lie at the heart of a holistic approach to education. Citing Gandhi, Miller alludes to the unity that may be found in all religions where there may be many forms but 'the informing spirit is one' (p. 17). Miller also points to the fact that wisdom or knowledge of this mysterious unity can be developed through various contemplative practices. He argues that this should be an important inclusion in education because it is from our realisation of the interconnectedness of reality that we develop the values that lead us to social action to counter injustice and human suffering.

To sum up, a concept of Timeless Learning is an appropriate approach to education for the contemporary world. It seeks to address the whole child, promotes connectedness, encourages passion and participation, creates a community of learners and is informed by the mystical dimensions of the Wisdom Traditions. Indeed, Timeless Learning reflects elements of a variety of approaches to education that have been inspired by well-known educationalists such as Steiner, Khrishnamurti, Montessori and others. Schools based on the philosophies of these people are found in many different countries and their links to the universal wisdom contained in the different traditions is discernible in their thinking and practice. In their publication, *Nurturing Our Wholeness: Perspectives on Spirituality in Education*, Miller and Nakagawa (2002) provide an illuminating account of some of these approaches from an array of writers. There are other lesser-known schools as well, which have developed as a result of a community's ideals, focus and intent.[5] Such schools draw their life from an alternative vision of education to that of the mainstream, and their primary aim is to provide an environment which encourages the child to grow and develop as a whole person and experience the full scope of their nature – intellectually, emotionally and spiritually.

## Two strands: A learning approach and a new discipline

In drawing the different threads of this discussion together, I would like to identify two strands that are distinct and, yet, interrelated. One is that broad approaches to education across different disciplines should be informed by an interspiritual approach which draws on the Wisdom Traditions of the world. This is what we have been discussing so far. The second is that there needs to be a distinct inclusion of a study of different belief systems and worldviews in the school curriculum to prepare today's students for the world of tomorrow. More importantly, it is not enough to distribute aspects of such a study to be incorporated into other subjects, such as literature, history, geography, social studies and/or politics. When that happens, learning dissolves into a rather 'hit and miss' affair, depending on the knowledge and skills of the classroom teacher. It can also result in a child receiving so many pieces of disjointed information so as to render them meaningless, thereby reducing the study or discipline to a series of topics or issues with little relevance to one another.

I am suggesting that in a global, plural world, the study of belief systems and worldviews is one that should be treated as a distinct discipline, one that requires as much acknowledgement and attention as that given to language, maths, science and technology. Of course, these traditional subjects continue to be of significance in assisting children and young people to communicate and negotiate their way through the world, especially in their future workplaces. Nonetheless, it is equally important that children have knowledge and understanding about the beliefs and practices of the people they live next to, encounter and interact with on their respective journeys. In a world suffused by diversity, such learning can remove fear of difference and so enrich and enliven the passage of each and every individual. Moreover, it will promote connectedness and wellbeing in all aspects of an individual's Being – physical, mental, emotional, psychological, ethical and spiritual – as well as at all levels of the individual's life: communal, societal, religious, political and global.

Such an education will not be restricted to preparing students for a future workplace. Rather, it is about preparation to be a well-rounded and well-adjusted citizen for a global, plural world, where there is an underlying recognition of a Universal Consciousness that connects all people, regardless of their religious or cultural heritage. It is a world where children will be able to grow up without a fear of the otherness of the Other, precisely because they know and understand the Other and have discovered their connectedness to them. The foundational idea for a vision of this kind of learning is that spirituality is innate: it is about belonging and connectedness; the experience of transcendence; of being part of the Whole; and about living as a relational Being. These elements are implicit in the way a large majority of individuals live in and perceive the world and therefore, they should play an intrinsic part in shaping future educational philosophies, practices and learning programmes and environments.

In Australia, as in many countries, a study of religion is not included in the core curriculum. Britain is one of the few countries that does offer it. However, in the current climate when religious fundamentalists and extremists have gained ground in the religious debate and religion and terror are spoken of in a single sentence, we can no longer neglect the role religion plays in the lives of people. I need to stress, however, that while there have been a variety of approaches to learning about religions, what I am proposing here is different.[6] I am talking about a study of the range of belief systems of which Australia and many other Western societies today are composed, and which motivate and determine the attitudes, behaviours and practices that can be observed in human actions every day. Such a study would necessarily be different to the traditional studies of religions, which tend to concentrate on a selection of the main world religions such as Buddhism, Christianity, Hinduism, Islam, Judaism, Sikhism and possibly other Eastern and Indigenous traditions. A study which restricts the content to the mainstream or traditional faiths is no longer appropriate in societies that are both multi-faith as well as secular. Instead, a study which includes religious and non-religious belief systems is more relevant because there is a greater chance that today's students, at some time in their lives, will engage with people whose beliefs and practices are different from their own. It is imperative, then, that children and young people today have a sound understanding of the diversity that exists in their communities so that the barriers that obstruct an understanding and acceptance of the Other are removed or, certainly, made less significant.

I believe, as well, that we need to move away from the concentration on the attainment of knowledge and skills or on formal assessment. Most approaches to a study of religions derive from a cognitive study, which begins at a point of divisiveness and compartmentalisation, where an identification of the various phenomena of different religions becomes the focus of the study. In other words, we start at the surface of the religion and we develop skills to analyse, categorise and evaluate the observable characteristics by which a particular belief system may be known. Given the constraints and reality of the classroom environment, for instance, the time allowed for the lesson, the interest of the students, the knowledge and enthusiasm of the teacher, the resources available and so on, it usually means that any experiential elements will be restricted to a visit to a sacred place or listening to a guest speaker from the tradition being studied. Understanding and appreciating a religion from the perspective and experience of an adherent is an aspect of the learning that is not always achieved, although there are some approaches that have incorporated this into their philosophy and practice; for instance, the interpretive approach (Jackson, 1997; Jackson & McKenna, 2005) and the interdisciplinary approach (Erricker, 2010). Generally, however, knowledge and understanding are about the memorisation of facts and figures that will be required for any subsequent assessment task. In other words, students' learning is reduced to a clinical and diluted experience, with little evidence of the emotion, passion and spirit that the faith tradition inspires in its followers.

What I am suggesting is an interspiritual approach that works in reverse; it is an 'inside out' process, whereby it begins at a point of unity that inspired the original vision of the tradition. Such an approach would draw on the thinking contained in Huxley's (1945) description of the two thought patterns that prevail in all the main religions as well as in many Indigenous systems of belief: the exoteric and the esoteric. The first is the outer appearance of the religion, the public face that allows it to be identified as a particular faith tradition. It is composed of the doctrines, the rules, the rituals and practices, as well as the buildings that signify the places of worship. It is the exoteric form of religion that provides the content that is foundational to the current approaches to religious education that were referred to earlier. The second face of religion is more secretive and has fewer followers than the exoteric version. It focuses on and is inspired by the spiritual consciousness that generates an understanding of a Universal Mind.

It is the exoteric form of religion that tends to exclusivity since it provides a boundary around its followers which promotes a sense of 'us' and 'them'. Newberg and Waldman (2006), writing from a neuroscientific perspective, highlight how brain research has shown that a belief system can encourage individuals to maintain a boundary to protect them from others who are different. They argue that emotions not only help us to maintain our beliefs but also defend us against other beliefs that threaten our worldview. When someone presents a different belief that may challenge our own, the first thing we do is to become dismissive of the Other. This is because our brain has already done a lot of work establishing what we should and should not believe in, and the neural circuits have been set: 'neurons that fire together wire together, or so we currently believe' (p. 34).

To further support their arguments, Newberg and Waldman refer to Spinoza's offer of an alternative theory to the Cartesian notion of dualism. It was Spinoza's contention that the human person could intuitively move beyond personal beliefs and draw closer to an Ultimate Reality and Truth. In such a state, the individual could experience 'the essence of an infinite, indivisible "substance", a term that Spinoza used to simultaneously embrace God, nature and the sum total of reality itself' (Newberg & Waldman, 2006, p. 41). Newberg and Waldman point out that while Spinoza's thinking was not well received in the seventeenth century, it is more appropriate to the understanding of spirituality in the contemporary world, particularly where people have moved away from religious influences and have begun to embrace different expressions of spirituality, which they appear to find more relevant and authentic (O'Murchú, 1997; Tacey, 2003). Newberg and Waldman also confirm that Spinoza's thinking correlates with the understanding today of the processes used by the brain to create a holistic image of the world, by assembling disparate pieces to compose a whole which is greater than the sum of its parts.

To sum up, the essence of the interspiritual approach is that it recognises the Universal Consciousness that is found in all religions, so that the concept of unity in diversity is foundational. The 'inside out' process begins with the search for meaning and transcendence, which is perceived as an innate characteristic of humankind. This will flow on to specific individuals, their visions and practices and finally, the communities that were formed by those who followed them and lived by their teachings. Next, the different ways and forms in which individuals and communities have framed their search will be examined, and recognition will be given to the particularity of each tradition as it developed and responded to regional, historical and cultural contexts that had an impact on its evolvement. Finally, the study will reach a point where it may address the doctrine, sacred texts, rituals, places of worship and so on that have become external or surface features of the belief system as it is identified today. Thus, the 'inside out' process is completed.

A further feature of this programme is that it should be designed to be taught across a range of year levels so that students of all ages have access to this learning. Another consideration is that there should be a recognition of the complementarity of different worldviews from East and West, which will promote an understanding of the human condition that led to the construction of religious frameworks. This should be an important deliberation in the contemporary world where Eastern and Western cultural traditions have constant exposure to one another, and may find themselves living as neighbours.

Such a recognition would also signal the shifting mindset from the twentieth to the twenty-first century. As discussed by Harman (1998), knowledge systems originated out of particular cultural beliefs and they are maintained precisely because they continue to reinforce the same beliefs which form the traditions, lifestyles and worldviews of a particular people. Thus, different systems originated across the West and East to reflect the different worldviews found in each of these regions. An interspiritual approach will encourage children to recognise such historical and cultural influences. They will also learn to bring a critical approach to their study in order to identify the strengths and weaknesses, as well as the relevance, of each belief system as it is being applied and practised in the contemporary world. Such a study has the potential to remove fear driven by ignorance; to promote acceptance generated by knowledge and understanding; and to further enhance peaceful community relations. As John Hull states:

> In spite of the difficulties in encountering them, we should take heart from the fact that the many human worlds remain human. After all what we have in common as human beings should enable us to enter every human world for nothing that is human is foreign to us.
>
> (Hull, 2009, p. 32)

## Concluding thoughts

To bring this discussion to a close, a study of the unifying principle that underlies different traditions will make a good starting point in a study of belief systems and worldviews. This is followed by the way and the reasons why religious frameworks developed and changed, depending on the cultural context within which they emerged. Such a study will not reduce knowledge of the differences inherent in the exoteric form of religions, but will emphasise them since they are what make the religion distinctive to others and by which the followers identify themselves.

However, by providing students with the opportunity to discover the underlying unity of thought that is at the core of the human person's search for a transcendent reality, there is less chance that 'us and them' attitudes will develop. The other possible outcome is that students may be more open to and accepting of the religious beliefs and practices of the Other. Education programmes that address these two faces of religion may lead to a change in consciousness where knowledge of the underlying unity that links Self with Other may promote respect for and inclusion of the Other.

In addition, it is important that learning programmes and environments are designed so that they attend to the spiritual dimension of students' lives to help them realise that they are not separate from the Other. Moreover, they may learn to recognise something of themselves in the Other and something of the Other in themselves – and appreciate that this helps to connect them to the Other. They should be encouraged to discover the mystical Element that resides at the core of their Being and they may even reach an understanding that the Other's final destination is likely to be the same as their own. By focusing on the connectedness between all individuals, a subject like this would have the potential to promote deeper knowledge and insightful understandings amongst students about the Other who is culturally, religiously and racially different. In addition, it could lead to changed attitudes as well as levels of empathy and compassion, thereby enhancing the social cohesion and the wellbeing of the future communities to which they belong. Ultimately, these are features that are essential in the education of our children and young people to enable them to take their rightful place and make an authentic contribution in the global, plural world of the twenty-first century.

## Notes

1 See Chapter 1 for a more expansive discussion.
2 A Google search showed 573,000 hits for 'interreligious' and 840 hits for 'interfaith' when combined with Australia on 26 May 2015.
3 See Chapter 3 for further discussion of Pratt's thesis.
4 This concept was discussed at more length in Chapter 1.
5 For instance, the St James School, London (www.stjamesschools.co.uk) and the Erasmus Primary School, Melbourne (www.schoolofphilosophy.org.au/features/erasmus). These are just two examples that reflect a much larger number of schools that have developed their philosophy, organisation and learning programmes along alternative lines to mainstream education.
6 I initially explored the seeds of this idea in an article published in 2011: Promoting inter-spiritual education in the classroom: Exploring the perennial philosophy as a useful strategy to encourage freedom of religious practice and belief. *Journal of Religious Education*, 59(1), pp. 27–37.

# Epilogue

The motivation for writing this book was to revisit and update my research into the role of spirituality in the lives of children and young people to demonstrate why educators need to consider addressing the spiritual dimension in the design of future learning programmes and environments.

At the turn of the century, the decline of religious and other community organisations that used to nurture children's sense of belonging, which afforded them a place in their communities, has meant that many young people today have not been grounded in any particular belief system. Instead, the sense of relativism appears to be a dominant value in the contemporary world, perhaps an accoutrement of a materialistic and consumeristic culture, and effortlessly transmitted through social media and other technological avenues of communication. Certainly, this has encouraged an attitude of 'anything goes' amongst many. Without a firm belief system and a secure sense of identity, children and young people are not always comfortably or safely placed to withstand outside pressures that reflect different viewpoints and practices. As societies have become increasingly multicultural and multi-religious, and where social attitudes and behaviours are heavily influenced by a powerful media, children and young people have much greater access to ways of being that are distinctly different from their own and that highlight the otherness of the Other. This can lead to confusion and bewilderment and a yearning to belong to one of the more attractive, popular or influential groups. In a plural world, this has led to children and young people embodying multiple identities, which enable them to belong to many different groups. This can trigger further difficulties for them when one or more of the identities conflicts with another. Misperceptions, turmoil, an underlying sense of loss and, perhaps, alienation can become possible outcomes.

The issue of prejudice and racism has continued to appear through these writings since it is a dominant feature in a plural world and a large part of the human shadow, the dark side of our spirituality. At our deepest core, our spiritual natures yearn for connectedness – but this longing is tempered by our physical natures and dominated by our sensory perceptions. At a non-conscious level, then, we are encouraged to reach out to those who look and live like ourselves, because it brings us feelings of acceptance and safety. This inclination suggests that developing prejudices and racist attitudes are a natural outcome of the complex processes that make us human, so that all humans can be socially and culturally programmed to develop prejudicial attitudes towards anyone who is different. At a conscious level, we prefer to reject any such notion, since we know that such attitudes are unacceptable. Instead, we look for other reasons to justify and explain any undesirable attitudes and behaviours that we project. In a world besieged by division, recognising our potential to be both compassionate and empathetic, as well as biased and racist, is an essential process in the nurturing of our self-understanding and our spiritual wellbeing.

Education is one avenue through which spiritual wellbeing may be fostered and enhanced. Nonetheless, despite the fact that there has been a singular amount of research and practice which has identified, clarified and concluded that spirituality is an innate human trait, and that the role of spirituality is a significant element in the wellbeing of the individual, there is, as yet, little evidence that this has been recognised and effectively addressed in mainstream education. As a result, most education systems and practices in Australia and other Western countries still reflect nineteenth century cultural attitudes, conditions and procedures, which concentrate on cognitive learning that leads to the development of knowledge and skills. While such attitudes dominate educational policies, it would seem that little progress is being made in adapting practices and processes to seriously prepare children for the global, pluralistic world of the twenty-first century.

There has been a wealth of ideas and research findings from many visionary educators over the past thirty or forty years, most of which focus on educating the whole child and enriching the child's relationship to the Self, others and the world. However, much of this does not appear to be widely reflected in current practices, where learning and assessment programmes are compartmentalised and dominated by examinations and testing of specific aptitudes and skills – ones that are perceived as being an appropriate preparation for the workforce. This is despite the fact that there is, as yet, little knowledge about just what a future workforce may look like, or feel like, or even sound like. In the process, the other characteristics, gifts and capacities that make us human – and which are necessary for the flourishing and prosperity of any community – are overlooked and neglected. Instead, the attempts to resolve current problems and issues in education today, ones which affect the health and wellbeing of children and young people, continue to be generated by leaders with mindsets that appear to be holding fast to the curriculum and pedagogical values and practices of a bygone era. Consequently, we are failing to prepare our students effectively to engage with and live well in their future worlds.

This book continues the trend to focus specifically on the spiritual dimension of the lives and education of our young as an element that is missing in current educational systems. A particular understanding of spirituality is articulated, which explains and interprets the ways that indicate its relevance to an educational approach, for religious or non-religious schools; one that recognises the child as a rational, emotional and spiritual being. Spiritual wellbeing as a factor in promoting social cohesion, a valuable element for a global, plural world, is also explored.

Finally, the various elements linked to spirituality that have significance for and impact on education have been visited, analysed and discussed, thereby confirming that education cannot exist in isolation. It cannot be compartmentalised into one area of human life, because its formative and generative qualities play a crucial role in assuring the interconnectedness, interdependence and blossoming of human societies. Thus, when we engage in a study of any aspect of education we need to attend to the cultural, social, historical, political, psychological, philosophical, technological and religious factors that contribute to creating the individual into the person that they become. And amidst all of this, the role of spirituality in education must be recognised and addressed if our education programmes and environments are to be truly responsive to and reflect the world of the twenty-first century.

# References

ABC News (2015). *NAPLAN: Queensland school's letter of affirmation to students facing test goes viral*, 12 May. Retrieved on 13 May 2015 from www.abc.net.au/ news/2015-05-12/qld-schools-letter-offering-naplan-support-goes-viral/6463644.

Abrams, J. (1998). Introduction. In D. Ford, *The Dark Side of the Light Chaser: Reclaiming Your Power, Creativity, Brilliance, and Dreams*, pp. xiii–xvi. New York: Riverhead Books.

Aly, W. (2014). Brandis' race hate laws are whiter than white. *The* Age, 27 March 27. Retrieved on 14 April 2014 from www.theage.com.au/comment/brandis-race-hate-laws-are-whiter-than-white-20140327-35lv7.html#ixzz2xbNuPmu5.

Anderson, C.A., Bushman, B.J., Donnerstein, E., Hummer, T.A. & Warburton, W. (2014). *SPSSI Research Summary on Media Violence*. The Society for the Psychological Studies of Social Issues. Retrieved on 19 April 2015 from www.spssi. org/index.cfm?fuseaction=page.viewPage&pageID=1899&nodeID=1.

Andreassen, C.S., Torsheim, T., Brunborg, G.S. & Pallesen, S. (2012). Development of a Facebook addiction scale. *Psychological Report 110*, pp. 501–517. www. amsciepub.com/doi/abs/10.2466/02.09.18.PR0.110.2.501–517, doi: 10.2466/ 02.09.18.PR0.110.2.501–517

Appiah, K.A. (2015). Race in the modern world: The problem of the color line. *Foreign Affairs, 92*(2), pp. 1–8.

Armstrong, K. (2009). *The Case for God: What Religion Really Means*. London: The Bodley Head.

Armstrong, K. (1993). *A History of God. From Abraham to the Present: The 4000-Year Quest for God*. London: Vintage.

Australian Bureau of Statistics (2014). 4102.0 – Australian Social Trends, November 2013: *Losing My Religion*. Retrieved on 3 April 2015 from www.abs.gov.au/ausstats/ abs@.nsf/Lookup/4102.0Main+Features30Nov+2013.

Australian Bureau of Statistics (2011). *Census of Housing and Population*. Retrieved on 28 March 2015 from www.abs.gov.au/census.

Australian Communication and Media Authority (2013). *Like, Post, Share: Young Australians' Experiences of Social Media*. Quantitative research report prepared for the Australian Communication and Media Authority, Newspoll Market and Social Research. www.cybersmart.gov.au/About%20Cybersmart/Research/~/media/ Cybersmart/About%20Cybersmart/Documents/Newspoll%20Quantitative%20 Like%20Post%20Share%20%20final%20PDF.pdf.

Australian Curriculum Assessment and Reporting Authority (n.d.). *National Assessment Program – Literacy and Numeracy*. www.nap.edu.au/naplan/naplan.html.

Australian Social Inclusion Board (2012). *Social Inclusion in Australia. How Australia is Faring*. 2nd Edition. Canberra: Department of the Prime Minister and Cabinet, Commonwealth of Australia.

Bagshaw, E. (2015). NAPLAN: Parents and teachers urged to calm students down. *The Sydney Morning Herald*, 11 May. Retrieved on 13 May 2015 from www.smh.com.au/national/naplan-parents-and-teachers-urged-to-calm-students-down-20150511-ggueta.html.

Bargh, J., Chen, M. & Burrows, L. (1996). Automaticity of social behaviour: Direct effects of trait construct and stereotype activation on action. *Journal of Personality and Social Psychology*, 71(2), pp. 230–244. Retrieved on 1 May 2015 from www.yale.edu/acmelab/articles/bargh_chen_burrows_1996.pdf.

Baron-Cohen, S. (2011). *Zero Degrees of Empathy: A New Theory of Human Cruelty*. London: Allen Lane.

Bauman, Z. (2004). *Identity*. Cambridge: Polity Press.

BBC Trending (2014). Sydney cafe: Australians say to Muslims 'I'll ride with you'. Retrieved on 26 March 2015 from www.bbc.com/news/blogs-trending-30479306.

Beaudoin, T. (1998). *Virtual Faith: The Irreverent Spiritual Quest of Gen X*. California: Jossey-Bass, Inc., Publishers.

Becker, K.A. (2003). History of the Stanford-Binet intelligence scales: Content and psychometrics. *Stanford-Binet Intelligence Scales, Fifth Edition Assessment Service Bulletin Number 1*. Retrieved on 22 October 2015 from www.assess.nelson.com/pdf/sb5-asb1.pdf.

Berryman, J.W. (2008). Speaking of evil: The struggle to speak no evil when teaching about it. In M. de Souza & W. Wing Ham Lamb (Eds). *Spirituality in the Lives of Children and Adolescents: Some Perspectives (Interface: A Forum for Theology in the World), 10*(2), pp. 57–67.

Bibby, R.W. (2009). *The Emerging Millennials: How Canada's Newest Generation is Responding to Change and Choice*. Lethbridge, AB: Project Canada Books.

Bloom, W. (2009). *The Complete Encyclopedia of Mind, Body and Spirit*. Retrieved on 7 March 2015 from www.f4hs.org/education/contemporary-spirituality-paper.htm.

Bly, R. 1988. *A Little Book on the Human Shadow*. New York: HarperCollins Publishers.

Bly, R. (n.d.). Three views of the shadow – Introduction. In M.R. Waldman (Ed.). *Shadow: Searching for the Hidden Self*, pp. 8–10. New York: Jeremy P. Tarcher/Putnam.

Bone, J. (2014). Spirituality and early childhood education in New Zealand and Australia: Past, present and future. In J. Watson, M. de Souza & A. Trousdale (Eds). *Global Perspectives on Spirituality and Education*, pp. 116–127. New York and Abingdon, Oxon: Routledge.

Borus, G. (1992). Irish Catholics in Australia: A brief survey up to 1945 ('rockchoppers'). *Hungarian Studies in English*, 23, pp. 119–123. Retrieved on 11 February 2015 from www.jstor.org/discover/10.2307/41273874?sid=21105316250301&uid=70&uid=3737536&uid=2129&uid=2&uid=4

Bouma, G., Cahill, D., Dellal, H. & Zwartz, A. (2011). *Freedom of Religion and Belief in 21st Century Australia*. A research report prepared for the Australian Human Rights Commission. Retrieved on 6 April 2011 from www.humanrights.gov.au.

Boyd, J.H. (2008). Have we found the Holy Grail? Theory of Mind as a unifying concept. In *Journal of Religion and Health*, 47(3), pp. 366–385. Retrieved on 2 April 2015 from library.acu.edu.au/.

Braggett, E. (1997). *The Middle Years of Schooling: An Australian Perspective.* Cheltenham, VIC: Hawker, Brownlow Education.

British Humanist Association (n.d.). *Religion and Belief: Some Surveys and Statistics.* Retrieved on 3 April 2015 from humanism.org.uk/campaigns/religion-and-belief-some-surveys-and-statistics/.

Brown, R. (2002). Self harm and suicide risks for same-sex attracted young people: A family perspective. *Australian e-Journal for the Advancement of Mental Health (AeJAMH)*, *1*(1). Retrieved on 5 May 2015 from www.opendoors.net.au/wp-content/uploads/2009/10/lgbt-youth-suicide.pdf.

Bucke, R.M. (1901). *Cosmic Consciousness: A Study in the Evolution of the Human Mind.* London: L.N. Fowler & Co.

Buzan, T. (2001). *The Power of Spiritual Intelligence: 10 Ways to Tap into Your Spiritual Genius.* London: Thorsons.

Capra, F. (2010). *The Tao of Physics: An Exploration of the Parallels Between Modern Psychic and Eastern Mysticism.* Boston: Shambhala Publications, Inc.

Carnagey, N.L., Anderson, C.A. & Bartholow, B.D. (2007). Media violence and social neuroscience. New questions and new opportunities. *Current Directions in Psychological Science*, *16*(4), pp. 178–182. Retrieved 19 April 2015 from public. psych.iastate.edu/caa/abstracts/2005–2009/07cab2.pdf.

Carpenter, D. & Ferguson, C.J. (2009). *The Everything: Parent's Guide to Dealing with Bullies.* Avon, MA: F+W Media, Inc.

Carroll, J. (1998). *Ego and Soul: The Modern West in Search of Meaning.* Sydney: HarperCollins Publishers.

Chittister, J. (1991). *Wisdom Distilled from the Daily: Living the Rule of St Benedict Today.* San Francisco: HarperCollins Publishers.

Chitwood, K. (2014). *Review and Commentary: Globalized Islam: The Search for a New Ummah by Olivier Roy.* Retrieved on 11 March 2015 from www.academia. edu/8873410/REVIEW_and_COMMENTARY_Globalized_Islam_the_Search_ for_a_New_Ummah_by_Olivier_Roy.

Claxton, G. (2008). *What's the Point of School: Rediscovering the Heart of Education.* Oxford: Oneworld Publications.

Claxton, G. (2005). *The Wayward Mind. An Intimate History of the Unconscious.* London: Abacus.

Claxton, G. (2000). The anatomy of intuition. In T. Atkinson & G. Claxton (Eds). *The Intuitive Practitioner: On the Value of Not Always Knowing What One is Doing.* Buckingham and Philadelphia: Open University Press.

Claxton, G. (1998). *Hare Brain Tortoise Mind: Why Intelligence Increases When You Think Less.* London: Fourth Estate.

Collins, M. (2007). Spirituality and the shadow: Reflection and the therapeutic use of self. *British Journal of Occupational Therapy*, *70*(2), pp. 88–90.

Collins-Mayo, S., Mayo, B. Nash, S. & Cocksworth, C. (2010). *The Faith of Generation Y.* London: Church House Publishing.

Cozolino, L. (2006). *The Neuroscience of Human Relationships: Attachment and the Developing Social Brains.* New York: W.W. Norton.

Crawford, M.L. & Rossiter, G.M. (1993). The spirituality of today's young people: Implications for religious education in church-related schools (also titled: Religious Education and the secular spirituality of youth). *Religious Education Journal of Australia*, *9*(2), pp. 1–8.

Csikzentmihalyi, M. (1992, 2002). *Flow: The Classic Work on How to Achieve Happiness.* London: Rider.

Culliford, L. (2011). *The Psychology of Spirituality: An Introduction.* London and Philadelphia: Jessica Kingsley Publishers.

Das, S. (2012). *Deranged Marriage: A Memoir.* North Sydney, NSW: Bantam Books.

Das, S. (2005). Between two worlds. *The Age,* 28 July. Retrieved on 28 July 2006 from www.theage.com.au/news/sushi-das/between-two-\worlds/2005/07/27/ 1122143904716.html.

Davies, O. (2006). *God Within: The Mystical Tradition of Northern Europe.* London: Darton, Longman & Todd.

Del Prete, T. (2002). Being what we are: Thomas Merton's spirituality in education. In J. Miller & Y. Nakagawa (Eds). *Nurturing Our Wholeness,* pp. 164–191. Rutland, VT: Foundation for Educational Renewal.

de Souza, M. (2014a). The empathetic mind: The essence of human spirituality. *International Journal of Children's Spirituality, 19*(1), pp. 45–54.

de Souza, M. (2014b). Religious identity and plurality in Australia: Inclusions, exclusions and tensions. *Journal for the Study of Religion,* South Africa, *27*(1), pp. 210–233.

de Souza, M. (2012a). The dual roles of unconscious learning in engendering and hindering spiritual growth: Implications for religious education in pluralist contexts. In J. Astley & L. Francis (Eds). *Teaching Religion, Teaching Truth,* pp. 185–204. Bern, Switzerland: Peter Lang AG International Academic Publishers.

de Souza, M. (2012b). Connectedness and *Connectedness.* The dark side of spirituality: Implications for education. *International Journal of Children's Spirituality, 17*(3), pp. 291–304.

de Souza, M. (2011). Promoting inter-spiritual education in the classroom: Exploring the perennial philosophy as a useful strategy to encourage freedom of religious practice and belief. *Journal of Religious Education, 59*(1), pp. 27–37.

de Souza, M. (2010). The roles of conscious and non-conscious learning in impeding and enhancing spirituality: Implications for learning and teaching. In M. de Souza & J. Rimes (Eds). *Meaning and Connectedness: Australian Perspectives on Education and Spirituality,* pp. 31–45. Melbourne: Australian College of Education.

de Souza, M. (2009). Promoting wholeness and wellbeing in education: Exploring aspects of the spiritual dimension. In M. de Souza, L. Francis, J. O'Higgins-Norman & D. Scott (Eds). *International Handbook of Education for Spirituality, Care and Wellbeing,* pp. 677–692. Dordrecht, Netherlands: Springer Academic Publishers.

de Souza, M. (2008). Spirituality in education: Addressing the inner and outer lives of students to promote meaning and connectedness in learning. In M. de Souza & W. Wing Han Lamb (Eds). *Children, Adolescents and Spirituality (Interface. A Forum for Theology in the World),* pp. 98–118. Adelaide: ATF Press.

de Souza, M. (2005). Engaging the mind, heart and soul of the student in religious education: Teaching for meaning and connection. *Journal of Religious Education, 53*(4), pp. 40–47.

de Souza, M. (2004). Teaching for effective learning in religious education: A discussion of the perceiving, thinking, feeling and intuiting elements in the learning process. *Journal of Religious* Education, *52*(3), pp. 22–30.

de Souza, M. (2003a) Contemporary influences on the spirituality of young people: Implications for education. *International Journal of Children's Spirituality, 18*(3), pp. 269–279.

de Souza, M. (2003b). Identifying the elements that shape spiritual development and a sense of the sacred: Tertiary students' perceptions of their spiritual journeys: Implications for lifelong learning. CD-ROM. *Proceedings of the Lifelong Learning Conference: Reaching the Unreached Learner.*

de Souza, M. (2001). Addressing the spiritual dimension in education: Teaching affectively to promote cognition. *Journal of Religious Education*, Australian Catholic University, *49*(3), pp. 31–41.

de Souza, M., Cartwright, P. & McGilp, E.J. (2004). The perceptions of young people who live in a regional city in Australia of their spiritual wellbeing: Implications for education. *Journal of Youth Studies, 7*(2), pp. 155–172.

de Souza, M., Francis, L., O'Higgins-Norman, J. & Scott, D. (Eds). (2009). *International Handbook of Education for Spirituality, Care and Wellbeing.* Dordrecht, Netherlands: Springer Academic Publishers.

Donaldson, M. (1987). *Children's Minds.* London: Fontana.

Donath, J.S. (1999). Identity and deception in the virtual community. In M.A. Smith & P. Kollack (Eds). *Communities in Cyberspace*, pp. 27–58. London: Routledge.

Dossey, L. (2010). Mind and neurons: Consciousness and brain in the twenty-first century. In D. Lorimer and O. Robinson (Eds). *A New Renaissance: Transforming Science, Spirit and Society*, pp. 105–119. Edinburgh: Floris Books.

Earl, M. (2001). Shadow and spirituality. *International Journal of Children's Spirituality, 6*(3), pp. 277–288.

Eckersley, R. (2004). *Well and Good: How We Feel & Why it Matters.* Melbourne: Text Publishing.

Eckersley, R. (1997). Portraits of youth: Understanding young people's relationship with the future. *Futures, 29*(3), pp. 243–249.

El-Haj, T.R.A., Wesley Bonet, S., Demerath, P. & Schultz, K. (2011). Education, citizenship, and the politics of belonging: Youth from Muslim transnational communities and the 'War on Terror'. *Review of Research in Education 35*, pp. 29–59.

Elliott, A. & Lemert, C. (2006). *The New Individualism: The Emotional Costs of Globalization.* London and New York: Routledge.

Emmons, R.A. (2000). Spirituality and intelligence: Problems and prospects. *The International Journal of the Psychology of Religion, 10*(1), pp. 57–64.

Engebretson, K., de Souza, M. & Salpietro, L. (2001). *Expressions of Religiosity and Spirituality Among Middle School Students in Victoria's Catholic Schools: A Research Project Conducted by the School of Religious Education, Victoria. Final Report.* Australian Catholic University, Melbourne. Unpublished.

Erricker, C. (2010). *Religious Education: A Conceptual and Interdisciplinary Approach for Secondary Schools.* London and New York: Routledge.

Erricker, C. (2008). In fifty years, who will be here? Reflections on globalization, migration and spiritual identity. *International Journal of Children's Spirituality, 13*(1), pp. 15–26.

Erricker, C., Sullivan, D., Ota, C., Erricker, J. & Logan, J. (1994). The development of children's worldviews. *Journal of Beliefs and Values: Studies in Religions and Education, 15*(2), pp. 3–6.

Evans, C. (2010). Religion and the Secular State in Australia: National Report. In *Religion and the Secular State: National Reports*. Paper presented at the 18th World Congress of the International Academy of Comparative Law, 2010. Retrieved on 10 March 2015 from www.iclrs.org/content/blurb/files/Australia%202014%20 FINAL.pdf.

Evans, G. (1995). Multiculturalism and Australian Foreign Policy. Sang Nguyen Support Dinner, Melbourne, 10 March. Retrieved on 13 February 2015 from www.foreignminister.gov.au/speeches/1995/multi.html.

Finnegan, J. (2008). *The Audacity of Spirit. The Meaning and Shaping of Spirituality Today*. Dublin: Veritas.

Ford, D. (1998). *The Dark Side of the Light Chaser: Reclaiming Your Power, Creativity, Brilliance, and Dreams*. New York: Riverhead Books.

Fordham, F. (1953). *An Introduction to Jung's Psychology*. 3rd edition. London: Penguin Books.

Francis, L. (1989). Drift from the churches: Secondary school pupils' attitudes towards Christianity. *British Journal of Religious Education, 11*(2), pp. 78–86.

Freire, P. (1970). *Pedagogy of the Oppressed*. London: Penguin Books.

Fukuyama, F. (2006). *Background Briefing on ABC Radio National*. Francis Fukuyama speaking at the Free Library of Philadelphia. Presenter: Kirsten Garrett. Interview transcript retrieved on 11 June 2006 from www.aba.net.au.

Gallimore, T. (2004). Unresolved trauma: Fuel for the cycle of violence and terrorism. In C. E. Stout (Ed.). *The Psychology of Terrorism: Coping with the Continuing Threat*. Condensed Edition, pp. 67–93. Westport, CT: Praeger Publishers/ Greenwood Publishing Group.

Gardner, H. (1999). *Optimizing Intelligences: Thinking, Creativity and Flow*. Video: in interview with Peter Salovey. New York: National Professional Resources, Inc.

Gardner, H. (1993). *Multiple Intelligences: The Theory in Practice*. New York: Basic Books.

Gardner, H. (1983). *Frames of Mind*. New York: Basic Books.

Gardner, H., Kornhaber, M.L. & Wake, W.K. (1996). *Intelligence: Multiple Perspectives*. Orlando, FL: Harcourt Brace College Publishers.

Gascoigne, J. (2002). *The Enlightenment and the Origins of European Australia*. Cambridge: Cambridge University Press.

Gilbert, P. (2010). *The Compassionate Mind: How to Use Compassion to Develop Happiness, Self-acceptance and Well-being*. London: Constable and Robinson Ltd.

Gladwell, M. (2005). *Blink: The Power of Thinking without Thinking*. London: Allen Lane.

Glatzer, N.N. (Ed.). (1966). *Martin Buber. The Way of Response: Selections from his Writings*. New York: Schocken Books.

Goleman, D. (1996). *Emotional Intelligence: Why it can Matter More Than IQ*. London: Bloomsbury Publisher, Inc.

Goleman, D. (1989). Researchers trace empathy roots to infancy. Retrieved on 8 April 2015 from www.nytimes.com/1989/03/28/science/researchers-trace-empathy-s-roots-to-infancy.html?pagewanted=2.

Gopnik, A. (2010). 'Empathic civilization': Amazing empathic babies. Retrieved on 8 April 2015 from www.huffingtonpost.com/alison-gopnik/empathic-civilization-ama_b_473961.html.

Greste, P. (2015). Peter Greste address to the National Press Club. Retrieved on 26 March 2015 from www.abc.net.au/news/2015-03-26/national-press-club-peter-greste/6350778.

Griffiths, B. (1994). *Universal Wisdom: A Sacred Journey Through the Sacred Wisdom of the World*. London: Fount.

Griffiths, B. (1989). *A New Vision of Reality: Western Science, Eastern Mysticism and Christian Faith*. London: Fount Paperbacks.

Griffiths, B. (1976). *Return to the Center*. Springfield, IL: Templegate.

Griffiths, M.D. (2012) Facebook addiction: Concerns, criticism, and recommendations – a response to Andreassen and colleagues. *Psychological Reports 110*, pp. 518–520. Retrieved on 15 April 2015 from doi: 10.2466/01.07.18.PR0.110.2.518–520.

Habermas, J. (2008). Notes on a post-secular society. Retrieved on 20 April 2015 from www.signandsight.com/features/1714.html.

Habermas, J., Brieskorn, N., Reder, M., Ricken, F. & Schimdt, J. (2011). *An Awareness of What is Missing: Faith and Reason in a Post-secular Age*. Cambridge: Polity Press.

Hamid, M. (2007). *The Reluctant Fundamentalist*. London: Penguin Books.

Hamilton, A. (2015). The Border Force Act's disquieting parallels. *Eureka Street, 25*(13). Retrieved on 8 July 2015 from eurekastreet.com.au/article.aspx?aeid=45107#. VZxozu8VirR.

Hannerz, U. (1996). *Transnational Connections: Cultures, Peoples, Places*. London and New York: Routledge.

Harman, W. (1998). *Global Mind Change: The Promise of the 21st Century*. San Francisco: Berrett-Koehler Publishers, Inc.

Harris, F.C. & Lieberman, R.C. (2015). Racial inequality after racism. *Foreign Affairs, 92*(2), pp. 9–20.

Harris, M. & Moran, G. (1998). *Reshaping Religious Education*. Louisville, KY: John Knox Press.

Harris, S. (2014). *Waking Up: A Guide to Spirituality Without Religion*. London: Transworld Publishers.

Hart, T. (2001). *From Information to Transformation: Education for the Evolution of Consciousness*. New York: Peter Lang.

Hay, D. (2006). *Something There: The Biology of the Human Spirit*. London: Dartman, Longman & Todd Ltd.

Hay, D. & Nye, R. (1998). *The Spirit of the Child*. London. Fount Paperbacks.

headspace National Youth Mental Health Foundation. *Why headspace?* Retrieved on 29 April 2015 from www.headspace.org.au/about-headspace/what-we-do/why-headspace.

Helms, J.E. (1993). Cultural racism: Conceptualization. *American Psychology Association Division, 38*. Retrieved on 7 May 2014 from www.health-psych.org/Cultural.cfm.

Hess, M. (2012). Mirror neurons: The development of empathy, and digital story-telling. *Religious Education: The Official Journal of the Religious Education Association, 107*(4), pp. 401–414.

Hillman, J. (1996). *The Soul's Code. In Search of Character and Calling*. Milsons Point, NSW: Random House.

His Holiness the Dalai Lama (2010). *Towards a True Kinship of Faiths: How the World's Religions can come Together*. New York: Doubleday Religion.

Hoffman, M.L. (2000). *Empathy and Moral Development: Implications for Caring and Justice*. Cambridge, MA: Cambridge University Press.

Hoffman, M.L. (1984). Interaction of affect and cognition in empathy. In C. Izard, J. Kagan & R.B. Zajonc (Eds). *Emotions, Cognition and Behaviours*, pp. 103–131. Cambridge, MA: Cambridge University Press.

Hogarth, R.M. (2001). *Educating Intuition*. Chicago and London: University of Chicago Press.

Holland, C. (2015). *Close the Gap: Progress and Priorities Report 2015*. Published by The Close the Gap Campaign Steering Committee in February 2015. Retrieved on 13 February 2015 from www.humanrights.gov.au/publications/close-gap-progress-and-priorities-report-2015.

Hollingsworth, A. (2008). Neuroscience and spirituality: Implications of interpersonal neurobiology for a spirituality of compassion. In *Zygon*, *43*(4), pp. 837–860. Retrieved on 2 April 2015 from library.acu.edu.au/.

hooks, b. (1994). *Teaching to Transgress*. London: Routledge.

Hughes, P. (2007). *Putting Life Together: Findings from Australian Youth Spirituality Research*. Nunawading, VIC: Christian Research Association.

Hughes, P., Thompson, C., Pryor, R. & Bouma, G.D. (1995). *Believe It or Not: Australian Spirituality and the Churches in the 90s*. Kew, Melbourne: Christian Research Association.

Hughes, R. (2003). *The Fatal Shore*. London: Vintage Books.

Hull, J. (2009). Religious education as encounter: From body worlds to religious worlds. In S. Miedema (Ed). *Religious Education as Encounter: A Tribute to John Hull*, pp. 21–34. Berlin: Waxmann.

Huxley, A. (1945). *The Perennial Philosophy*. Reprinted 1985. London: Triad Grafton.

Hvidt, N.C. (2013). Making meaning of meaning-making research: The background of key dimensions. In J.L. Hochheimer & J. Fernandez-Goldborough (Eds). *Spirituality in the 21st Century: Conversations*, pp.103–120. Oxford: Inter-Disciplinary Press.

Hyde, B. (2008). *Children and Spirituality: Searching for Meaning and Connectedness*. London: Jessica Kingsley Publishers.

Iacoboni, M. (2008). *Mirroring People: The Science of Empathy and How We Connect with Others*. New York: Picador.

Illich, I. (1970). *Deschooling Society*. Middlesex: Penguin Books Ltd.

Jackson, R. (2005). Intercultural education, religious plurality and teaching for tolerance: Interpretive and dialogical approaches. In R. Jackson & U. McKenna (Eds). *Intercultural Education and Religious Plurality*, pp. 5–13. Oslo: The Oslo Coalition on Freedom of Religion or Belief.

Jackson, R. (1997). *Religious Education: An Interpretive Approach*. London: Hodder Murray.

Jackson, R. & McKenna, U. (2005). *Intercultural Education and Religious Plurality*. Oslo: The Oslo Coalition on Freedom of Religion or Belief.

Johnson, K. & Ord, D.R. (2012). *The Coming Interspiritual Age*. Vancouver: Namaste Publishing.

Johnston, W. (2000). *Mystical Theology: The Science of Love*. Maryknoll, NY: Orbis Books.

Karaiskos, D., Tzavellas, E., Balta, G. & Paparrigopoulos, T. (2010). P02–232 – Social network addiction: A new clinical disorder? *European Psychiatry*, *25*(1), p. 855. Retrieved on 15 April 2015 from www.sciencedirect.com.ezproxy2.acu.edu.au/science/article/pii/S0924933810708464,doi:10.1016/S0924-9338(10)70846-4.

Kay, W.K. & Francis, L.J. (1996). *Drift from the Churches: Attitude Toward Christianity During Childhood and Adolescence*. Cardiff: University of Wales Press.

Keane, J. 2012. Your body's search for spirit: Focusing through the felt-sense for children's wellbeing – a biospiritual journey. *Keynote Address* (with Dr Peter Campbell) *at the 12th International Conference for Children's Spirituality*.

Kenneally, T. (2011). *Australians: Eureka to the Diggers*. Crows Nest, NSW: Allen & Unwin.

Kenneally, T. (2009). *Australians: Origins to Eureka*. Crows Nest, NSW: Allen & Unwin.

Kessler, R. (2000). *The Soul of Education. Helping Students Find Connection, Compassion and Character at School*. Alexandria, VA: Association for Supervision and Curriculum Development.

Keysers, C. (2011). *The Empathic Brain: How the Discovery of Mirror Neurons Changes our Understanding of Human Nature*. Social Brain Press.

King, M. (2009). *Postsecularism: The Hidden Challenge to Extremism*. Cambridge: James Clark & Co.

Klein, G. (2003). *The Power of Intuition: How to Use your Gut Feelings to Make Better Decisions at Work*. New York: Currency DoubleDay.

Koleth, E. (2010). *Multiculturalism: A Review of Australian Policy Statements and Recent Debates in Australia and Overseas*. Research Paper No 6 2010–2011. Retrieved on 31 March 2015 from www.aph.gov.au/About_Parliament/Parliamentary_Departments/Parliamentary_Library/pubs/rp/rp1011/11rp06.

Laszlo, E. (2008). *Quantum Shift in the Global Brain: How the New Scientific Reality can Change Us and our World*. Rochester, VT: Inner Traditions.

Law, S. (2006). *The War for Children's Minds*. Abingdon, Oxon: Routledge.

Lindqvist, C. (1991). *China: Empire of Living Symbols*. Translated by J. Tate. New York: Addison-Wesley.

Lovat, T. (2010). Spirituality and the public school. In M. de Souza & J. Rimes (Eds). *Meaning and Connectedness: Australian Perspectives on Education and Spirituality*, pp.19–30. Mawson, ACT: Australian College of Educators.

Lovat, T. & Toomey, R. (Eds) (2007). *Values Education and Quality Teaching: The Double Helix Effect*. Macksville, NSW: David Barlow Publishing.

Lucas, B. & Claxton, G. (2010). *New Kinds of Smart: How the Science of Learnable Intelligence is Changing Education*. Berkshire: McGraw-Hill Education, Open University Press.

Lyons, D. (2000). *Jesus in Disneyland: Religion in Postmodern Times*. Cambridge: Polity Press.

Mackay, H. (2007). *The Good Life. What Makes Life Worth Living?* Sydney: Pan Macmillan.

Mackay, H. (1993). *Reinventing Australia: The Mind and Mood of Australia in the 90s*. Pymble, NSW: Collins Angus & Robertson Publishers.

Maitra, S.K. (2000). *The Meeting of the East and the West in Sri Aurobindo's Philosophy*. Pondicherry: Sri Aurobindo's Ashram.

Mansouri, F., Jenkins, L., Morgan L. & Taouk, M. (2009). *The Impact of Racism Upon the Health and Wellbeing of Young Australian: A Research Project*. Melbourne: The Foundation for Young Australians and the Institute for Citizenship and Globalization, Deakin University.

Maslow, A. (1968, 1999). *Towards a Psychology of Being*. 3rd Edition. New York: John Wiley & Sons, Inc.

Mason, M., Singleton, A. & Webber, R. (2007). *The Spirit of Generation Y: Young People's Spirituality in a Changing Australia*. Melbourne: John Garratt Publishing.

Mayer, J.D. & Salovey, P. (1997). What is Emotional Intelligence? In P. Salovey & D. Sluyter (Eds). *Emotional Development and Emotional Intelligence: Implications for Educators*. New York: Basic Books.

Mayer, J.D., Salovey, P. & Caruso, D. (2000). Models of emotional intelligence. In R. Sternberg (Ed.). *Handbook of Intelligence*, pp. 396–420. Cambridge: Cambridge University Press. Retrieved on 26 May 2015 from www.unh. edu/emotional_intelligence/EI%20Assets/Reprints...EI%20Proper/ EI2000ModelsSternberg.pdf.

Mercer, J.A. (2008). Children, Church and the problem of boredom. In M. de Souza & J. Rimes (Eds). *Children, Adolescents and Spirituality (Interface. A Forum for Theology in the World)*, pp. 23–40. Adelaide: ATF Press.

Merton, T. (2005). *No Man is an Island*. Boston: Shambhala Publications, Inc.

Metzinger, T. (2009). *The Ego Tunnel: The Science of the Mind and the Myth of the Self*. New York: Basic Books.

Miller, J. (2006). *Educating for Wisdom and Compassion: Creating Conditions for Timeless Learning*. Thousand Oaks, CA: Corwin Press.

Miller, J. (2000). *Education and Soul: Towards a Spiritual Curriculum*. Albany, NY: State University of New York Press.

Miller, J. & Nakagawa, Y. (Eds) (2002). *Nurturing Our Wholeness: Perspectives on Spirituality in Education*. Brandon, VT: Foundation for Educational Renewal.

Mission Australia (2014a). *Youth Mental Health Report 2014*. Mission Australia in Association with the Black Dog Institute. Retrieved on 6 July 2015 from www. missionaustralia.com.au/component/search/?searchword=mental%20health%20 report&searchphrase=all.

Mission Australia (2014b). *Youth Survey 2014*. Retrieved on 22 January 2015 from www.missionaustralia.com.au/what-we-do-to-help-new/young-people/ understanding-young-people/annual-youth-survey.

Moffett, J. (1994). *The Universal Schoolhouse*. San Francisco: Jossey-Bass, Inc.

Moore, M.E. & Wright, A.M. (Eds) (2008). *Children, Youth and Spirituality in a Troubling World*. Danvers, MA: Chalice Press.

Myers, D.G. (2002). *Intuition: Its Powers and Perils*. New Haven and London: Yale University Press.

Nakagawa, Y. (2000). *Education for Awakening: An Eastern Approach to Holistic Education*. Brandon, VT: Foundation for Educational Renewal.

Nangle, P. (2014). *The Transition of the Spirituality of the Christian Brothers in Australia from a Traditional to a Contemporary Mode*. Unpublished PhD thesis. Melbourne: Australian Catholic University.

Newberg, A. & Waldman, M.R. (2006). *Why We Believe What We Believe*. New York: Free Press.

Newberg, A., D'Aquili, E. & Rause, V. (2001). *Why God Won't Go Away*. New York: Ballantine Books.

Noddings, N. (1992). *The Challenge to Care in Schools*. New York: Teacher's College Press.

O'Connell Consultancy (2000). *Evaluation of the Community Response to Six Incidents of Youth Suicide in Hume Region, June – September 1999: Community Document*. Victoria: O'Connell Consultancy for Human Services.

O'Connor, P. (1996). *Understanding Jung*. Melbourne: Mandarin.

O'Keefe, G.S. & Clarke-Pearson, K. (2011). Clinical report: The impact of social media on children, adolescents and families. *Pediatrics*, pp. 800–804, doi: 10.1542/peds.2011-0054.

Oldmeadow, H. (2010). Crossing religious frontiers: Editorial. In H. Oldmeadow (Ed.). *Crossing Religious Frontiers: Studies in Comparative Religion*, pp. vii – ix. Bloomington, IN: World Wisdom, Inc.

O'Murchú, D. (1997). *Reclaiming Spirituality*. New York: Crossroad Publishing Company.

Oriti, T. (2015). Muslim youth pushed to 'the margins of society', Islamic spokesman Keysar Trad tells forum on radicalisation. Retrieved on 10 April 2015 from www.abc.net.au/news/2015-04-09/muslim-forum-told-australia-alot-learn-understand-radicalisation/6379384.

Overholt. L.D & Penner, J.A. (2005). *Soul Searching the Millennial Generation: Strategies for Youth Workers*. Toronto: Novalis/St Paul University.

Palmer, P. 2000. *Let Your Life Speak. Listening for the Voice of Vocation*. San Francisco: Jossey-Bass.

Paton, G. (2012). Overexposure to technology 'makes children miserable'. *The Telegraph*, 26 October. Retrieved on 13 April 2015 from www.telegraph.co.uk/education/educationnews/9636862/Overexposure-to-technology-makes-children-miserable.html.

Pearce, J.C. (2002). *The Biology of Transcendence: A Blueprint of the Human Spirit*. Rochester, VT: Park Street Press.

Pearce, J.C. (1985, 2003). *From Magical Child to Magical Teen*. Rochester, VT: Park Street Press.

Pearce, J.C. (1977). *Magical Child*. New York: Plume.

Peguero, A.A. (2008). Is immigrant status relevant in school violence research? An analysis with Latino students. *Journal of School Health, 78*(7), pp. 397–404. Retrieved on 17 April 2015 from onlinelibrary.wiley.com.ezproxy2.acu.edu.au/doi/10.1111/j.1746–1561.2008.00320.x/full, doi: 10.1111/j.1746–1561.2008.00320.x.

Persinger, M.A. (1996). Feelings of past lives as expected perturbations within neurocognitive processes that generate the sense of self: Contributions from limbic liability and vectorial hemisphericity. *Perceptual and Motor Skills, 83*(3) (part 2), pp. 1107–1121.

Pitman, S. (2008). The impact of media technologies on child development and well-being. Ozchild. Retrieved on 15 April 2015 from www.pdc.org.au/scarf/res/file/Resources%20and%20Useful%20Links/ImpactOfElectronicMedia.pdf.

Pratt, D. (2015) Islamophobia as reactive co-radicalization. *Islam and Christian–Muslim Relations, (26)*2, pp. 205–218, doi: 10.1080/09596410.2014.1000025.

Public Affairs, Department of Immigration and Multicultural and Indigenous Affairs (2005). *Fact Sheet 6. The Evolution of Australia's Multicultural Policy*. Revised 10 May 2005. Canberra: Commonwealth of Australia. Retrieved on 28 June 2006 from **www.immi.gov.au/facts/06evolution.htm**.

Ramachandran, V.S. (2012). *The Tell-tale Brain: Unlocking the Mystery of Human Nature*. London: Windmill Books.

Ramachandran, V.S. & Blakeslee, S. (1998). *Phantoms in the Brain*. London: Fourth Estate.

Rideout, V. (2012). *Social Media, Social Life: How Teens View Their Digital Life. A Commonsense Media Research Study*. San Francisco: Common Sense Media.

Rivett, G. (2014). Neuroscientist Susan Greenfield warns young brains being re-wired by digital technology. 891 ABC Adelaide. Retrieved on 13 April 2015 from www.abc.net.au/news/2014-11-20/neuroscientist-warns-young-brains-being-reshaped-by-technology/5906140.

Rizzolatti, G. & Sinigaglia, C. (2008). *Mirrors in the Brain. How We Share our Actions and Emotions*. Oxford: Oxford University Press.

Robinson, J.A.T. (1963). *Honest to God*. Adelaide: SCM Press.

Robinson, K. (2001). *Out of Our Minds: Learning to be Creative*. Chichester, West Sussex: Capstone Publishing Limited.

Robinson, K. with Aronica, L. (2009). *The Element: How Finding Your Passion Changes Everything*. Melbourne: Penguin Books.

Rosenstreich, G. (2013). *LGBTI People Mental Health and Suicide. Briefing Paper*. Revised 2nd Edition. National LGBTI Health Alliance Sydney. Retrieved on 5 May 2015 from www.beyondblue.org.au/docs/default-source/default-document-library/bw0258-lgbti-mental-health-and-suicide-2013-2nd-edition.pdf?sfvrsn=2.

Rossiter, G. (2014). A perspective on spiritual education in Australian schools: The emergence of nonreligious personal development approaches. In J. Watson, M. de Souza & A. Trousdale (Eds). *Global Perspectives on Spirituality and Education*, pp. 140–152. New York and Abingdon, Oxon: Routledge.

Rossiter, G. (2013). Perspective on the use of the construct 'Catholic Identity' for Australian Catholic schooling: Areas in the discourse in need of more emphasis and further attention – part 2. *Journal of Religious Education, 61*(2), pp. 17–29.

Roth-Hanania, R., Davidou, M. & Zahn-Waxler, C. (2011). Empathy development from 8 to 16 months: Early signs of concern for others. *Infant Behaviour and Development, 34*, pp. 447–458, doi: 10.1016/j.infbeh.2011.04.007.

Roy, O. (2004). *Globalised Islam. The Search for a New Ummah*. London: Hurst & Company.

Rymarz, R. (2006). Drifting from the mainstream: The religious identity of Australian core Catholic youth. *International Journal of Children's Spirituality, 11*(3), pp. 371–383.

Sagan, C. (1996). *The Demon Haunted World: Science as a Candle in the Dark*. New York: Ballantine Books.

Sagiolou, C. & Greitmeyer, T. (2014). Facebook's emotional consequences: Why Facebook causes a decrease in mood and why people still use it. *Computers in Human Behaviour, 35*, pp. 359–363.

Salovey, P. (1998). *Optimizing Intelligences: Thinking, Emotion and Creativity*. Video. New York: National Professional Resources, Inc.

Salovey, P. & Mayer, J.D. (1990). Emotional intelligence. *Imagination, Cognition and Personality, 9*, pp. 185 – 211.

Sheldrake, R. (2012). *The Science Delusion: Freeing the Spirit of Enquiry*. London: Coronet.

Smetar, M. (2000). *Spiritual Intelligence: What We Can Learn from the Early Awakening Child?* New York: Orbis Books.

Smith, C. (2005). *Soul Searching: The Religious and Spiritual Lives of American Teenagers*. New York: Oxford University Press.

Smith, H. (1976). *Forgotten Truth: The Common Vision of the World's Religions*. New York: HarperOne.

Sternberg, R.J. (1985). *Beyond IQ: A Triarchic Theory of Human Intelligence*. New York: Cambridge University Press.

Tacey, D. (2006). *How to Read Jung*. London: Granta Books.

Tacey, D. (2003). *The Spirituality Revolution: The Emergence of Contemporary Spirituality*. Sydney: HarperCollins Publishers.

Tacey, D. (2000). *ReEnchantment: The New Australian Spirituality*. Sydney: HarperCollins Publishers.

Tagore, R. (1931). *The Religion of Man*. New York: The Macmillan Company.

Teasdale, W. (2003). *Bede Griffiths: An Introduction to his Interspiritual Thought*. Woodstock, VT: Skylight Paths Publishing.

Teasdale, W. (1999). *The Mystic Heart: Discovering a Universal Spirituality in the World's Religions*. Novato, CA: New World Library.

Tsiolkas, C. (2008). *Tolerance, Prejudice and Fear: Sydney Pen Voices – The Three Writers' Project*. Crows Nest, NSW: Allen & Unwin.

Tu, W. (1998). The continuity of being: Chinese visions of nature. In M.E. Tucker & J. Berthrong (Eds). *Confucianism and Ecology: The Interrelationship of Heaven, Earth and Humans*, pp. 105–121. Cambridge, MA: The Harvard University Centre for the Study of Religions.

Turkle, S. (2011). *Alone Together: Why We Expect More from Technology and Less from Each Other*. New York: Basic Books.

Turpin, K. (2008). Princess dreams. In M.E. Moore & A.M. Wright (Eds). *Children, Youth and Spirituality in a Troubling World*, pp. 45–61. St Louis, MO: Chalice Press.

Underhill, E. (1993). *Mysticism: The Nature and Development of Spiritual Consciousness*. Oxford: Oneworld Publications.

Watson, J., de Souza, M. & Trousdale, A. (Eds) (2014). *Global Perspectives on Spirituality and Education*. New York and Abingdon, Oxon: Routledge.

Wilber, K. (2006). *Integral Spirituality: A Startling New Role for Religion in the Modern and Postmodern World*. Boston and London: Integral Books.

Wilber, K. (2001). *The Eye of Spirit: An Integral Vision for a World Gone Slightly Mad*. Boston and London: Shambhala Publications, Inc.

Wilber, K. (1999). *The Collected Works of Ken Wilber. Volume 1*. Boston and London: Shambhala Publications, Inc.

Wilber, K. (1998). *The Marriage of Sense and Soul: Integrating Science and Religion*. Dublin: Gateway.

Williams, R. (2014). Children using social networks underage 'exposes them to danger'. *The Telegraph*, 6 February. Retrieved on 14 April 2015 from www.telegraph.co.uk/technology/news/10619007/Children-using-social-networks-underage-exposes-them-to-danger.html.

Wilson, L.E. (2005). Listening to ancient voices: Reaching hearts and souls through benchmarks and rites of passage experiences in schools. In J.P. Miller, S. Karsten, D. Denton, D. Orr & I. Colalillo Kates (Eds). *Holistic Learning and Spirituality in Education*, pp. 167–180. Albany, NY: State University of New York Press.

Wilson, T. (2002). *Strangers to Ourselves: Discovering the Adaptive Unconscious*. Cambridge, MA and London: The Belknap Press of Harvard University Press.

Wong, P. (2005). The Chinese approach to learning: The paradigmatic case of Chinese calligraphy. In C. Ota & C. Erricker (Eds). *Spiritual Education: Literacy, Empirical and Pedagogical Approaches*, pp. 154–170. Brighton: Sussex Academic Press.

Wright, A. (2007). Hospitality and the voice of the Other: Confronting the economy of violence through religious education. In J. Asley, L.J. Francis & M. Robbins

(Eds). *Peace or Violence: The Ends of Religion and Education?* pp. 64–80. Cardiff: University of Wales Press.

Zohar, D., & Marshall, I. (2000). *SQ: Spiritual Intelligence, the Ultimate Intelligence.* New York: Bloomsbury Publishing.

Zubrick, S.R., Silburn, S.R., Lawrence, D.M., Mitrou, F.G., Dalby, R.B., Blair, E.M., Griffin, J., Milroy, H., De Maio, J.A., Cox, A. & Li, J. (2005) *The Social and Emotional Wellbeing of Aboriginal Children and Young People: Vol. 2.* Perth: Telethon Institute for Child Health Research and Curtin University of Technology; Australian Indigenous Health*InfoNet.* Retrieved on 13 February 2015 from www.healthinfonet.ecu.edu.au/health-facts/health-faqs/sewb.

Zull, J.E. (2002). *The Art of Changing the Brain: Enriching the Practice of Teaching by Exploring the Biology of Learning.* Sterling, VA: Stylus Publishing, LLC.

Zweig, J. & Abrams, J. (Eds) (1991). *Meeting the Shadow: The Hidden Power of the Dark Side of Human Nature.* New York: Jeremy P. Tarcher/Penguin.

# Index